THE INVISIBLE FRENCH

The French in Metropolitan Toronto

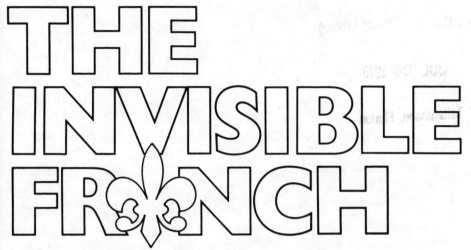

THE INVISIBLE FRENCH

The French in Metropolitan Toronto

Thomas R. Maxwell

Canadian Cataloguing in Publication Data

Maxwell, Thomas R., 1911-
    The invisible French

Originally presented as the author's thesis (Ph.D.),
University of Toronto, 1971, under the title: The
French population of metropolitan Toronto.

Bibliography: p.
ISBN 0-88920-029-7 bd.   ISBN 0-88920-028-9 pa.

1. Canadians, French-speaking - Ontario - Toronto
metropolitan area.* 2. French in the Toronto metropolitan area, Ont. 3. Canadians, French-speaking -
Ethnic identity.* 4. Minorities - Ontario - Toronto
metropolitan area. I. Title.

FC3097.9.F85M39   971.3'541'00441   C77-001357-0
F1059.5.T689M39

Copyright © 1977

Wilfrid Laurier University Press
Waterloo, Ontario, Canada
N2L 3C5

Cover Design: Michael Baldwin

To Reta, my wife, with love and appreciation
for her patience and good humour
while husband and father
was preoccupied with
this inquiry

Foreword

Forthcoming efforts to assess the future shape of the Canadian nation will be required to give careful consideration to the findings of this study by Professor Maxwell. Professor Maxwell's study grew out of the thinking that lay behind the establishment of the Royal Commission on Bilingualism and Biculturalism. It was one of a number of enquiries directed to the end of seeking to discover what was happening to that large French-speaking population which had spread out from the old settled parishes of Quebec into urban-industrial communities dominated by English-speaking business interests, not only beyond the borders of the province but in the newer areas of industrial development in Quebec itself. The examination by Professor Maxwell of the position of the French origin population in the urban community of Toronto was intended to complement the examination of the position of this population in such northern Quebec and Ontario industrial communities as Dolbeau-Misstassini, Noranda-Rouyn, Timmins and Kapuskasing.

What these various studies, including this one by Professor Maxwell, revealed was both the strength and the weakness of the growing movement of national self-consciousness of the Canadian Francophone population. The "quiet revolution" in French Canada was an outgrowth of the strengthening position of the French-speaking middle class in the Province of Quebec. It was within the ranks of this middle class that gathered the major support for those forces of change in the society of Quebec which have led today to the challenge to the dominant position in the province of the English-speaking business establishment.

In the shift of the French-speaking population out of the rural areas of Quebec into the urban-industrial communities growing up in Northern Quebec and Ontario and into such large urban complexes as Toronto, however, there was lacking the resources to support any sort of movement of national self-consciousness. These were not middle-class people. Rather, they were people predominantly who were attracted by the opportunities for industrial employment which such areas offered. For them, as a consequence, economic advancement involved the acceptance of the dominant position of the English-speaking establishment.

In time there did grow up, wherever there was a gathering in substantial numbers of people of French origin, a French-speaking middle class, and in those industrial communities in Northern Quebec where the English-speaking population had long held a dominant position the influence of this French-speaking middle class came to make itself felt to the point where the society was ultimately made over. Beyond the borders of the Province of Quebec, however, the French-speaking middle class, in areas of concentration of a French origin population, could command only very limited political support from the Quebec Government. Efforts here, thus, as in the industrial communities of Northern Ontario or in the city of Toronto, to develop among the French origin population a sense of national self-consciousness depended upon the support of a provincial government only very slowly awakening to the importance of building a social-political structure to accommodate its citizens of French origin.

Professor Maxwell has done an important service in bringing up to date and securing the publication of his study of the position of the French origin population in the Toronto urban community. The final chapter of the study was written after the November 15 election in the Province of Quebec. To persons concerned with maintaining a united Canada it would have been comforting had Professor Maxwell discovered that recent years had brought about a great change in the position of the French in Toronto. He found, however, little evidence that such had occurred. Developments in Quebec had led to a significant strengthening of the Toronto French-speaking middle class, and to increased efforts on the part of this class to extend the range of French cultural institutions, but the "invisible French" of the 1960s and earlier remained invisible still. Herein lies the challenge posed by Professor Maxwell's study. Advocates of Quebec separatism can argue seemingly convincingly that the overpowering position occupied by the English-speaking population outside Quebec inevitably means that the population of French origin can never be more than an ethnic minority, preserving like other ethnic minorities certain cultural traditions, but failing ever to become equal partners with the English-speaking population in a Canadian national community. Thus out of the forces which have made the French in a community like Toronto invisible have developed those forces which have made highly visible the French of Quebec, the Quebecois. The fate of the Canadian nation will be very largely decided by the French people of Quebec. But not wholly unimportant in determining that fate will be the willingness of the English-speaking people outside Quebec to accept within the nation their French-speaking compatriots as equal partners.

—S. D. Clark

Preface

"Why doesn't someone find out what is happening to the French in Toronto?" remarked a panelist on a television program in the early seventies in which French-English relations in Sudbury, Ontario, were discussed. Curiosity about francophones in Toronto was evident in the panel, but the comment revealed that few people were aware that such a study had already been completed in 1964-1966 as a project of the Royal Commission on Bilingualism and Biculturalism. But the Report on the Toronto project submitted to the Commission was one of a number which were not published in its proceedings, and its emergence as a doctoral thesis was not in a form available to the general public. That is one reason why it was recommended to the Social Science Council of Canada that a revised and updated version of the research should be published in order to close this gap in our knowledge of what is happening to French-Canadian minorities outside of the Province of Quebec.

The study could not have been completed without the warm welcome and often enthusiastic cooperation of francophones in Toronto, both in 1964-1966 when the original research was carried out and in 1975-1976 when the study was brought up to date by the author. It was a gratifying experience in interviews to find, with few exceptions, keenly interested respondents among the clergy, administrators in the French-language division of the Ontario Department of Education, principals, and secretaries of French-language schools, francophone officials in government at both the municipal and provincial levels, francophone executives in business and industry, radio, television and publishing, the executive officers of French voluntary associations, and francophones chosen randomly from every walk of life who were part of the representative sample spread across the city. The interpretation of the information and materials acquired, and the conclusions drawn, however, are the responsibility solely of the author.

The author is deeply grateful to Dr. S. D. Clark for writing the foreword as it was through his encouragement, sympathetic guidance, and knowledge of Canadian society, that the study was initiated. The opportunity to work as a research assistant for Dr. Oswald Hall, Director of Community Studies for the Royal Commission on Bilingualism and Biculturalism, as well as his role as thesis advisor while Dr. Clark was on sabbatical, has been much appreciated. To Dr. Jean Burnet is owed an involvement in the field of race and ethnic relations, and an editorial pencil to which the readability of this study is much indebted. The other member of my committee, Dr. Raymond Breton, through his advice and research on institutional completeness has added a new dimension to the interpretation of francophone life in Toronto.

A special vote of appreciation is due to Mrs. Danièle Juteau Lee, my official assistant on the project, for her field work, collation of data, translations, and other meaningful collaboration. Dr. Richard Carlton and Professor Henry Cooperstock gave invaluable assistance, as did the team of interviewers who were an essential part of the inquiry.

The author wishes to thank the Department of the Secretary of State, Social Action Branch, through Dr. John Petrolias, for permission to use three confidential reports to the Department, namely, the Appraisal of La Chasse-Galerie of August, 1972, and the Appraisal of La Maison Française de Toronto of July, 1973, both by Gladys Hitchman of York University, and the Appraisal of the contribution of the parish of the Sacré-Coeur to the francophone working class, by Claire Pageau in April, 1975.

The original study was financed by the Royal Commission on Bilingualism and Biculturalism, to whom is due appreciation for the use of the data gathered under its auspices; and to Waterloo Lutheran University (now Wilfrid Laurier University) for financial assistance in the preparation of the thesis manuscript.

The book has been published with the help of a grant from the Social Science Council of Canada, using funds provided by the Canada Council.

Appreciation is also due to Dr. Norman Wagner, Director of Wilfrid Laurier University Press and his staff, for their patience while preparation of the revision was delayed by unusual circumstances; to Mrs. Doreen Armbruster and Mrs. Reta Lienhardt for their accurate typing, and to Mrs. Bonnie Quinn and Mrs. Heather Blain for their efficient preparation of the manuscript for the printer.

Table of Contents

FOREWORD vii

PREFACE ix

LIST OF TABLES xiii

LIST OF ILLUSTRATIONS xvii

I.   WHY INVISIBLE? 1

II.   SOCIAL PARTICIPATION AND ETHNIC IDENTITY 5

III.   HISTORICAL PERSPECTIVES 17
        A.   The Settlement of the French in Toronto
        B.   The Origins of the French Population
        C.   The Development of Parish Organization

IV.   PATTERNS OF SETTLEMENT IN TORONTO 37
        A.   The Spatial Pattern
        B.   The Occupational Pattern
        C.   The Pattern of Stratification

V.   THE MAGNET OF ECONOMIC SECURITY 57

VI.   RELIGIOUS VALUES AND ETHNIC NATIONALISM 71

VII.   BETWEEN TWO CULTURES: THE BILINGUAL SCHOOLS . . 79
        A.   Separate School Boards of Education
        B.   Social Class and Bilingual Education
        C.   Academic Proficiency and Bilingual Education
        D.   The Bilingual High School
        E.   Ethnic Identity and Bilingual Education

VIII.   FRENCH AS MOTHER TONGUE 93

IX.   CHOOSING ASSOCIATES AND FRIENDS 107
        A.   Formal Associations
        B.   Immigrant French Associations
        C.   Informal Associations
        D.   Kinship Networks

X.   USE OF THE COMMUNICATIONS MEDIA 125
        A.   The French-Language Newspaper
        B.   French Magazines
        C.   French Books
        D.   French Radio
        E.   French Films
        F.   Television
        G.   Patterns of Mass Media Use

XI.   PROSPECTS FOR SURVIVAL 137

XII.   POSTSCRIPT 1976: THE TRENDS OF A DECADE, 1966-1976 . 141

BIBLIOGRAPHY 169

List of Tables

Table

1 Comparison of the Place of Origin of the Adult Population of French Origin in Metropolitan Toronto with the Place of Origin of Respondents in the Toronto Sample of that Population . . . 14

2 Growth of the Main Minority Ethnic Groups, City of Toronto, From 1901 to 1961 23

3 Growth of Main Minority Ethnic Groups, Metropolitan Area of Toronto, 1941 to 1961 24

4 French Adult Population of the Metropolitan Area of Toronto According to Place of Origin 25

5 Occupations of the Fathers of Respondents in the Metropolitan Toronto Sample 27

6 Comparison of the Growth of the Total Population with the Population of French Origin, 1951 to 1961, for (1) The Metropolitan Area, (2) the City of Toronto and the Twelve Suburban Municipalities, (3) the Largest Suburbs: Scarborough, North York, and Etobicoke 41

7 Reasons Given by the French for Settlement in the Toronto Area 45

8 Occupations of the Sample of Gainfully Employed Males of French Origin, 1965, Compared With Total Labour Force, Metropolitan Toronto, 1961 47

9 Length of Time Living in Toronto and Job Mobility for Male and Female Respondents Who Were Gainfully Employed . . . 59

10 The Occupational Distributions of Ninety French-Speaking Fathers and Sons and Ninety-Nine Fathers-In-Law and Sons-In-Law of the Toronto Sample 61

11 Amount of Education in the Various Occupational Categories of Employed Male Respondents 63

12 Family Income of the 252 Respondents in the Toronto Sample . 65

13 Family Income from all Sources of Respondents in the Toronto Sample Who Grew Up in Ontario, Quebec and the Maritime Provinces 68

14 Church Attendance 72

15 Reasons for Not Attending the French Parish 73

16 Areas of Residence and Attendance at the Sacré-Coeur 74

17   Reason for Choosing Area of Residence 74

18   A Comparison of Family Income and Attendance at the
      Sacré-Coeur French Parish 76

19   The Various Types of Schools Available for the Education of
      Children in the Toronto Area, and the Number of Children
      from the Toronto Sample Who Attend Such Schools 81

20   A Comparison of Family Income and Place of Residence of
      the Forty-Nine Families Who Sent Children to Bilingual
      Schools, From the Toronto Sample 82

21   The Amount of Education and the Type of Schools in Which
      It Was Received, for Respondents in the Toronto Sample Who
      Were Asked the Question: "How Much Education Did You
      Have the Opportunity to Get Yourself?" 86

22   How Much Education Respondents Felt Most Young Men
      Should Have Today 87

23   Comparative Percentages of the French and English Languages
      Spoken in Various Circumstances by the Toronto Sample of
      the Population of French Origin 96

24   The Ethnic Origin of Fellow Workers at Place of Employment
      For Both Men and Women Among Respondents in the Toronto
      Sample Who Are Gainfully Employed, and the Opportunities
      to Speak the French Language Where There are Some French
      Fellow Workers 98

25   Comparative Percentages of the French and English Languages
      Spoken in Various Circumstances by the French in the Sample
      Who Were Born and Grew Up in Toronto 99

26   Comparative Percentages of the French and English Languages
      Spoken in Various Circumstances: (A) By Families in Which
      Both Spouses Were French, and (B) By Families Where One
      Spouse is French and one Non-French 100

27   Comparative Percentages of the French and English Languages
      Spoken in Various Circumstances By Families From Quebec,
      With: (A) Both Spouses French, and (B) One Spouse French,
      and One Non-French 102

28   Comparative Percentages of the French and English Languages
      Spoken in Various Circumstances By the Children in Families
      Where: (A) the Father French, the Mother Non-French, and
      (B) the Father Non-French, the Mother French 103

29 Comparative Percentages of the French and English Languages
    Spoken in Various Circumstances by the Children in Families
    Where One Spouse is Catholic and One Spouse is Protestant . . . 104

30 Memberships of Respondents in French, English and Bilingual
    Formal Organizations 111

31 Toronto Sample—Frequency Distribution of Friendships by
    Ethnicity of Friends, By Intimacy or Closeness of Relationship . 120

32 Regular Reading of French and English Newspapers, Magazines
    and Books by Respondents in the Toronto Study 127

33 Patterns of Radio Listening Among Those of French Origin in
    Toronto 131

34 The Ten Most Significant Patterns of French Mass Media Usage
    Among the 145 Toronto Families of French Origin Who
    Report 331 Usages of One or More of the French Mass Media . . 135

35 Table Showing Growth Rates of the Six Largest Minority
    Ethnic Populations in Metropolitan Toronto in Order of
    Mother Tongue Spoken Most Often in the Home 159

36 Table of Major Subdivision of Metropolitan Toronto Showing
    (A) Densities of the French Population, and (B) Percentage
    of the French Mother Tongue Spoken Most Often at Home . . . 162

List of Illustrations

Distribution of the Population of French Origin 38-39

Growth of the Francophone Population in the Toronto Core
(Metropolitan Corporation) and the Fringe Area 145

A Comparison of Francophone Children Enrolled in French-
Language Schools and the Potential Enrollment in
Three Categories 149

Residential Distribution of the French and Italian Populations
Over 10% Density in Census Tracts 161

Chapter I

Why
Invisible?

Since World War II, Toronto's image as a rather staid, predominantly British community, has been transformed through massive immigration into what has been aptly described as a "salad bowl" of identifiable ethnic communities with their characteristic languages, neighbourhoods, shops, newspapers, radio programs and sporting events. Such drastic changes in the composition of the population prompted the City of Toronto Planning Department to prepare a series of maps showing the initial staging areas and the areas of more permanent settlement of the majority of Toronto's ethnic populations.[1] But, unaccountably, the French were missing from the maps, even though they were the third largest ethnic minority in the metropolitan region. Where were the French located within this cosmopolitan scene?

University students, majoring in French language and literature at a local university, were anxious to find out. While filming a documentary on French life in Toronto, they interviewed pedestrians of various ages and both sexes as they streamed along the sidewalks of some of Toronto's main streets. They discovered that Torontonians were almost totally unaware of the presence of the French in their midst, let alone having personal acquaintance with residents of French ancestry.[2] In fact, few of the French themselves, when interviewed in a previous survey, had any clear idea of the extent of French settlement in Toronto, or where they were located within the metropolitan area. Even the priest at the French parish, La Sacré Coeur, was unable to provide information about the French population beyond the few hundred who attended the downtown parish.[3] It is no wonder that one of the pedestrians described the French as "invisible."

The anonymity of the French poses the question of how a large minority population which claims a distinctive culture, and has grown from over sixty thousand in 1961 to over ninety thousand in 1971, can virtually disappear within the two million residents of Metropolitan Toronto.[4] An illuminating

[1]City of Toronto Planning Board, *Ethnic Origins of the Population of Toronto, 1960* (Toronto, 1961), Figs. D-1 to D-17.

[2]A documentary film entitled, "The Invisible French," produced by the Department of Instructional Aid Resources of York University, Downsview, Ontario, in collaboration with the Department of French Literature, 1971; funded by the Department of the Secretary of State, Social Action Branch, Ottawa. The film is available from the Department of Instructional Aid Resources, York University.

[3]From the research reported in subsequent chapters of this volume, conducted under the auspices of the Royal Commission on Bilingualism and Biculturalism, 1964-1966.

[4]*Census of Canada, 1961* and *1971*.

comment came from a French university professor when he was asked, "To what extent do you feel yourself to be a member of Toronto's French community?"

Well, I guess it depends on what you mean by French community in Toronto. If you mean only French-speaking people living in Toronto, then of course, I am part of such a community. But if you mean a social or political community, I don't believe there is such a community in Toronto. As a matter of fact, I don't think you have a French community. You have a group of French-speaking people living in Toronto. And I think if you have a community, all these people should have, to a certain extent, ties together. But as it is now, the French-speaking people are coming from France, from Quebec, from New Brunswick, from Belgium, or elsewhere, and don't seem to have much in common but certain interests, cultural interests.[5]

What has been described so far seems to confirm the fears voiced over the last decade or so in the Province of Quebec that the French-Canadian minorities outside of that province are being lost to the French-Canadian linguistic and cultural heritage. Toronto provides an opportunity to explore the social processes which may or may not be leading to a loss of ethnic identity by members of the French population. Metropolitan Toronto, the most populous urban area in English-speaking Canada, houses the largest population of French origin outside of the Province of Quebec, with the exception of the federal capital, Ottawa.[6] Its total population (2,628,130 in 1971) so overshadows the French population (91,975) that the latter represents only 3.49 per cent of the total population. Accentuating minority status within the host population is the position of the French within the Roman Catholic Diocese of Toronto, where they are also a minority of only 8 per cent of the Catholic residents of the area.[7] Furthermore, other characteristics of French life in the metropolis, to be discussed in subsequent chapters, strongly suggest that the French situation in Toronto represents an almost maximal exposure of the French language and culture to the influence of a majority English-speaking culture.

Toronto, however, is only one example of a trend in Canada, the development of large urban areas to the degree that the entire society may be thought of as falling within the orbit of identifiable urban regions.[8] In 1961, when Canada's population was 72.3 per cent urban, over one-half of the total population (54%) and three-quarters of its urban population lived within thirty-seven metropolitan

[5]From the sound track of the film "The Invisible French," noted above.

[6]The City of Ottawa constitutes a special case for two reasons: (1) it is situated on the border of Quebec while Toronto is a considerable distance away; and (2) a large number of French-Canadians are employed in the federal bureaucracy which seeks to equalize employment of the French on a proportional basis according to population, although it is not always successful.

[7]Census of Canada, 1971.

[8]Delbert C. Miller and William H. Form, Industrial Sociology (2nd ed.; New York: Harper and Row, 1964), p. 43.

and other large urban areas.[9] In 1971, when Canada's population was 76.1 per cent urban, and its French population 68.2 per cent urban, one-half of the total population was concentrated in only twenty-two metropolitan areas, accentuating the influence of increasingly larger urban regions upon the ethnic minorities within their boundaries.[10]

Almost one-quarter of the population of French origin in Canada lives outside of the Province of Quebec, spread across the other nine provinces. Over the first seven decades of the twentieth century this segment of the French population has increased more rapidly than the French population of the Province of Quebec, and is still growing. Only in the decades of the 1920's and the 1960's was there a slight reversal of this trend. The Province of Ontario is the home of just over one-half of the French minority population. It is predominantly urban in character, with 69.5 per cent living in Ontario's nine metropolitan areas and many more in smaller urban communities.[11]

What has been happening to the French minority population of Metropolitan Toronto may be symptomatic of what is happening in other urban areas, not only in Ontario but across Canada. It is the contention of this study that many of the cultural and social problems confronting such minorities may be brought into focus by considering the relationship between ethnic identity and social or institutional participation. Consequently, Chapter II presents a brief sociological analysis of ethnic relations, concentrating in particular upon the social processes which determine the locus of social participation and thus influence the retention or the loss of ethnic identity by an ethnic minority.

[9]*Census of Canada, 1961.*
[10]*Census of Canada, 1971.*
[11]Ibid.

Chapter II

Social Participation and Ethnic Identity

In the last half of the nineteenth century and the first quarter of the twentieth century, when good arable land became too scarce to support the growing rural population, French-Canadians migrated in considerable numbers from the Provinces of Quebec and New Brunswick into the cities and towns of New England where employment opportunities abounded. As four out of five of the immigrants settled within an urban environment, they became an urban minority within the majority, English-speaking, American society. Its members found themselves oriented at one and the same time to several different cultural worlds.[1] Their leaders were concerned for the survival of the French language and culture within this multicultural milieu. An effective strategy was necessary to ensure the retention of the French ancestral heritage.

The basic goal of retaining the identity of the Franco-Americans as a group was visualized by their leaders as attainable through the three crucially important institutions of the Church, the school, and the home. The long experience of the Franco-Americans as a minority group disposed them to believe that if these three institutions, closely integrated one with the other, could be formed into havens of refuge impenetrable to outside influences, where the Catholic faith, the French language, and the French-Canadian culture were cherished and nurtured, they could thrive, even in the midst of an alien and mildly hostile milieu.[2]

But this goal was attainable only during the early period of settlement when successive waves of mainly rural migrants, homogeneous in background, education and economic status as unskilled factory workers, formed compact French-speaking neighbourhoods in urban areas of New England. The multiplication of ethnic parishes, establishment of small businesses, professional services, and welfare agencies, along with the appearance of various types of associations and societies, served to channel primary social interaction within ethnic social institutions.

The cessation of group migration in the 1920s, however, was followed by socio-economic differentiation of an increasingly mobile French population. The transition was evident in marked changes in the range of occupations in which the French were employed, residential dispersion beyond French-speaking neighbourhoods, and the expansion of the class structure. Franco-Americans who had grown up in New England with little contact with French-Canada were increas-

---

[1]George F. Theriault, "The Franco-Americans of New England," in Mason Wade, ed., *Canadian Dualism* (Toronto: University of Toronto Press, 1960), p. 393.

[2]Ibid., p. 403.

ingly reluctant to identify with the French culture. They tended to adopt the outlook and attitudes of the majority population and participate in the social institutions of the American society.

Such cultural diversity developed at the same time as the ethnic alliance of Church, school and home was seriously weakened by the action of the American Roman Catholic Episcopate in limiting the expansion of ethnic parishes and the use of the French language in parochial schools. In this changing milieu, dependence upon the triad of Church, school and home, as integrators of community life and guardians of the French language and culture, proved ineffective in preventing the accelerating rate of participation[3] of Franco-Americans within the social structures of the majority, host society.[4]

Exact parallels with Canadian settings cannot be drawn from the Franco-American experience since urban communities vary widely in their characteristics: size, location, composition of the population, degree of industrialization, economic and political importance. But the social processes which were crucial to the survival of the French language and culture in New England, or conversely, to their dissolution, are also operative in the Canadian situation and therefore are relevant to an analysis of ethnic minorities in Canada.

In the first phase of French settlement in New England, "the interaction of like-minded persons in some numbers . . . the fundamental requirement of all societies,"[5] was fulfilled. The wave-like character of French-Canadian immigration made possible the establishment of closely-knit French-speaking neighbourhoods in which the institutional structure was complete enough to ensure the continuity of the French language and culture. But in the second phase, beginning early in the twentieth century and continuing to the present day, increasing participation by the French in the institutional structures of the majority society, especially by those who grew up in New England, led to substantial assimilation to the host, American society.

In many ways, these two aspects of Franco-American experience correspond to the two types of assimilation distinguished by Milton M. Gordon in his classic treatment of the concept. Utilizing Robert E. Park's classic definition of assimi-

---

[3]The root meaning of the word "participation" in Webster's Dictionary is "To have a share in common with others, or to take part with others." *Dictionaries of Sociology* such as Fairchild (Paterson, N.J.: Littlefield, Adams and Co., 1961), p. 213, define participation as "Entry into, identification with, as through communication or common activity, some defined social situation"; p. 287, "Social participation is sharing by sentient beings in social interaction." Theodorson and Theodorson in their *Modern Dictionary of Sociology* (New York: Thomas Y. Crowell & Co., 1969) define the concept as "The participation of the individual in social groups." In the above senses of the term there is the implication of a parallel with the enactment or taking of a role. As Olsen comments: "Participation is a dynamic aspect of status and thus would correspond to role playing or enactment . . . . To enact a role a person must act as a relatively involved part of an established social organization" (*The Process of Social Organization* [New York: Holt, Rinehart and Winston, 1968], pp. 105, 107).

[4]George F. Theriault, "The Franco-Americans of New England," pp. 392-411.

[5]Ibid., p. 398.

lation, "the process of interpenetration and fusion by which persons or groups acquire the values, attitudes and behaviour patterns of other persons or groups," Gordon argues that the process of assimilation can take place on two levels, either as "cultural assimilation" or as "structural assimilation."[6]

In cultural assimilation, the traditional institutional structures of the minority population such as family and occupational patterns, religious organizations, class structure, education and recreation, etc., are not altered in any significant way. Consequently, there is "a situation in which primary group contacts with the majority community are held to a minimum even though secondary contacts on the job, on the civic scene, and in the areas of impersonal relationships may abound."[7] It involves accommodations to the majority society such as the use of the majority language and the typical norms of etiquette which are commonly practised in normal social intercourse throughout the entire community.

In structural assimilation, the traditional institutional structures of the minority population are partially or wholly lacking or have become irrelevant for a substantial number of that population and therefore cannot function as a viable organizational system. Members of an ethnic minority which thus lacks the organizational means to focus participation within cultural boundaries, stimulate interest in issues pertaining to ethnic survival, and provide opportunities for the recruiting and training of ethnic leadership, have no alternative but to identity outside the society of origin.[8]

Recent research has demonstrated that the degree of institutional completeness within an ethnic minority population determines the extent to which participation takes place within ethnic boundaries.[9] In this respect ethnic minorities vary widely, ranging at one extreme from minorities in which social structure is essentially no more than informal networks of relatives and friends, to the other extreme of highly organized minorities which approximate institutional completeness.[10] The significance for ethnic identity of such variation is that:

[6]Milton F. Gordon, *Assimilation in American Life* (New York: Oxford University Press, 1964), Chap. 3.

[7]Ibid., p. 235.

[8]Horace Miner, *Saint-Denis, A French-Canadian Parish* (Chicago: The University of Chicago Press, 1963), p. 235: "It is a commonplace that social systems change to meet their structural problems. When the traditional ways cease to solve the problems of life, social behaviour varies from the old ways until a solution is found. If the new ways are successful, they in turn will become traditional." Fredrick Barth, *Ethnic Groups and Boundaries* (Boston: Little, Brown and Company, 1969), p. 25: "The incentives to a change of identity are thus inherent in the change of circumstances. . . . Since ethnic identity is associated with a culturally specific set of value standards, it follows that there are circumstances where such an identity can be moderately successfully realized, and limits beyond which such success is precluded. . . . Ethnic identities will not be retained beyond these limits. . . . "

[9]Raymond Breton, "Institutional Completeness of Ethnic Communities and the Personal Relations of Immigrants," in Bernard Blishen, *et al.*, eds., *Canadian Society* (3rd ed.; Toronto: Macmillan of Canada, 1968), p. 77.

[10]Ibid., pp. 84, 88.

Ethnic populations with the highest degree of institutional completeness have a much greater proportion of their members with most of their personal relations within the ethnic group; 89 per cent of the members of highly institutionalized communities as compared with 21 per cent of those from ethnic groups with few or no formal organizations.[11]

Identifying outside of the society of origin, however, implies a change of identity, and raises the question of what is meant by the statement that a member of a certain group has a particular "ethnic identity", and the further question of how such an identity can be changed. In discussing social identity, Erving Goffman has suggested that identity as a social reality has two aspects. It involves not only personal attributes such as "honesty" which are individualistic in character, but also structural attributes such as "occupation" which are group oriented.[12] One could add to occupation other structural attributes such as ethnicity, religion, class, and so on, which are similarly group oriented. Group identification has been defined as:

A process in which an individual incorporates within himself the expectations, standards, values and goals of a group, and utilizes them in the organization, reorganization, or stabilization of his social self.[13]

In such group identification, the patterns of social participation tend to reflect the structural rather than the personal attributes of ethnic identity.

In general terms, a sociological definition of ethnic identity embraces the idea of a "consciousness of kind." This includes not only an awareness of shared origin, tradition, language and culture, but also a conception of how one is typed by members of the surrounding population.[14] The consciousness of identity normally is created within the family,[15] reinforced by social interaction within the larger context of the local community, and maintained by continued partici-

---

[11]Ibid., p. 82. Breton's research in Montreal indicates that "religious institutions have the greatest effect in keeping the immigrants personal associations within the boundaries of the ethnic community." Newspapers and periodicals have the second most important effect, and welfare organizations the least of the institutions studied. Pp. 87, 88. These findings are quite relevant to the Toronto situation.

[12]Erving Goffman, in *Stigma* (Englewood Cliffs, N.J.: Prentice-Hall, Inc., 1963), pp. 2-3.

[13]Theodorson and Theodorson, *Modern Dictionary of Sociology*, p. 180.

[14]Barth, *Ethnic Groups and Boundaries* pp. 11, 13. Tamotsu Shibutani and Kian M. Kwan, *Ethnic Stratification* (New York: The Macmillan Company, 1965), p. 47. Will Herberg, *Protestant, Catholic, Jew* (New York: Doubleday and Company, Inc., 1955), p. 25. "The way in which one identifies and locates himself ('Who, what, am I?') is closely related to how one is identified and located in the larger community ('Who, what, is he?'). Normally they reflect, sustain, and illumine each other; it is only in abnormal situations that they diverge and conflict."

[15]Emile Durkheim, *Suicide*, trans. by John A. Spaulding and George Simpson (Glencoe, Ill.: The Free Press, 1951), p. 202.

pation in communal social structures. The most important element in this view of identity is that it is shaped by those persons and groups with which the members of a society "participate frequently and share close behavioural similarities," a process which has been labelled "participational identification."[16] Thus identity can vary significantly with the kind and degree of social participation habitual to the members of the ethnic group, depending upon the permeability of cultural boundaries.

Participational identification with a particular group, community or society creates a cultural boundary, or "invisible wall"[17] which differentiates its members from the members of other societies. Such boundaries are the product of the relative isolation of most societies from each other during their growth and development. Tangible geographic and political boundaries are invariably accompanied by intangible cultural and social boundaries which are apparent in the different languages, customs, values and beliefs which distinguish one society from another.

Cultural boundaries are not only operative between societies but exist within societies. Within a single society with a common language, a region may be so isolated from other regions by geographic barriers or local circumstances, that linguistic dialects and other differences in styles of life develop which hinder communication and understanding within the society. And when a society, such as Canada, is composed almost wholly of migrants from various societies with divergent cultures, the importance of cultural boundaries is accentuated. Where geographic and cultural boundaries coincide, as in the Province of Quebec, or on Indian reservations, there is reciprocal reinforcement of the "invisible wall" between French and English Canada, or between the Indian peoples and Euro-Canadians. Where many ethnic groups exist within the same geographic boundaries, the retention of traditional cultures becomes a matter of concern for each of the immigrant minorities.

Continued social participation within cultural boundaries is therefore necessary to preserve the solidarity, identity and cultural patterns characteristic of a particular society.[18] Just as identity is shaped by general conformity to the cultural norms, values and beliefs indigenous to the society, with virtual absence or rejection of alternatives, so identity is perpetuated through continuing involvement in a network of social relations sustained by the social organizations traditional to the society.[19] There are usually rewards for respecting cultural

[16]Gordon, *Assimilation in American Life* pp. 51, 53.

[17]David R. Hughes and Evelyn Kallen, *The Anatomy of Racism: Canadian Dimensions* (Montreal: Harvest House Ltd., 1974) in which the concept of the "invisible wall" and its implications for various aspects of ethnic relations is discussed in considerable detail from the theoretical point of view with relevant illustrations from the Canadian scene. Cf. pages 95, 115, 132, 136, 146, 167, 186, 200.

[18]Charles F. Loomis and Zona K. Loomis, *Modern Social Theories* (Toronto: D. Van Nostrand Co., Inc., 1965), p. 16.

[19]Ibid., p. 304, where the authors maintain that in Robert K. Merton's conception of

boundaries in the form of social acceptance and the expectations of present and future advantage, while penalties such as the withdrawal of such privileges await the individual who ignores cultural boundaries. Even more important for the integration of the community or society is a general ideological commitment, religious, moral or political, which undergirds ethnic identification. The cumulative influence of some or all of these integrative pressures upon members of a community or society creates a comparatively homogeneous culture, and a strong, unitary sense of ethnic identity.[20]

But when an ethnic minority has settled within a multiethnic urban community, such as Toronto, any local conditions or circumstances which encourage the members of the minority to participate in the social structures of the majority society in preference to their own, weaken cultural boundaries and are a potential threat to the cultural survival of the ethnic minority.

For instance, the pattern of residential settlement may scatter members of the minority throughout the urban area rather than concentrating them in neighbourhoods, thus maximizing their exposure to the majority culture and isolating them from contact with their own. The host society may offer opportunities for social and/or material advantages which are not available within the minority population. Lack of a viable leadership élite may stifle the growth of ethnic organizations which normally channel social interaction within ethnic boundaries. The absence or cessation of ethnic discrimination or conflict between majority and minority populations may create a climate favourable to accommodation to another culture.

Participational identification is also influenced by the pattern of social stratification. Social classes do become sources of group identity, and to some members of a minority "differences of class are more important than differences of ethnic group."[21] People tend to confine social participation in primary groups and relationships within their class segment of the minority population. Social participation may even cross the boundaries of an ethnic minority to identify on a class basis with members of other societies, thus weakening the ethnic bonds of their own minority population.

> The social class, in other words, while not formally delineated, tends to have its own network of characteristic organizations, institutional activities, and social cliques. These are created because people who are approximately in the same social class have similar interests and tastes, have a common educational background, and work at occupations which bring them in touch with one another in various ways and which involve com-

---

boundaries, social cohesion involves three aspects of social systems, namely, culture, social organization, and social structure.

[20] Percy S. Cohen, *Modern Social Theory* (London: Heinemann Educational Books Ltd., 1968), pp. 130-31.

[21] Gordon, *Assimilation in American Life*, pp. 46, 52.

mon types of experience. Thus they feel "comfortable" with each other.[22]

When class participation becomes dominant over ethnic participation it influences "the ability of a minority group to generate effective leadership in its relations with a majority alien population."[23] Socio-economic differentiation accentuates status differentials such as education, residence and associational affiliations, and thus tends to isolate the upper and middle classes from the lower class in terms of attitudes and values. When communication between classes is blocked it generates suspicion and distrust of higher class leadership.

The minority leader must be acceptable to his own people, but his position depends ultimately on his acceptance by the majority. . . . In his tenuous position he must pacify both groups. He must integrate their conflicting demands, those of the minority group requiring commitment to its most cherished values, including claims for social equality, and those of the majority group requiring acceptance of its values, including maintenance of its dominant position. The minority leader must negotiate between "selling out" his own people by overcompromising their demands and threatening the power of the majority by overdemanding social equality. Although his position rests on "two centres of gravity," it is the majority group whose judgment of his acceptability ultimately matters. In making the demands of both groups palatable to each other, the minority leader therefore must pay more homage to the majority since it is the group that "runs things" in society.[24]

Any restriction of leader-follower relationships within an ethnic minority limits proportionately the growth of the social structures which enable the various strata in the class structure to participate together within ethnic boundaries.[25] Class divisions encourage participation across ethnic boundaries and create a climate favourable to the "passing" of members of the ethnic minority into the corresponding strata of the host society and thereby to disappear ethnically, except for an ethnic name.[26]

Within a multiethnic community, therefore, a variety of alternative identifications, both ethnic and class, is available to members of an ethnic minority

[22]Ibid., p. 46.

[23]James B. Watson and Julian Samora, "Subordinate Leadership in a Bicultural Community," *American Sociological Review*, XIX (1954), 413.

[24]Seymour Leventman, "Minority Group Leadership: The Advantages of the Disadvantaged," in Bernard Rosenberg, *et al.*, *Mass Society in Crisis* (New York: The Macmillan Co., 1964), pp. 604-605.

[25]S. D. Clark, *The Developing Canadian Community* (rev. ed.; Toronto: University of Toronto Press, 1968), p. 239.

[26]Nathan Glazer and Daniel P. Moynihan, *Beyond the Melting Pot* (Cambridge: The M.I.T. Press, 1963), p. 111; Shibutani and Kwan, *Ethnic Stratification*, p. 50; Herbert Gans, *The Urban Villagers* (Glencoe: The Free Press of Glencoe, 1962), p. 31.

population such as the French. The research reported here was initiated as a project of the Royal Commission on Bilingualism and Biculturalism. No one seemed to know, not even the French themselves, what was happening to the French population resident in Toronto in relation to the English-speaking population. The Commission was interested in finding out. In the research, two considerations have been kept in mind. First, what have been the circumstances surrounding French settlement in Toronto which have culminated in the contemporary situation? And second, how have the existing patterns of participation, either within or without ethnic boundaries, affected French identity?[27]

Consequently, Chapters III to V examine the various factors within the history of French settlement in Toronto which have determined the composition of the French population, and the patterns of residential distribution, parish organization, social stratification, and occupational structure. Chapters VI to X seek to determine both the extent of participational identification by the French within their own institutional structures or those of the majority society, and the reasons for such patterns of behaviour. Chapter XI evaluates these findings in terms of the prospects for survival of the French language and culture in Toronto. The final chapter is a postscript to the original research, summarizing the author's impressions, gained through further investigation, of the progress of a decade in establishing a viable French identity within the Toronto milieu.

The Process of Inquiry[28]

The data upon which this study is based were derived from over three hundred interviews with residents of Toronto of French origin, of which 252 constituted a representative sample. Utilizing previous research in the field, assisted by preliminary unstructured interviews, a precoded interview schedule was constructed which took from one to one and a half hours to complete. It was printed in English and conducted in that language in the majority of cases for two reasons: only two of the ten experienced interviewers, all graduates or graduate students in sociology, were fluent in French, although others had some facility in the language; secondly, the expressed opinion of both clerical and lay French leaders was that interviewers would find minimal difficulty arising from the inability of respondents to express themselves in English. This proved to be the case. The main survey was conducted during the month of May, 1965, preceded and followed by supplementary interviews, mainly with the middle class.

Two sources were used for the sample: the parishes of the Catholic Diocese of Toronto and the Metropolitan City Directory. The first source had two aspects: one, a participant-observer study of the French national parish, the Sacré-Coeur,

---

[27]For a different approach and a somewhat expanded theoretical treatment see the Introduction to: Thomas Robert Maxwell, "The French Population of Metropolitan Toronto: A Study in Social Participation and Ethnic Identity" (unpublished Ph.D. dissertation, The University of Toronto, 1971).

[28]The Process of Inquiry may be skipped by those not interested in methods of social research or the empirical basis for the research reported in this volume.

conducted by a French-Canadian graduate student over a period of almost a year. Two, an attempt to secure the names and addresses of families and individuals of French origin attending non-French parishes. Inquiry revealed that a negligible number of the French were associated with non-French immigrant parishes. Consequently, all the English-speaking parishes in the Diocese were contacted by letter, telephone and interviews, with 61 per cent responding, supplying over one thousand names and addresses, varying in each case from two or three to over one hundred names. The major gaps were in the older, central areas of the city and suburbs, the areas of highest concentration of the French population, where priests reported high residential mobility and consequent difficulty in maintaining contact with French families and individuals. This problem was overcome by the use of the Metropolitan City Directory.

The Metropolitan City Directory was utilized to scrutinize every address in the five areas in the city and suburbs where the population of French origin constituted 4 per cent or over of the total population of census tracts,[29] as shown on the accompanying map.[30] Selection of this universe was by simple recognition of French names by a French-Canadian graduate student. Certain biases were introduced into the universe by this method. Names are not always a reliable guide to ethnic origin because some French names have been anglicized.[31] French males who were heads of households tended to be overrepresented while French wives of non-French husbands were underrepresented. Parishes had supplied names of French wives of non-French husbands but these were used only in spot-sampling outside of the five areas of concentration of the French population. Lower age groups also tended to be underrepresented because most of the interviewing was carried out during the day when younger people were at places of employment, although evening interviewing compensated to some degree. Over one thousand names were secured from the Metropolitan Directory.

The total universe obtained from these two sources consisted of well over two thousand names, from which a sample was drawn for four of the five areas of concentration by the use of random sampling tables. In the fifth area, Riverdale, a total sample was derived from the single census tract of highest French density, using both the Directory and parish lists,[32] while the remainder of Riverdale was spot-sampled. A spot-sampling technique was utilized for all of Metropolitan Toronto outside of the five areas of concentration, using parish and bilingual school lists and random sampling tables, as time and available assistance did not permit otherwise.

[29]*Census of Canada*, Bulletin CT-15, 1961.

[30]See Chapter IV, pp. 38-39, for this map.

[31]A. R. M. Lower, *Canadians in the Making* (Toronto: Longmans, Green, 1958), p. 109. "Mere names no longer are entirely safe guides to racial origin or to religion."

[32]The study of the single census tract in Riverdale was the subject of an M.A. thesis by a graduate student who was one of the team of interviewers in the Toronto study. See article by John A. Lee, "The Greendale Canadians: Cultural and Structural Assimilation in an Urban Environment," in Bernard Blishen, *et al.*, eds., *Canadian Society* (3rd ed.; Toronto: Macmillan of Canada, 1968), pp. 636-47.

Only respondents who claimed French origin were interviewed. All interviews were arranged by telephone where a listing existed, and interviews were conducted in the homes. House calls were made to addresses with no telephone listing. Ten per cent of those with French names who were telephoned declared that they were not French, or were no longer French in terms of language, and declined to be interviewed. Residential mobility was high during the ten months since the Metropolitan City Directory used had been issued, with removals averaging 25 per cent for the entire sample, reaching as high as 37 per cent in one area, Parkdale.

Completed interviews totalled 252, 108 males and 144 females.[33] When this sample was compared in terms of place of origin with the total adult population of French origin in 1961, as can be seen in Table 1, there was an overrepresentation in the sample of respondents from New Brunswick and Quebec when compared to the total French population. This was probably due to the choice of the sample, except for spot-sampling, from the areas of highest French density in the city. The profile of the Toronto sample, however, appears sufficiently similar to

Table 1

Comparison of the Place of Origin of the Adult Population of French Origin in Metropolitan Toronto with the Place of Origin of Respondents in the Toronto Sample of that Population

Place of Origin	Metropolitan Area[a]		Sample	
		%		%
New Brunswick	4,078	10.32	51	20.81
Other Atlantic Provinces	3,482	8.81	14	5.71
Quebec	7,660	19.39	60	24.49
Ontario	19,609	49.63	102	41.63
Western Provinces and Territories	1,525	3.86	8	3.26
United States of America	835	2.11	2	.82
Other Countries	2,323	5.88	8	3.27
Total French Born in Canada	36,354	92.00	235	95.91
Total French	39,512	100.00	245[b]	97.22

[a]Census of Canada, 1961; the population fifteen years and over.

[b]Place of origin of seven respondents was not ascertainable, bringing the total respondents in the sample to 252.

[33]Appendix A is a summary of the sampling statistics of the Toronto study.

that of the entire French adult population in 1961 to be considered a representative sample.

In seeking to determine the class structure within the representative sample the framework used was dictated more by necessity than by choice, the socio-economic categories of males of French origin in the labour force. Some sociologists claim that socio-economic categories represent only strata of social inequality rather than a class structure; they are merely statistical constructs.[34] This view finds some confirmation in the fact that within the changing French-Canadian social structure the middle class at the present time is somewhat indeterminate in form.[35] With this stricture in mind, an effort was made by means of supplementary interviews, especially of middle-class respondents, to clothe the bare bones of socio-economic status with the flesh of further criteria of social status, such as styles of life as reflected in place of residence, memberships in voluntary and professional associations, ascription of status by peers, which supplement such categories as occuption, education, income, and prestige.

Therefore, in addition to the representative sample of 252 respondents, interviews were conducted with the following: contemporary and former priests and parishioners of the French parish; the principals of the two bilingual primary schools, and the private bilingual secondary school; the superintendent for Ontario of bilingual schools, the bilingual school inspector for the Toronto area, and the chairman (a Franco-Ontarian) of the Metropolitan Separate School Board; the Director of the Association canadienne-française d'Education d'Ontario; French university professors; highly-placed executives in the business and industrial world; presidents and some past presidents of French and French-English voluntary associations; the programme director of the French-language radio station CJBC; former editors of two of the defunct French newspapers; plus other contacts and attendance at meetings and one national convention of French voluntary associations.[36]

Overall, there are at least four areas in which the sample is biased. All have been referred to above. One is the limitation of simple recognition of French names. Another is the overrepresentation of males who were heads of house-

---

[34]Dennis H. Wrong, "Social Inequality without Stratification," *Canadian Review of Sociology and Anthropology*, I, No. 1 (February, 1964), 5-16.

[35]Jean-Charles Falardeau, "The Changing Structures of Contemporary French-Canadian Society," in Marcel Rioux and Yves Martin, eds., *French-Canadian Society* (Toronto: McClelland and Stewart, 1964), p. 117.

[36]Some thirty-five interviews additional to the sample were conducted with members of the French middle class. This number included one-third of the membership of the Club Richelieu. Two methods were used in conducting these interviews. In some the interview schedule used for the representative sample was utilized buth the exact words of the respondent not always recorded. Other interviews were conducted without a schedule in order to elicit a freer response. In the latter, hastily scribbled notes, or none at all, were taken, and immediately after the interview a tape recorder was used to record the substance of the interview. Direct quotations are used in this study where the exact words of the respondent were available. Otherwise, where accurate records of the substance of what was said can be secured from the tape record, the third person is used to communicate information.

holds and the underrepresentation of French wives of non-French husbands. A third is the underrepresentation of respondents in the age brackets under thirty years of age, both married and unmarried. This resulted partly from the usage of the Toronto Directory which lists mainly heads of households, and partly from the conduct of interviews during the day when those under thirty years of age are usually at work.

The fourth bias has implications throughout the study. The sample was chosen from the five major areas of concentration of the French population, supplemented by spot-sampling. The proximity to the French parish and bilingual school of such areas within the city has given a definite bias in favour of higher attendance at the French parish, at bilingual schools, at French voluntary associations, a greater use of the French language in all circumstances, and greater recognition of French leadership than are probable throughout the entire French population of Metropolitan Toronto. Attention has been drawn to this bias throughout the study.

Chapter III

Historical Perspectives

This chapter surveys the historical background of French settlement in Toronto with three objectives in mind: to discover the basic characteristics peculiar to Toronto as a community which have determined the slow rate of growth and low density of the French population throughout the history of settlement in the area; to trace the origins of the French migrants which have contributed to the existing heterogeneity of cultural background within the French minority; and to analyze the development of parish organization in quest of the reasons why the French parish system has remained at the level of a single parish in spite of the tremendous increase in the French population since the parish was founded in 1887.

A. The Settlement of the French in Toronto

"Toronto" was the name given to the "carrying place" or portage route which Indians had used for generations in travelling from Lake Ontario to Lake Huron, via the Humber and Holland Rivers, Lakes Simcoe, Couchiching and Sparrow, and the Severn River. Samuel de Champlain reached the midpoint of this route from the north in the year 1615 and sent his young interpreter, Etienne Brulé, with a small band of Indians on an errand to the south. He thus bestowed upon the young man the honour of being the first recorded white man not only to gaze over the broad expanse of Lake Ontario, but to stand upon the site of the future city of Toronto. Subsequently Robert de La Salle used the route a number of times in the course of his explorations, so the French became aware of the strategic importance of this short-cut to the upper lakes, especially since the Toronto Carrying-Place was a channel of the Indian fur-trade with the Dutch and English at Albany, and later Oswego. In the later part of the seventeenth century the Sulpician missionary Père Joseph Mariet established the first settlement on the site of Toronto.[1]

Intermittent warfare with the Iroquois Federation, however, whose Seneca tribe had established the village of Teiaiagon at the mouth of the Humber River during the seventeenth century, effectively restricted French movements in the area. Not until after the Treaty of Utrecht in 1713 restored peace with the English did the French return to the west end of the lake. By this time the Iroquois had disappeared from the north shore of Lake Ontario and an Algonquin tribe, the Mississaugas, had established a new village at the foot of the Carrying-Place. The name Toronto, which had been applied to the whole route, now became localized at the mouth of the Humber River.[2]

[1]D. C. Masters, *The Rise of Toronto, 1850-1890* (Toronto: University of Toronto Press, 1947), p. 3.

[2]Katherine Hale, *Toronto* (Toronto: Cassell and Co. Ltd., 1956), pp. 11-12.

In 1720, the French built a fur-trading post, known as "le poste du fonde du lac" or "le poste de Toronto," not far from the Indian village. At first trade flourished, then languished, and finally the post was abandoned in 1730. Another twenty years elapsed before the French made a determined effort to control the Indian fur-trade with the English colonies by building Fort Toronto on the site of the old fur-trading post. The following year it was found expedient to build a larger and more adequate structure three miles to the east, at the foot of what is now Dufferin Street. It was named Fort Rouillé, after the French Minister of Marine and Colonies, but was still known locally as Fort Toronto. Its existence was short, however, as the French period was brought abruptly to a close in 1759 when Fort Rouillé was burned by orders of its commandant, Captain Alexander Donville, in order to prevent its capture by the British.[3]

From the beginning of the British regime the eclipse of the French has been almost complete. Very little has been recorded from 1760 until the present day regarding the nature and size of the French population apart from the decennial census reports beginning in 1851. It is known that the French fur-trading family of Bâby from Detroit established a trade-store on the Humber in 1762, and its location is still indicated by the Baby Point district in West Toronto. Jean Baptiste Rousseau arrived from Montreal in 1770 and opened a second store nearer the mouth of the Humber. He had considerable influence on the development of the future settlement of the area as he was an Indian linguist like his father before him, and acted as a government interpreter on many occasions and as an intermediary in negotiations between the British, French and Indians.

In 1787, Lord Dorchester, the Governor-General, having become aware of the potentialities of the Toronto site with its excellent harbour and wishing to ensure the future expansion of the fur-trade westward through the strategically located route to the upper lakes, arranged to purchase a tract of land from the Mississauga Indians at Toronto, and in the following year it was surveyed for a town site. Settlement became a reality only in 1793, however, when Lieutenant Governor Simcoe, having decided that Toronto possessed the finest harbour and was potentially the most easily defensible location on the north shore of the lake, chose it for the establishment of the capital of Upper Canada and renamed it York. With its British garrison and its coterie of government officials, York possessed a thoroughly British character from the very beginning. As a provincial capital it soon gained importance for the role of government was far-reaching, and alongside it a business, industrial and financial community soon grew up. In 1803 the population numbered only 456, but had risen to 2,500 by 1815. The only allusion to the French during this period is a passing reference in a document that some twenty-five French families lived in York prior to the War of 1812.[4]

[3]Masters, *The Rise of Toronto*, p. 3.

[4]Edith G. Firth, ed., *The Town of York, 1793-1815, A Collection of Documents of Early Toronto* (Toronto: The Champlain Society for the Government of Ontario, 1962), p. lxxviii.

The town of York was incorporated as a city in 1834, with a population of 9,265, and its former name, Toronto, restored. The city was well on its way to dominating the economy of Upper Canada by 1850, when its population reached 30,775, and its influence was being felt in the westward expansion of settlement. As the century advanced the overwhelming British character of the population became more and more evident. In 1851 the English (including Welsh), Scottish and Irish represented 91 per cent of the total population and by 1881 it had reached its peak at 93 per cent. From then on the British proportion steadily declined, slowly at first, to 90 per cent in 1901, then more rapidly with the massive immigration of other ethnic groups in the twentieth century. In 1951 the British represented only 69 per cent of the total population in the city of Toronto, and 73 per cent in the metropolitan area. A further decline came during the 1950s, the period of greatest non-British immigration, when the British population slumped to 52 per cent within the city and 61 per cent in the metropolitan area.

The Growth of the French Population

The population of French origin in 1851 numbered only 467, or 1.5 per cent of the population of Toronto, which was 30,775. As the population of the city grew rapidly in the ensuing decades, the French proportion remained fairly stable, with 1.4 per cent (572) in 1871 and 1.2 per cent (2,526) in 1901. It was still only 1.6 per cent (8,350) in 1921, but climbed to 2.3 per cent (15,135) by 1941. The next two decades showed the greatest proportional growth, still inconsequential in actual density, from 3.2 per cent (21,865) in the city and 2.8 per cent (31,853) in the metropolitan area in 1951, to 4.1 per cent (27,564) in the city and 3.3 per cent (61,421) in the metropolitan area in 1961. It is true that the French population increased as the British population decreased, but this growth was more than counterbalanced by the large non-French immigration. As a result the low ratio of the French population to the total population has been maintained.

The significance for the French culture of a low ratio of the French population to the total population is reflected in the 1961 census record of French as mother tongue. Only three metropolitan areas, Ottawa, Timmins, and Sudbury, had minority French populations numbering more than one-third of the total population of their respective areas (40.8%, 38.8%, 36.1%), and in each case the retention of French as mother tongue has been high (92.4%, 88.4%, 85.0%). But when the proportionate size of the French population drops, as it has in the other fifteen metropolitan areas of Ontario, curtailing the possibilities of social interaction among the members of such minority populations, the retention rate of French as mother tongue also drops, sometimes drastically. In all but one case[5] it has dropped below 50 per cent, even as low as 15 per cent, with

---

[5] James Robert Wilkins, "The French-Canadians of Sarnia" (unpublished undergraduate thesis in Geography, Waterloo Lutheran University, 1967). A homogeneous French-

variations between the areas which are probably due to local patterns of settlement.

In 1961 Metropolitan Toronto occupied a median position among the metropolitan areas of Ontario with a retention rate of French as mother tongue of 42.3 per cent. A proportion of those who no longer claimed French as mother tongue would, of course, maintain French as a second language. This implies potential channels of ethnic communication via the French language among only a part of the French population, even without taking into consideration the social barriers to communication erected by class differences, cultural heterogeneity of background and affiliation with the English Catholic parish system.

The predominantly British character of the city of Toronto throughout its history has been the main deterrent to the growth of the population of French origin. Toronto from its very inception was meant to serve as a bulwark against the expansion of the American colonies northward, and the high proportion of United Empire Loyalists within its population ensured the prevalence of anti-American sentiment. But the overwhelmingly Protestant population tended to be anti-French as well. The hostility toward the French and toward Roman Catholicism appeared early in the growth of the settlement and gradually hardened into a local tradition. The War of 1812, the Rebellion of 1837, and the Fenian Raids of the 1860s all served to crystallize the strongly British and fervent Protestant traditions among the largely homogeneous, English-speaking community. Closely linked by blood and sentiment to Britain, the population reacted militantly to events which in any way challenged the British hegemony, such as the North-West Rebellion of Louis Riel.[6]

A second factor of importance was the strength of the Irish immigration during the nineteenth century. The Irish proportion of the total population was 36 per cent in 1851 and it had grown to 43 per cent by 1871, a larger proportion than that of the English. By 1881, however, the Irish had subsided to 37 per cent of the population, further to 31 per cent in 1901, and continued its gradual decline in the twentieth century. It has been suggested that the decline may be explained partially by the failure of many of the Irish to designate themselves as such and their consequent merging into the population as English.

The Irish influence in the development of Toronto had a double significance for the French-Canadian population. On the one hand, the Irish were responsible for the growth of the Roman Catholic Church, over which they soon established hierarchical control, and through which they became responsible in large measure for the treatment accorded Catholic ethnic minorities such as the French in both parish life and parochial education. On the other hand, the considerable

Canadian neighbourhood existed close to the Polymer Corporation in Sarnia until after the census of 1961, when redevelopment spread the French-speaking community across other areas of the city. The higher rate of retention of French of 54 per cent in spite of the low density of 8.74 per cent in comparison to the total population is probably due to this local variation in distribution of the population.

[6]Masters, *The Rise of Toronto*, pp. 20-21, 211.

influx of Irish Protestants from Northern Ireland transplanted to the Canadian scene the Orange Order which had caused so much trouble between the Protestant and Catholic Churches in their homeland. The Orange Order served to unite Protestants against both Roman Catholics and French Canadians. Parades or special events arranged by either side were often the occasions of scenes of bitter animosity in which the smaller Catholic population was often at a disadvantage.[7]

The political climate in Toronto in the nineteenth century and on into the twentieth was a third factor which was in general harmony with the attitudes of British Protestants and particularly of Orangemen. The prevailing and at times rabid Toryism of the population exalted the Empire and especially the monarchy, and was coupled with a marked antipathy for Americans and the Roman Catholic Church, as well as hostility toward Lower Canada or Quebec. The last of these attitudes appeared to have been shared by both political parties during the Red River Insurrection when the general outcry could be summed up as ". . . no compromise with the French."[8] A Canada First movement which tended to exalt the British and intensify hatred of the French was a product of this period of Toronto's history. The cause was bolstered by the fiery editor of the Toronto *Globe*, George Brown, who wielded a wide influence for many years. He shared with Toryism a fervent loyalty for things British, and his strong anti-French and anti-Catholic sentiments were widely propagated through his newspaper.[9]

In spite of such opposition the Roman Catholic Church grew steadily. According to an early Toronto historian, Robertson, the first Catholic services were held in the town of York as early as 1797-1798. The community's first priest, later Bishop Macdonnell, arrived in 1805, although the first permanently-resident priest, James Crowley, was not stationed in York until 1821. St. Paul's Catholic Church was built on Power Street near the Don River in 1826, and when the Diocese of Toronto was erected in 1841 it served as the Cathedral Church until St. Michael's Cathedral was completed in 1848.[10] By 1851, Roman Catholics constituted 26 per cent of the population of Toronto, of which 6 per cent were French Canadians. By the end of the century in 1901, the Catholic proportion had dropped to 15 per cent but the French proportion in the Church had climbed to 11 per cent. At the mid-point of the present century in 1951, both proportions had climbed to some degree, the Catholic proportion of the population up to 20 per cent, of which the French constituted 17 per cent. The latest census in 1961 shows the results of the massive influx of European Catholics, for the Roman Catholic proportion of the metropolitan population had climbed to 26 per cent, of which the Italians represented 30 per cent, the French Catholics dropping to 13 per cent.

[7]Ibid., p. 38.
[8]Ibid., pp. 27, 128.
[9]Ibid., p. 29.
[10]Ibid., p. 38.

A fourth consideration of significance as an environmental factor for the population of French origin has been the nature of the city as a trading and commercial center. From its earliest days Toronto served as the market place for a vast hinterland which continually expanded both northward and westward to eventually include the new provinces of the prairies. Transportation played its part as the early roads were built out from the harbour and helped to develop trade, government and defense. Railways brought a dramatic change, accelerating the growth of Toronto as the center of the region. The rise of the motor vehicle resulted in both people and industry gradually spreading outwards as congestion increased in the expanding city. At the present time one-third of the purchasing power of all of Canada is within one hundred miles of the downtown area of Toronto. This provides a firm foundation for Toronto's diversified industry and strong support for its business and financial community.[11]

As a national center of trade and commerce Toronto early developed a rivalry with Montreal for control of the westward expansion of Canada in the sphere of finance, commerce and industry. The failures in Upper Canada of important financial institutions such as banks during the nineteenth century were blamed with some justification on the tactics of Montreal financial interests. It did little to encourage harmonious relationships between Ontario and Quebec, although the increasingly interlocking character of the capital structures of both cities has tended to mitigate the tensions of the rivalry.[12]

The financial, commercial and industrial characteristics of Toronto during most of its history held little attraction for the French Canadian reared in the traditional rural parish. If he sought employment in Toronto he had to contend with a hostile atmosphere in which his language, culture and religion were a constant source of discomfort, discrimination and, occasionally, of deliberate insult. A French Canadian who has resided in Toronto for over forty years claimed that few of the French could endure the cultural climate of Toronto for more than three years. They migrated to New England, and later to Northern Ontario, but by-passed British and Protestant Toronto. But the growing industrialization and urbanization of Quebec, as well as of Ontario, has spawned a different type of French Canadian, the urban worker, who has been more willing to seek employment wherever he can find the highest wages, even if it has meant forsaking his traditional cultural environment. This has become increasingly evident as the twentieth century moved along, especially in the last two decades.

Finally, immigration drastically altered the composition of the population and hence of the relationship of the French to the British population during the last part of the nineteenth and throughout the twentieth century. Beginning as a mere trickle prior to the turn of the century, it quickened almost to flood proportions after the new century began, subsided during both world wars with some expansion in between them, and then became a flood again after World

[11]City of Toronto Planning Board, *A New Plan for Toronto* (Toronto, 1966), pp. 9-10.
[12]Masters, *The Rise of Toronto*, pp. 70, 112, 115, 119, 165.

War II. The opportunities for employment presented by the vast financial, commercial and industrial complex which developed in Southern Ontario around Toronto as its center proved so attractive to immigrants that by 1960 thirty-four minority ethnic groups were of sufficient size to be included in a special study by the City of Toronto Planning Board,[13] while several others were noted as being present in smaller numbers. The largest of such groups are shown in relation to the population of French origin in Tables 2 and 3 below.

Table 2

Growth of the Main Minority Ethnic Groups, City of Toronto, From 1901 to 1961

Ethnic Group	1901	1911	1921	1931	1941	1951	1961
Italian[a]	1,025	4,617	8,217	13,015	9,328	18,441	77,898
German	4,728	9,775	4,689	9,343	3,084	11,585	30,748
French	2,526	4,886	8,350	10,869	15,135	21,865	27,564
Polish	138	700	2,380	8,483	10,317	20,857	27,191
Ukrainian	n.a.	n.a.	1,149	4,434	10,479	23,383	26,097
Jewish	3,043	18,237	34,619	45,305	39,663	40,809	11,264

[a]Arranged in order of their size in 1961.
Source: *Census of Canada* for the years 1901, 1911, 1921, 1931, 1941, 1951, and 1961.

The German minority was the largest during the last three decades of the nineteenth century ending with the census of 1901. Then they were displaced through the heavy Jewish immigration which took place just after the turn of the century, a position of numerical superiority which the Jews maintained for half of the century, before moving almost en masse to the suburbs during the decade of the fifties. The French minority became the second largest with the census of 1921 and remained so until after 1951. In the meantime both German and Italian populations suffered depletion during the two world wars when many left Canada and none came in, although moderate expansion took place in the peace years of the twenties and thirties. It was not until the massive influx of the Italians in the fifties that their numbers soared to three times that of the French in the city and almost that proportion in the metropolitan area. Post-war German immigration also expanded rapidly, surpassing the number of the French in the city and becoming one-third larger in metro. The position of the French in 1961 was that of the third largest minority ethnic group, closely followed by the Polish, Jewish and Ukrainians, as seen in Table 3.

[13]City of Toronto Planning Board, *Ethnic Origins of the Population of Toronto, 1960.*

Table 3

Growth of Main Minority Ethnic Groups,
Metropolitan Area of Toronto, 1941 to 1961

Ethnic Group	1941	1951	1961
Italian[a]	17,887	27,962	140,378
German	11,529	19,329	80,300
French	19,423	31,853	61,421
Polish	13,094	26,998	58,578
Jewish	52,779	59,448	53,123
Ukrainian	11,823	29,262	46,650

[a]Arranged in order of their size in 1961.
Source: *Census of Canada*, 1941, 1951, and 1961.

B. The Origins of the French Population

A major characteristic of the members of the French population of Toronto
has been their diversity in terms of place of origin. The migrants have come from
all parts of Canada: Acadians from the Maritime Provinces, Quebeckers from
various areas in that province, Franco-Ontarians from both northern and southern regions, and from Western Canada. Franco-Americans have moved to Toronto from the United States, and the immigrant French from France and other
European countries such as Belgium. Because of this regional diversity of origin,
significant differences in social background divide the French population in spite
of common ethnic origin. This lack of social homogeneity is further complicated
by cultural differences between urban and rural migrants, and by economic
differentiation arising out of social and occupational mobility.

The primary cleavage is that between the French Canadians and the French
immigrants from France or adjoining countries in Europe. The evidence on
which this rests is the incompatibility of the two groups. Even though both share
a remote ancestral background, the long separation of centuries between the
continental and Canadian segments of the French people has not only permitted
the North American environment to modify the language, values, norms and
goals of French Canadians, but it has also isolated them from the liberalizing
currents of thought in France since the French Revolution in 1789. As a result,
little fraternization takes place between them with the exception of a few of the
French-Canadian middle class. When it does occur the French Canadian com-
plains that there is condescension on the part of the immigrant French as if the
French spoken in Canada as well as French-Canadian culture are somehow infe-
rior to the European. The continental Frenchman appears very conscious of his
status as an immigrant, and seeks through his numerous clubs and organizations

to preserve his identity in ways common to most ethnic groups. On the other hand, the French Canadian is proud of his status as a native Canadian and makes every effort to avoid classification as an immigrant. He resents being identified, as he often is by language, with immigrants from another country, even though they come from the same parent stock.

Table 4

French Adult Population[a] of the Metropolitan Area of Toronto According to Place of Origin

Place of Origin	Number	Percentage
New Brunswick	4,078	10.32
Other Atlantic Provinces	3,482	8.81
Quebec	7,660	19.39
Ontario	19,609	49.63
Western Provinces and Territories	1,525	3.86
United States of America	835	2.11
Other Countries	2,323	5.88
Total French Born in Canada	36,354	92.00
Total Adult French	39,512	100.00

[a]Includes only those fifteen years of age and over.
Source: *Census of Canada, 1961.* A special summary of the French ethnic group by census tracts—birthplace, for Metropolitan Toronto, compiled by the Dominion Bureau of Statistics for the Royal Commission on Bilingualism and Biculturalism.

A second source of differentiation within the French population has been the regionalism by province or smaller area which has isolated many of the French groups represented in Toronto from one another for a long time, allowing the development of divergent interests, attitudes and values. For instance, the Acadians have led a largely separate existence in the Maritimes almost as long as the continental separation of the French of Quebec from their homeland in Europe. Their unique historical experience, coupled with a low level of education and retarded urbanization and industrialization has resulted in a minimum of interests being held in common with the urbanized French from Quebec or Southern Ontario. They feel more at home with those from Gaspé or Northern Ontario who are not typical of the French urban dweller. The principal of the bilingual school associated with the Sacré-Coeur parish in Toronto attributed the quarrelsomeness of the Acadian children in the school to a basic insecurity arising out of an inadequate grasp of the French language and culture and the poverty which kept many of their parents on city welfare. Consequently Acadians do not feel at ease with Quebeckers or Franco-Ontarians and in spite of efforts to encourage attendance at each other's social events and other functions little fraternization has taken place.

The French from Quebec and those from Southern Ontario tend to be much more on a par educationally and share more common interests, working together to a much greater degree in the Toronto milieu. But the latter resent the implication subtly communicated by Quebeckers that they have sold out to the English in terms of both language and culture. They dislike the claim that Quebec speaks for all French Canadians throughout the country, and have often expressed their inability to understand viewpoints current in Quebec regarding the French "nation" in Canada. Much of the leadership in the Toronto population comes from Quebec along with a few Franco-Ontarians, which means that they are over-represented in positions of authority while the Acadians and those from Northern Ontario are underrepresented, another cause of division among the various groups. Those from Western Canada and the United States are only a very small proportion of the French population, and being more anglicized tend to disappear in the English population. This variety and range of regional background has made the attainment of consensus within the French minority a rather remote possibility.

A third form of population differentiation is also present in the form of the contrast in life styles between an urban and a rural background prior to coming to Toronto. On the whole the French population is more representative of the urbanized and industrialized French than it is of the traditional rural French from Quebec, the Maritimes and Ontario. Only 44 per cent of the representative sample interviewed grew up in a rural or semi-rural background. In the suburban areas the rural proportion dropped to 32 per cent. Only one of the five areas of concentration of the French population, Riverdale, had a majority with a rural background, and this was small, 55 per cent.

The occupations of the fathers of respondents provide confirmation of this general picture. Only 25 per cent of the fathers were farmers or fishermen with another 10 to 15 per cent engaged in non-urban occupations. As is evident in Table 5 below, 60 to 65 per cent of the fathers were in urban-type occupations. Among non-farm unskilled labourers were a few bushworkers, and in the skilled category there were sawyers and blacksmiths, but the largest proportion were industrial workers. The proprietors of small butcher, grocery and hardware stores, or small lumber mills, which could be either urban or rural, have been grouped in the table with executives and public officials who are usually located in urban areas. Clerical, sales and services occupations are found in rural areas, but they are more common in urban centres. Ten per cent of those interviewed reported that they had been born and grew up in Toronto. It seems reasonable to conclude that the families in which respondents grew up were predominately urban in background.

Table 5

Occupations of the Fathers of Respondents
in the Metropolitan Toronto Sample

Occupations	Number	Percentage
Professionals, Technicians and Kindred	6	2.38
Proprietors, Managers and Officials	24	9.52
Clerical and Sales	13	5.16
Skilled (Craftsmen and Foremen)	70	27.78
Semi-Skilled (Operators and Kindred)	23	9.13
Service (Protective, Public and Private)	12	4.76
Unskilled (Labourers, Non-Farm)	39	15.48
Farmers and Fishermen	63	25.00
Not Ascertainable	2	.79
Totals	252	100.00

The presence of migrants from both types of backgrounds, however, has affected to some degree their patterns of living after reaching Toronto. Franco-Ontarians from Northern Ontario have usually been reared in a rural environment whose focal centre is the bilingual parish and school, while those from Southern Ontario have been scattered among an English population which is predominantly urban, and therefore tend to be more urbanized and anglicized. Migrants from the Province of Quebec illustrated the same dichotomy. The urbanites from Montreal, Quebec and other large centres display very different life styles from their rural counterparts from the eastern and northern townships and the Gaspé. The tendency has been for those who grew up in rural areas with their lower level of education and lack of industrial skills to congregate in the lower-class districts of the city where housing was cheaper and where there is a greater demand for unskilled labour. The more occupationally-mobile urbanites have preferred the suburbs as a place of residence.

A fourth source of differentiation has been the socio-economic, the stratification of the migrant population in terms of occupation, education, income and residence, which adds the dimension of social class to an already diversified French population.

In summary, two major patterns have emerged in the history of French settlement in Toronto which have influenced the development and maintenance of ethnic identification among the migrants. One is the slow, gradual growth of the French population due to the various factors which have tended to inhibit French migration to a British, Protestant city. The other pattern has been the fragmentation of the French population through regional diversity of origin with consequent disparities of cultural background. Among the French migrants to

Toronto there has existed little of the cultural homogeneity which is necessary to the formation and maintenance of a collective sense of ethnic identity.

C. The Development of Parish Organization

The French parish of the Sacré-Coeur was the first national or ethnic parish in Toronto when it was established in 1887. A national parish provides means of ethnic identification for both individuals and families in multiethnic communities because its activities are conducted in the mother tongue and follow the distinctive cultural patterns familiar to its parishioners, all within the religious heritage of minority group members. Such parishes therefore impart a sense of belonging in the midst of an alien majority culture.[14] Consequently, as immigration contributed both to the growth of the city and of the Roman Catholic Church, other minorities established national parishes.

By the mid-1960s when Metropolitan Toronto had grown to a population of over two million, the Roman Catholic Diocese of Toronto possessed seventy-two parishes within the boundaries of the Metropolitan Corporation and several others in the fringe areas beyond. Twenty-one of these parishes were national or ethnic parishes, of which the Italians had four, the Polish three, the Lithuanians and Slovenians two each, and ten single parishes, the Croatian, Czech, Dutch, French, German, Hungarian, Latvian, Maltese, Portuguese, and Slovak.[15]

It is evident that in spite of its early beginning when the French population numbered less than two thousand, the Sacré-Coeur remained the only French parish when the French population was well over sixty thousand. When one considers the strategic role which the Catholic Church has performed within French-Canadian society[16] it is relevant to ask, why has the French parish system in Toronto remained at the level of a single parish in spite of the vast increase in the French population of the area?

A brief historical survey suggests possible answers as it follows the development of the Sacré-Coeur through three phases of its existence: the initial communal phase preceding and following the turn of the century; the transitional phase as continuing growth of the urban-industrial community brought ecological changes and socio-economic differentiation to the parish constituency; and the present phase beginning in the 1950s which has culminated in the contemporary downtown urban parish.

[14]At different times the Holy See at Rome has safeguarded the rights of immigrants to worship in their mother tongue, thus helping to preserve their allegiance to the Roman Catholic Church. See T. J. Harte, "Racial and National Parishes," in L. J. Nuesse and T. J. Harte, eds., The Sociology of the Parish (Milwaukee: The Bruce Publishing Company, 1951), pp. 159-60.

[15]The Catholic Directory for Ontario, a publication produced and sold by the Newman Clubs of the universities, which lists each diocese in the province, all diocesan office holders, parishes and their priests, hours of services, parish organizations, and other information.

[16]In brief "the religious ideology expresses the ultimate values of the society and supports the forms of life of that society." Miner, Saint-Denis, p. 104.

Until nearly the end of the nineteenth century, French-speaking residents of Toronto had no alternative but to attend English parishes. At the mid-point of the century the French population was small, numbering 467, and only 572 two decades later. So the English parishes of St. Patrick's on McCaul Street and St. Basil's off Bay near Bloor Streets made provision from time to time for the services of a French-Canadian priest.[17] French Canadians, however, were not satisfied with this arrangement because in addition to language, significant differences in religious and cultural traditions exist between the French and the English branches of the Roman Catholic Church,[18] the product of Quebec's virtual isolation from both Europe and the rest of North America until well into the nineteenth century.

The situation continued unchanged until further migration more than doubled the French population in the 1870s and 1880s. While preaching a retreat at St. Patrick's parish in May, 1887, the Reverend Father Déféanse, C.S.S.R., noticed the number of French Canadians present and suggested that they seek the establishment of a parish of their own. Responding to a petition, Msgr. Lynch, then Archbishop of Toronto, requested Msgr. Fabre of Montreal to send a French-Canadian priest to Toronto.[19]

> At length a French-Canadian priest was brought from Montreal and given special charge over all the French Catholics of the City. On the 26th of June he held his first services in the St. Vincent-de-Paul Chapel, in St. Michael's Palace, where they remained for fifteen months. Then an old Presbyterian Church on King Street, between Power Street and the Don was purchased, and having been refitted, was blessed on October 7th, 1888, by the late Vicar-General Laurent.[20]

The Communal Phase

As a national parish the Sacré-Coeur differed from the surrounding territorial English parishes because its boundaries were not a circumscribed area of the city within which all Catholics are members of one parish. The French parish included all those of French origin throughout the city and even beyond who sought to use their mother tongue in their religious duties. Thus ethnic homogeneity was substituted for territorial homogeneity, facilitating the maintenance

---

[17]This arrangement served two purposes within the Diocese: priests representing more than one ethnic group could serve the needs of a mixed population when the ethnic proportions warranted such provision; and second, the constant exposure to the English language in a mixed parish usually led to the gradual phasing out of any language other than English.

[18]Harte, "Racial and National Parishes," p. 157.

[19]Part of the material on the development of parish organization was gathered by Mrs. Danièle J. Lee, French-Canadian assistant to the present study, who did a participant-observation study of the Sacré-Coeur as part of her responsibilities. For a full treatment of her study see her M.A. thesis entitled "The Evolution of an Ethnic Parish" (Department of Sociology, University of Toronto, 1967).

[20]A. Lamarche, O.P., "La Paroisse du Sacré-Coeur, 1887-1933" (a small pamphlet telling of the history and major events and personalities of the Sacré-Coeur).

of the French language and culture by providing a milieu in which ethnic solidarity could be expressed, and assimilation to the majority culture retarded.

During the early years just before and after the turn of the century the identification of ethnicity and religion was easily perpetuated because the French population served by the parish came from similar backgrounds in the largely rural parishes of Quebec and the Maritimes. They shared almost identical status as unskilled, poorly-educated wage workers. They faced similar problems in finding jobs, in securing housing for large families in working-class districts, and in adapting to the language handicap in a predominantly English-speaking, Protestant environment. As a consequence the parish developed many of the characteristics usually associated with the communal type of parish in rural areas. The parish priest dominated the scene, organizing associations and multiplying both religious and social activities in order to draw the French migrants within the orbit of parish life.

One of his first concerns was the organization of a bilingual school,[21] utilizing the basement of the church building as a classroom. Initially he assumed the role of teacher but within three years there were seventy-six pupils enrolled and he had to turn to the ranks of his parishioners for teaching assistance. He maintained a relationship to his flock as counsellor and educator, not only in the things of the spirit but also in the concerns of everyday living. A commemorative pamphlet issued on an anniversary in 1933 sought to capture in print the family-like atmosphere of the communal phase of the Sacré-Coeur:

> La paroisse de Sacré-Coeur, par bon église, par son école à formation française, par ses cercles et ses différentes organizations est réellement le centre de la vie française à Toronto et par son rôle social elle s'imposes à l'admiration de tous.[22]

The Transitional Phase

A gradual weakening of the communal nature of the parish came as urban expansion continued to scatter French migrants over an increasingly wider area of the city, making distance to the Sacré-Coeur a major problem for newcomers. When the French population expanded from 4,886 in 1911 to 8,350 in 1921, more and more of the migrants attended English parishes instead of affiliating with the Sacré-Coeur. Instead of increased attendance at the French parish commensurate with the growth of the French population there were repeated de-

---

[21]Only the French parish possessed the legal right in the Province of Ontario to establish bilingual schools supported by public funds up to and including Grade 10. In Toronto the Italians, Polish, Germans, Slovenians, and other immigrant groups who established national parishes sent their children to English-speaking parochial schools. Private schools had to be supported entirely by parish funds.

[22]Lamarche, "La Paroisse du Sacré-Coeur, 1887-1933." Even as late as the 1940s it was written that: "Pour les Canadiens français, cependant, selon l'antique tradition toujours vivante, tout se centralise dans la paroisse, autour au clocher." C. Lachapelle, "La vie française à Toronto," in Documents Historiques, No. 13 (Sudbury: La Société Historique du Nouvel-Ontario), p. 44, quotation in Lee, "Evolution of an Ethnic Parish," p. 49.

mands for the establishment of a west-end parish closer to the industrial area in Parkdale where so many of the French migrants had found employment and residence.

In 1919, plans were implemented to establish a west-end parish at 96 Indian Grove where the parish of St. Joan of Arc is now situated. But the project was beyond the financial resources of French-Canadian parishioners with their mainly low-income, unskilled employment. Part of the building collapsed during construction and then the post-war depression set in. By 1930, the parish had been taken over completely by English-speaking parishioners. It was a serious setback for the French in West Toronto who had agitated for a national parish more conveniently located. It had already become evident that a single French parish could not effectively serve the rapidly-growing and thinly-scattered French population.

A second departure from the original communal parish pattern developed through a change of clerical leadership in the mid-1920s. The degree to which an ethnic parish performs an ethnic role depends to a large extent upon the parish priest's conception of the dual nature of an ethnic parish, both religious and ethnic. The dual role of the parish was perpetuated during the communal phase of the Sacré-Coeur because the priest accepted as an integral part of his religious ministry the ethnic role of making sure that the traditional unity of the Catholic faith with the French language and culture was not broken. But the different personality of his successor and the changing nature of the parish environment combined to produce in practice a different conception of the role of the French parish.

On the one hand, the influence upon clerical leadership of the failure of the west-end parish led to a policy of seeking to maintain the Sacré-Coeur as the one centre of French Catholic life and bilingual education in Toronto. Subsequent actions of the clergy were geared to this strategy in spite of the radical changes in the urban milieu which went on during the next four decades. On the other hand, the parish priest and his curates became involved daily with "typically urban problems, such as family disorganization, over-crowding, inadequate provision for health and recreation, racial tensions, labor-management conflict, unemployment and poverty."[23] During the Great Depression of the 1930s these problems were so multiplied that ethnic concerns were relegated to a secondary place or ignored entirely. The ethnic role of the parish suffered eclipse at the very time when the Sacré-Coeur was the only focal point of French identification in Toronto.

This preoccupation of the clergy with social and welfare problems created division within the parish because another social process, the socio-economic differentiation which is characteristic of industrial communities, was changing the earlier class homogeneity of the French population. A growing middle class,

[23]D. H. Fosselman, C.S.C., "The Parish in Urban Communities," in L. J. Nuesse and T. J. Harte, eds., *The Sociology of the Parish* (Milwaukee: The Bruce Publishing Company, 1951), p. 151.

chiefly migrants from Quebec, visualized the Sacré-Coeur as more than a religious welfare agency, necessary as this was to the community. They believed that the survival of the French language and culture required implementation of an ethnic role by the national parish if it were to justify its existence within a French-speaking population.

The development of such class divisions can be attributed in large part to the ethnic nature of national parishes within an expanding urban environment. In large cities the territorial limits which define the boundaries of the ordinary urban parish ensure a certain degree of residential and hence class homogeneity. But ethnic parishes lack closely-defined territorial limits. The homogeneity gained in terms of ethnicity tends to be lost in terms of class because parishioners may come from all areas of the city and suburbs. This has been particularly true of Toronto where a single parish has sought to serve an urbanized area of over 240 square miles. In these circumstances, the ethnic nature of the Sacré-Coeur, which had been its strength during the initial communal phase of its existence, now became a divisive influence. Ethnically-oriented class values were now competing with religiously-oriented welfare values.

The disunity arising out of divergent class values was sharpened when factories began to proliferate in the area of the parish in the early 1930s and threatened to engulf the parish buildings. Housing deteriorated and parishioners moved from the district. Permission was given to erect a new church in another location.[24] A site at the upper end of the parish neighbourhood, located at the corner of Sherbourne and Bloor Streets, was offered to the parish free of charge. It was conveniently situated across the road from a desirable middle and upper-class residential area, Rosedale. But the parish priest declined the offer on the grounds that it was too far from the poor and indigent of his flock, although the actual distance was only a few city blocks. So the yellow brick church and presbytery were erected at the corner of Sherbourne and Carlton Streets, much to the disappointment of middle and working-class parishioners who had opposed relocation within an obviously declining neighbourhood.

When the new parish buildings were completed in 1937, Sherbourne and nearby Jarvis Streets were still lined with the former mansions of Toronto's upper class, with a few of the families still in residence. But the same ecological changes which had sent most of the wealthy in flight to the suburbs earlier in the century were still operative in reducing the parish district to lower-working-class status. Stately houses were taken over one by one for conversion to temporary offices or rooming houses during the 1940s and 1950s, while housing in general assumed a slum-like character. Those who remained in the neighbourhood were mainly Acadians from New Brunswick along with the more poorly educated from Northern Ontario and Quebec.

[24]Permission to relocate was granted provided the new parish was free of debt from the beginning, a serious handicap during depression years of widespread unemployment. Well-to-do parishioners assisted with large contributions, but it was the heavy investment by the parish priest of an inheritance which enabled this condition to be met.

The French parish still continued to serve as a staging or reception agency for French-speaking newcomers to the city. French residents who had settled in Toronto in the 1940s and 1950s stated in interviews that they went to the Sacré-Coeur when they first arrived in Toronto. But after a period of time, sometimes quite short, they turned to English parishes in spite of the urging of the French clergy to settle close to the national parish. Members of the middle class, with few exceptions, refused to live in the midst of commercial and institutional establishments where housing was substandard. Even the working class who had settled in the area moved to other parts of the city and suburbs as soon as economically feasible. From there they seldom travelled to the Sacré-Coeur.

A number of attempts were made by members of the middle class in the 1940s to have the parish priest replaced by one who was more nationalistically-minded, and who was less authoritarian in his leadership role, but without success.[25] Indifferent to this current of dissatisfaction, the parish priest devoted himself almost exclusively to his religious duties and welfare responsibilities. He continued to identify with his lower-class parishioners, who constituted the majority of his flock, while a succession of curates, all but one of them Franco-Ontarians, compensated by sponsoring organizations which catered to middle-class parishioners. Class divisions were thus introduced into the clerical leadership of the parish and resulted in controversy over the roles of both clergy and parishioners in an ethnic parish.[26]

One result of this situation was an attempt by a number of the French middle class in the 1950s to promote the establishment of a west-end parish which would fulfill what they considered to be lacking in the Sacré-Coeur, the ethnic role of ensuring the survival of the French as a distinct cultural entity in Toronto. Apparently they had received some assurance from the Diocese that the project would be viewed with favour if a sufficient number of French-speaking families were interested both spiritually and financially. A curate of the Sacré-Coeur who was sympathetic to these aspirations visited French families throughout the west-end and found about 500 families who expressed interest and pledged $30,000 toward the purchase of a Protestant church building made available by the merger of two Protestant congregations.

But clerical leadership when apprized of the plan still favoured a single centre of French parish life in Toronto, so the project never developed beyond the survey stage. Ignored was the fact that in spite of every effort to concentrate the French population near the parish they had scattered throughout the city and

[25] The following comment of a prominent member of the French middle-class probably represents an extreme but prevalent point of view among some of the migrants: "If the personality of the French priest had been more welcoming to stray French it would have been different. He turned them away. He was hard to get along with, a real dictator. Why go to the French parish and get abused? Go to an English parish and be a nonentity but welcomed. I brought it to the attention of Cardinal M. He told me to be careful of the priest as he was not well. The Father had built the church with his own funds and he couldn't put him out. The Cardinal would not do anything."

[26] Lee, "Evolution of an Ethnic Parish," p. 52.

suburbs. Very few of the families who had signified interest in the new parish attended the Sacré-Coeur, even sporadically. The same policy was also evident in 1961 in clerical opposition to the establishment in the suburb of Scarborough of a bilingual school which would be independent of the Sacré-Coeur. But in this case the middle-class sponsors were successful in persuading the Separate School Board of Education in the municipality to go ahead with the project.

The Contemporary Phase

The culmination of the gradual process of displacement of the ethnic role of the national parish by its religious role was the appointment in 1962 of a Franco-Ontarian as parish priest. It was both logical and practical for a Catholic diocese situated in the Province of Ontario to appoint a Franco-Ontarian to a Toronto parish. But the move was viewed with suspicion by members of the middle-class who had migrated from Quebec. The greater acculturation of Franco-Ontarians to English-speaking society was interpreted by them as indifference to the survival of the French language and culture.

The new parish priest did little to allay their fears. He had been born and educated in Ontario and had taught in English for thirty years. Consequently he was more at home in English than in French, although he spoke the latter fluently. But his relatives who looked after the Presbytery spoke only English, and when his curate spoke to him in French he was almost invariably answered in English. Thus while his religious qualifications were beyond question, many of his parishioners regarded him as an English Canadian and therefore unqualified to exercise a leadership role in a French parish.

Some parishioners even argued that his nomination represented a subtle method of limiting French culture in Toronto.[27] In his study of the Franco-Americans of New England, Theriault points out that priests appointed to Franco-American parishes were often approaching the end of their careers and were given secure posts with curates as assistants. He comments:

> Since these appointments were in the hands of the hierarchy of the Church, it appears likely that the absence of vigorous leadership in the "national" parishes reflected a basic policy of not encouraging the further development of such parishes.[28]

Neither the Franco-Ontarian parish priest nor his curate adjusted his clerical role to harmonize with the ethnic nature of the parish which they served. Both interpreted their roles in strictly religious and not ethnic terms. As a conse-

---

[27]Official Catholic policy regarding national parishes in North America was that "the Church intends it to be an exceptional organizational device. The Code of Canon Law lays down the general norm that such parishes may not be established without a special indut from the Holy See (not necessary for territorial parishes). There exists a decided preference of the Church for the territorial type of organization." Harte, "Racial and National Parishes," p. 158.

[28]Theriault, "Franco-Americans of New England," p. 406.

quence, the formal organization of the parish deviated only linguistically from the established blueprint for the typical territorial parish, especially the pattern of downtown urban parishes. The Sacré-Coeur had now become a specialized urban institution in terms of both its clerical leadership and parish organizations, performing its functions for only a segment of the French-Canadian population.

From the foregoing it is evident that the contemporary French parish epitomizes the end product of a trend of development which has been controlled by two major influences within the Toronto milieu, the Diocese of Toronto and the urban-industrial environment. On the one hand, the French parish could not evade the impact of the larger English Catholic diocesan structure within which it had been shaped and must function. The appointment of its clerical leadership rested with the English-speaking hierarchy. It was surrounded by English parishes to which it suffered the constant loss of an acculturating membership. On the other hand, the parish symbolizes the ways in which industrialization and urbanization have left their marks on every urban Catholic parish. Even French-Canadian parishes in urban areas, which have retained the traits of rural parishes to an unusual degree, cannot escape the effects of urban sprawl, of socio-economic differentiation with resultant changes in residence, outlook, associational affiliations, and cultural values. The urban parish, unlike its rural counterpart, neither encompasses the whole community, nor absorbs more than a part of the interests of its parishioners.

> The more secular urbanite remains satisfied with a minimum of religious practices; the community to which he feels bound is not the parochial group, but the whole urban community. . . . Except for a small nucleus of devout people who focus their social life on active participation in parochially organized, religious associations, the majority of the people in urban parishes are only nominal members of these associations and set a higher value on membership in associations organized around secular interests.[29]

[29]J. C. Falardeau, "The Parish as an Institutional Type," in B. R. Blishen, et al., eds., Canadian Society (Toronto: The Macmillan Company, 1961), p. 426.

Chapter IV

Patterns of Settlement in Toronto

The historical context of French migration to Toronto has conditioned the spatial, occupational and social class distribution of the French population in such a way as to encourage social participation within the English host society rather than the French minority population. In this chapter these three dominant group patterns, residence, occupation and social status, are discussed in relation to their influence upon social participation and consequently upon ethnic identity.

A. The Spatial Pattern

The distribution of the French population within Metropolitan Toronto is unusual for a large ethnic minority. In 1961, 65 per cent of the French residents were spread so evenly across the metropolitan area that French population densities fell routinely between 1 and 3 per cent in most census tracts. Only three clusters of census tracts within the city, located in the Don, Riverdale and Parkdale districts, and two clusters in the suburbs, in the Lakeshore and Scarborough municipalities, showed higher densities. As shown on the accompanying map of Metropolitan Toronto, they ranged from 4 to 15 per cent,[1] and accounted for a further 30 per cent of the French population. The remaining 5 per cent were in widely-scattered, isolated census tracts with low densities of 4 to 5 per cent of French residents.

In contrast to ethnic minorities such as the Jews or Italians, none of these areas of concentration has taken the form of an ethnic enclave where the French constitute a large proportion of the local population, with characteristic stores, restaurants and social clubs, newspapers and other services, which function as a focus for ethnic group activities. Instead, the French have settled in areas where the majority of the residents were of British origin.[2] Even in their place of residence French Canadians wish to be recognized as native Canadians. They dislike being classified as "immigrants" from another country and therefore avoid predominantly immigrant areas. They also share a common substratum of Canadian culture with English Canadians which is the product of two centuries and more of living in Canada isolated in large measure from European culture and its subsequent developments.

[1]*Census of Canada, 1961*, Bulletin CT-15. See map of Metropolitan Toronto showing the percentage distribution of the French within census tracts.

[2]City of Toronto Planning Board, *Ethnic Origins of the Population of Toronto, 1960*, Figs. D-1 to D-17, which locate both the staging areas and the areas of more permanent settlement of the majority of Toronto's ethnic groups. When the map of the French concentrations is compared with the concentration maps prepared by the City of Toronto Planning Board for seventeen other ethnic minority groups, there is little or no overlapping in areas of residence.

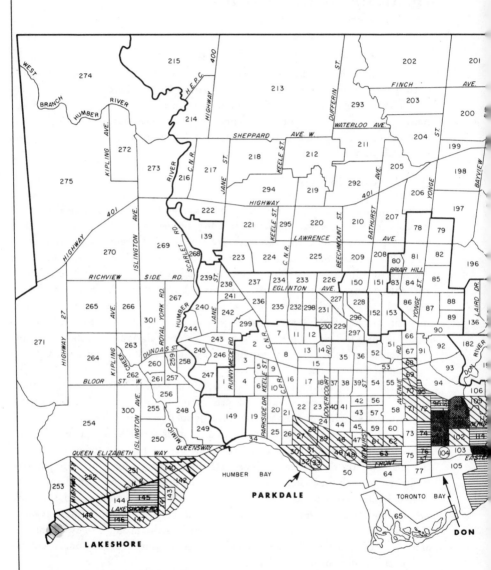

**DISTRIBUTION OF THE POPULATION
OF FRENCH ORIGIN**

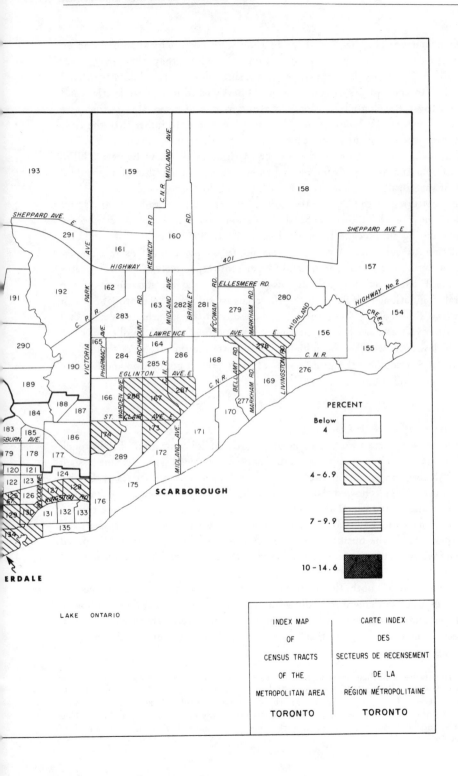

When members of the French population were asked why they had chosen the particular area of Metropolitan Toronto in which they then lived, over one-half (55%) emphasized the type of housing which they could afford, and proximity to their places of employment. Others wished to be near relatives and friends (15%). Residential location was also a matter of personal taste for those who liked a particular house or neighbourhood, the suburbs rather than the city, the convenience of nearby shopping areas or public transportation (13%). Ten per cent, all migrants from Quebec or the Maritimes, wished to be near a bilingual school. Another 5 per cent wanted to be near a Catholic Church, but only 2 per cent specifically mentioned the French parish, the Sacré-Coeur.

The scattering of the French throughout the entire area can be illustrated by the way the French followed general population movement from the city to the suburbs during the decade from 1951 to 1961. In 1951 the ratio of total city population to suburban population was 60 to 40 per cent. This was almost reversed during the decade, to 41 and 59 per cent respectively. Table 6 indicates how the French have not only followed but surpassed the movement of the general population, especially to the three largest suburbs, Scarborough, North York, and Etobicoke.[3] The result of this exodus to the suburbs for the general population was a heavy loss to the city of both population and families. For the French, however, who had been highly concentrated in the city prior to 1951, it served only to equalize the proportions of both French population and families between city and suburbs.

The Areas of French Concentration

Some conception of the character of the areas of concentration of the French is necessary as 80 per cent of the respondents interviewed were resident in such areas. All five concentrations were in the old, longer-settled districts of the city and suburbs. They followed the original band of settlement along the waterfront both east and west from the commercial centre of the city into the suburbs. In the city, the Don, Riverdale, and Parkdale areas were part of the transitional zone just outside the business core, characterized by aging and often dilapidated housing whose market values had fallen with the encroachments of business and industry.

In the suburbs, both the Lakeshore and Scarborough areas developed as ribbon types of settlement, initially with cottages along the waterfront, followed by the erection of a heterogeneous mixture of housing, retail stores and commercial establishments along the main highways from the city, and the lining of the

---

[3]The twelve suburban areas included: Leaside, Weston, Mimico, New Toronto, Long Branch, Swansea, Forest Hill, Scarborough, York, York East, York North, Etobicoke. In 1967 the twelve municipalities in the suburbs were merged into five large boroughs with the city of Toronto as the sixth borough. The three small lakeshore municipalities of Mimico, New Toronto and Long Branch, mentioned in the study, were merged with the larger suburb of Etobicoke.

Table 6

Comparison of the Growth of the Total Population with
the Population of French Origin, 1951 to 1961, for
(1) The Metropolitan Area, (2) the City of Toronto
and the Twelve Suburban Municipalities, (3) the
Largest Suburbs: Scarborough, North York, and
Etobicoke

Area	Total Population	French Population	
	% Gain	% Gain	Numerical Gain
(1) Metropolitan Area[a]	44.8	72.0	31,853 to 54,804
(2) City of Toronto	-.5	26.0	21,865 to 27,564
Suburban Area[a]	114.2	172.7	9,988 to 27,240
(3) Largest Suburbs:			
Scarborough	285.9	416.2	1,421 to 7,331
North York	214.2	284.5	1,836 to 7,161
Etobicoke	190.1	244.5	1,231 to 4,241

[a]Census tracts added after 1951 deleted leaving only the city and the twelve suburbs in both
census years, namely, the Metropolitan Corporation of Toronto, in 1961.
Source: *Census of Canada, 1951, 1961.*

railways with industries.[4] Growth of the city consolidated the original residential districts, replacing the cottages with luxury homes and apartments along the
lake, and filling the farmlands to the north with middle and upper-class housing
projects.

In spite of marked ecological changes over the years, however, all five areas of
the concentration of the French have maintained a typically working and lower-
class character.

The Don Area

The most important concentrations of the French for this study has been the
Don area because the French parish, the Sacré-Coeur, has always been located
within its boundaries. Consequently, the parish has never been able to escape the
influence and reputation of its own immediate neighbourhood. Some sections of
the Don area have gone through the various stages of an ecological cycle of

[4]S. D. Clark, *The Suburban Society* (Toronto: University of Toronto Press, 1966),
p. 27.

change, from the exclusive residential mansions of the wealthy early in the century, to the ramshackle dwellings of a virtual slum at its midpoint. Stretching northward from the extensive industrial basin on the lakefront to Bloor Street, and west from the factory-lined Don River to Toronto's main north-south artery, Yonge Street, the Don has been one of the most heterogeneous, densely-populated districts in the city. Over five thousand of the French migrants have been drawn there by prospects of employment in its many industries, resulting in the highest French concentration in the metropolitan area, reaching 15 per cent of the population in some census tracts.

The characteristics of the Don area which have moulded attitudes of many of the French population toward the French parish can be illustrated from an intensive study of the Don area published by the City of Toronto Planning Board in 1963.[5] The study was stimulated not only by the necessity of redeveloping blocks of deteriorating and condemned housing, but also by the search for ways of controlling deviant behaviour among residents of the area. Families in the Don district in 1963 were significantly larger than in most of Toronto, with 20 per cent of families having three or more children compared to the city average of 12 per cent. Overcrowding existed in 22 per cent of the properties, with doubling up of families common. Incomes in the district, according to the Planning Board report, were much lower than the average for the city, especially in the range below $3,000 per year. Employment in high-status occupations such as the professions, proprietors, managers and officials was much lower than in the total city labour force, while those employed in service and unskilled occupations were proportionately higher. There was a considerable overrepresentation in the Don area of reported cases of crime, delinquency, social welfare and vagrancy.[6] Such characteristics are often identified with lower-class urban areas.

The Other Areas of Concentration of the French Population

The Riverdale and Parkdale areas of concentration within the city, situated on the eastern and western fringes of Toronto's downtown transitional area, were more residential and hence less heterogeneous than the Don area, although redevelopment has been taking place along the inner boundaries of each area.[7]

[5]City of Toronto Planning Board, *Don Planning District Appraisal* (September, 1963).

[6]Judging by statistics gathered by welfare and police departments, social problems appear to be more intense in the Don than in other parts of the city, although distributed in pockets rather than over the whole area. With 6 per cent of the population of the city in 1963, the Don had 11 per cent of all Children's Aid cases, 12 per cent of juvenile offenders, 19 per cent of welfare recipients, 17 per cent of Neighbourhood Worker cases, 34 per cent of drunkenness offenders, and 65 per cent of old, homeless and transient men. Traffic in drugs and prostitution tended to be centralized in the Don area at that time.

[7]The writer has been on nearly every street of the areas of concentration of the French within the city as part of a University of Toronto research team which interviewed a random sample of several hundred homeowners from the eastern end of Riverdale to the western

The railroads which bisect each area at an angle were lined with industries which have attracted French residents. In Riverdale the density of this French population ran from 4 to 11 per cent, while in Parkdale it was 6 to 9 per cent.

The Scarborough and Lakeshore municipalities, situated just outside the eastern and western boundaries of the city along the lakeshore, possessed somewhat lower concentrations of the French. In Scarborough, with a population of over 200,000, French density was low, averaging 3 per cent, rising to 5 per cent in some census tracts, while it was slightly higher, 5 to 7 per cent in the Lakeshore. In both areas the French residential areas were hemmed in between the luxury homes and apartments which have replaced the cottages on the lakefront, and the middle and upper-class housing developments to the north of the provincial highway and major railway lines which bisect each area. Industries such as the Goodyear Tire and Rubber Company and the Continental Can Company, located on the railway lines, have provided the employment which has concentrated the French working class in these areas.

The most significant development, apart from the five areas just described, has been a growing concentration of the French middle class on the northern fringe of Scarborough where they have been responsible within the last decade for the establishment of a second bilingual primary school, Ste. Madeleine.[8]

The Residents of the Areas of Concentration

The characteristics of the residents of the areas of French concentration are important because four-fifths of the respondents in this study lived in such working and lower-class areas of the city and suburbs. Less than one-third of the middle class had taken up residence in these areas and with few exceptions they were lower-middle class, employed mainly in clerical and sales occupations. Their incomes ranged from low to average, which is typical of the lower-middle class whose incomes are often lower than skilled manual workers. The other two-thirds of the middle class and well over two-thirds of the working class were scattered throughout the remainder of the city and suburbs.

In general, residents of the five areas were a stable, established segment of the French population. Well over one-half (62%) had been living in Toronto over ten years, with a quarter of them resident over twenty years. Only 20 per cent were newcomers, living in Toronto less than five years, with another 18 per cent resident from five to ten years. The age spread confirms the predominance of older residents as less than 12 per cent of respondents were under thirty years of

---

end of Parkdale and north from the waterfront to Gerrard Street in the east and Dundas Street in the west. This took place during the summer of 1964 just prior to beginning the study of the French. It was under the auspices of Central Mortgage and Housing Corporation, Ottawa, and was carried out through the City of Toronto Planning Board.

[8] Clark, *Suburban Society*, p. 99. This is in spite of the fact that in Scarborough 75 per cent of the population was British and 70 per cent Protestant.

age. The median age of such respondents was in the low forties.[9] Respondents living in the suburbs tended to be a somewhat younger group, with a median age in the thirties,[10] and with a higher proportion of newcomers, especially among the middle class.

The stability of the residents of areas of concentration is also evident from their lack of residential mobility, as 23 per cent claimed to have lived in the same house or on the same street since moving to Toronto. Only 26 per cent reported one move, and 19 per cent two moves, since arriving in Toronto. Residential mobility of any significance was reported by only 32 per cent of the respondents. Home ownership by 52 per cent of respondents may partially explain the lack of mobility,[11] but it is not the whole story as 25 per cent of the sample chosen from the Metropolitan City Directory had moved in the ten months since the Directory was issued. Changes of residence reached as high as 37 per cent in Parkdale.[12] The mobile French population appears to be the apartment dwellers, as only 13 per cent of those interviewed were resident in this type of domicile.

Implications of the Spatial Pattern

It is significant that no single motive provided a focus for French settlement in Toronto. Rather, the predominance of economic motives has tended to disperse the French throughout the metropolitan area in conformity with the widely-spread character of Toronto's industrial development. This geographic dispersion of the French population has two implications for social participation within the French population. First is the virtual isolation of French families from one another even in areas of concentration while in constant social interaction with the surrounding English-speaking population both in the neighbourhood and on the job. Second, the absence of any significant concentrations of the French population has left its members without a central focus for ethnic participation and consequent identification within the boundaries of their own culture.

B. The Occupational Pattern

The magnet which has drawn most of the rather heterogeneous French population to Toronto and scattered them throughout the metropolitan area has been

---

[9]In the working class 12 per cent were under thirty years of age, 34 per cent in their thirties, 30 per cent in their forties, and 20 per cent over fifty years of age, with a few cases not ascertainable.

[10]In the middle class 13 per cent were in their twenties, 46 per cent in their thirties, 34 per cent in their forties, and only 7 per cent over fifty years of age.

[11]Thirty-two per cent were renting all or part of a house, and 13 per cent were renting an apartment, with a few cases not ascertainable.

[12]Removals within less than a year were 37 per cent for Parkdale, 31 per cent in the area just north of Parkdale, 32 per cent on the Lakeshore, 24 per cent in the Don, 17 per cent in Scarborough, and 15 per cent in Riverdale.

the abundant opportunities for employment within Toronto's industrial complex. Table 7 shows why employment within the Toronto work world has been the major point of articulation of the French with the host English-speaking population. Respondents mentioned not only the availability of jobs, but the attraction of the higher wage scales prevailing within the Toronto industrial area.[13]

Table 7

Reasons Given by the French for Settlement in the Toronto Area

Reasons	Number	Percentage
In order to find work	141	55.95
Transferred by employer	31	12.30
To join relatives and/or friends	32	12.70
Miscellaneous	24	9.52
Born and grew up in Toronto	24	9.52
Totals	252	99.99

Transfers to Toronto by employers, chiefly of executives in business and industry, either for experience in the English-speaking sector of the Canadian economy, or to supervise French interests within work organizations, was a second motive for entry into the Toronto labour force. Less than one-quarter of the French population has settled in Toronto for non-economic reasons such as joining relatives and friends, seeking to further education or learn English, and so on.

The French Labour Force

The increasing pace of French settlement in Toronto since World War II has resulted in a French labour force in the middle sixties of around 25,000, which was approximately 5 per cent of the total Toronto labour force.[14] The distribution of the French within the occupational structure is shown in Table 8.[15] The

[13] A skilled tradesman from New Brunswick found he could almost double his income in Toronto. A factory worker, idled by a strike in Moncton, New Brunswick, visited his daughter near Toronto and immediately found employment. He returned to the Maritimes only to move his family to Toronto. Such incidents as recorded above could be multiplied many times over.

[14] *Census of Canada, 1961*, Bulletin CT-15, Table 3.

[15] The representative sample from which the statistics regarding occupations were drawn consisted of 252 respondents, of whom 108 were males and 144 were females. In addition to seeking information on female employment, married women were requested to supply

location of most of the French work force exemplifies the traditional overrepresentation of the French in the manual segment of the occupational ladder, the
categories of skilled, semi-skilled, service and unskilled. But it also presents a
contrast between the contemporary French labour force, which is concentrated
at the top end of the manual category in skilled and semi-skilled occupations,
and the labour force earlier in the century which was concentrated in the unskilled category. The latter arrived in Toronto lacking the kind of education
needed for skilled occupations, and with experience restricted mainly to primary
occupations such as farming, lumbering, fishing and mining. They filled the need
for unskilled labour, however, at a time when Toronto had embarked upon
massive civic construction.

During the last thirty years, according to Porter,[16] as the lower levels of the
occupational ladder have been flooded by massive immigration from eastern and
southern Europe, the French labour force has moved towards a more normal
type of distribution. A larger proportion of the French labour force has moved
into the semi-skilled and skilled jobs to the extent that in Toronto, at least, the
French have an overrepresentation in these categories of 13 per cent in comparison with the parallel segment of the total labour force in Toronto. Porter points
out that Franco-Ontarians are still as overrepresented in the manual segment as
they ever were,[17] but in Toronto there has been at least the shift, perhaps due
to apprenticeship and on-the-job training programmes, to the upper end of the
manual sector.

This upward mobility within the manual sector may have been the result of a
change in the areas of employment of the French work force. The earlier concentration of the French in the construction industry has declined, leaving only
13 per cent in occupations which have been virtually taken over by Italians and
eastern Europeans. The French have moved into employment characteristic of
the secondary phase of industrial development, manufacturing, transportation
and communication. They have been only sparsely represented in the fast-
growing tertiary field of service occupations with one-half of the proportion
existing within the total Toronto labour force.

The most significant occupational development has taken place in one sector
of the non-manual or white-collar segment of the French labour force. The

---

the details of the occupations of their husbands. Since twenty-one of the French wives had
married non-French husbands, which was significant for social status but irrelevant to the
occupational status of those of French origin, these were deleted, leaving only French males
included in the totals. Of the 252 males, twenty-eight were not gainfully employed at the
time of the survey. But none of them were unemployed. The majority of this group belonged to the 11 per cent of the sample who were over sixty years of age, and except for
one or two students, all were retired from regular employment. There were fourteen cases
where the female respondent was either not married, separated from her husband, or the
husband was deceased. Consequently the total number of French males who were gainfully
employed from whom the details of the occupational structure could be gained was 189.

[16]John Porter, *The Vertical Mosaic* (Toronto: University of Toronto Press, 1965), p. 86.

[17]Ibid., p. 98.

Table 8

Occupations of the Sample of Gainfully Employed Males of French Origin, 1965, Compared With Total Labour Force, Metropolitan Toronto, 1961[a]

Occupational Category	French Males		Total Male Labour Force[b]	
	No.	%	No.	%
Professional, Semi-Professional and Technician	13[c]	6.87	51,518	11.18
Proprietor, Manager, and Official	24	12.69	63,763	13.84
Clerical and Sales	22	11.64	89,142	19.36
Skilled (Craftsmen and Foremen)	73	38.62)		
		)	184,545	40.07
Semi-Skilled (Operators and Kindred)	28	14.81)		
Service (Protective, Public and Private)	7	3.70	40,971	8.89
Unskilled	22	11.64	26,042	5.65
Primary (Farming, Fishing, Logging, Mining, etc.)	—	—	4,455	.96
Total gainfully employed	189	99.97	460,436	99.95
Not gainfully employed	28		12,870	
Not ascertainable	14			
Totals	231		473,306	

[a]Includes only the metropolitan corporation; the city and twelve suburbs.
[b]*Census of Canada, 1961.*
[c]No semi-professionals; one technician.

occupations of proprietors, managers and officials has expanded to within 1 per cent of the proportion in the same occupational category of the total labour force in Toronto. Only 2 per cent of this category were self-employed as proprietors, and less than 1 per cent were officials, so almost all were executives who have migrated to Toronto in recent years. According to informants, none of this group were indigenous to Toronto but came in the main from Quebec, with some from elsewhere in Ontario, and a few from the Maritimes.

These executives represent what Hubert Guindon in his study of the social evolution of Quebec has called the new middle class, the élite which has been giving leadership in recent years in the religious and governmental bureaucracies of that province.[18] In contrast to Quebec, however, the new middle class in Toronto were executives in business and industry with scarcely any representation in church or government except for a few in the Bilingual School Division of the Ontario Department of Education.[19]

When location in the occupational structure is related to the region from which workers have come, certain implicit differences in education and occupational experience emerge. For instance, migrants from Quebec, although represented on all occupational levels, occupied the greatest proportion of white-collar positions such as professionals and executives, in comparison with Ontario and the Maritimes. Acadians, scarcely represented at all in white-collar occupations, supplied the largest proportion of skilled workers. Franco-Ontarians, while represented throughout the occupational hierarchy, were concentrated to a greater degree than either Quebeckers or Acadians in the semi-skilled and un-skilled occupations. This distribution does not substantiate the popular stereotype of the Acadians as inevitably occupying the lowest rungs on the occupational ladder.

Female employment among the French was considerably lower than the 39 per cent of females employed within the total female population of Metropolitan Toronto.[20] Out of 144 females interviewed, 123 (85%) indicated that they were housewives exclusively. Working females were located as operators in factories, as bookkeepers, section supervisors, sales clerks, stenographers, and teachers. Or they worked part-time in pursuits such as dressmaking, cosmetic representatives, or translating. In view of the low rate of female employment among the French it has simply been assumed that the social status of the family was dependent upon the occupation of the husband rather than the wife when both were working.[21]

---

[18]Hubert Guindon, "The Social Revolution of Quebec Reconsidered," in Marcel Rioux and Yves Martin, eds., *French-Canadian Society* (Toronto: McClelland and Stewart, 1964), pp. 155-56.

[19]Jacques Brazeau, "Quebec's Emerging Middle Class," in Marcel Rioux and Yves Martin, eds., *French-Canadian Society* (Toronto: McClelland and Stewart, 1964), p. 322.

[20]*Census of Canada, 1961,* Bulletin CT-15.

[21]Bernard Blishen, "A Socio-economic Index for Occupations in Canada," *Canadian Review of Sociology and Anthropology,* IV, No. 1 (February, 1967), 42.

In summary, the occupational pattern shows only one exception to the traditional overrepresentation of the French in manual occupations and underrepresentation in non-manual occupations.[22] The near parity of the executive level with the corresponding segment of the Toronto labour force appears to be a clear-cut case of vertical occupational mobility. Otherwise, however, French white-collar workers are proportionately 6 per cent below the parallel sector of the Toronto labour force, because professionals, semi-professionals, technicians, and clerical and sales occupations are all underrepresented. The fields of finance, insurance and real estate are not represented at all.[23] The scant 2.3 per cent of the French in wholesale and retail trade perhaps reflects the absence of a French quarter or enclave in Toronto. The majority both of the French labour force and of the respondents in this study were in skilled or semi-skilled occupations, members of the working class.

C. The Pattern of Stratification

Occupation in industrial societies is so closely related to education, income, and prestige that it has become the major determinant of social status. Position in the system of social stratification, apart from ascribed statuses such as sex, age, and ethnic origin, rests upon achievement within the work world. In the case of ethnic populations such as the French in Toronto, however, its members find their place in the class structure through a shifting combination of both ascribed and achieved statuses. As long as linguistic and cultural differences distinguish the minority population from the host society, status or social position tends to be ascribed on the basis of ethnic origin.[24] But if such differences become minimal or disappear through acculturation, participation in the occupational structure opens up the mobility chances of achieving status within the larger society.[25]

The outlines of the pattern of stratification of the French population of Toronto are typical of many ethnic minorities, but its internal structure is different because so few of the French are immigrants. It is doubtful if there is an upper class among the French in Toronto. There was little evidence that any of the French population possessed the combination of wealth and social position which would qualify them for membership in an upper-class élite. The middle class, on the other hand, embraced at least 30 per cent of the French population, some seven or eight thousand of the French labour force, which with dependents would aggregate just under twenty thousand persons. The remaining 70 per cent

[22]Bernard C. Rosen, "Race, Ethnicity, and the Achievement Syndrome," in Milton L. Barron, ed., *Minorities in a Changing World* (New York: Alfred A. Knopf, 1967), pp. 151-72; Porter, *Vertical Mosaic,* pp. 85-90.

[23]Porter, *Vertical Mosaic,* p. 84.

[24]Ibid., pp. 73ff.; Rosen, "Race, Ethnicity," pp. 151ff.

[25]Everett C. Hughes and Helen M. Hughes, *Where Peoples Meet* (Glencoe, Ill.: The Free Press, 1952), p. 114.

of the French were working or lower class, embracing over eighteen thousand of the French labour force plus dependents for a total of over forty thousand persons.

The Upper Middle Class

Almost two-thirds of the middle class can be considered an upper middle class, composed of a number of disparate elements. It has been typical of most ethnic migrations that traditional élites seldom join the migrants.[26] But in Toronto the upper middle class has always included a few of the traditional or "old" middle class who embodied characteristics of the social and economic élites of pre-industrial Quebec. It included members of the historic professions, clerical, legal, medical, and educational, the French consuls and other government officials, and the proprietors of commercial establishments which conformed to the familial model of business activity characteristic of French Canada.[27]

Usually educated in the classical colleges and universities of the Roman Catholic Church, members of the old middle class have not been prepared either by education or outlook to adopt middle class roles consonant with a rationalized, bureaucratic industrial society. The models were Protestant and involved the adoption of Protestant values and goals.[28] But their professional, entrepreneurial and official statuses have provided a measure of insulation against conformity to the urban-industrial system while at the same time enabling them to be active in sectors of non-articulation with the host society such as the French parish and French associations.[29] Some of the old middle class were charter members of the Sacré-Coeur from its earliest beginnings, and over the years have provided leadership for its organizations, financial support for its projects, and representation on Separate School Boards of Education for bilingual schools.

The vast majority of the upper middle class, however, were executives in business and industry along with a few professionals in the more technical fields. This "new" middle class began to trickle into Toronto in the 1940s, became a flow in the 1950s, and a stream in the 1960s, bringing with them the initiative for action and independence of judgment which had been part of their experience in the economic sphere. On the whole they were fairly young with over half of their number (54%) in the thirty to forty age group, most of them fairly recent arrivals on the scene in Toronto. Very much like the emergent new

[26] Ibid., p. 85.

[27] N. W. Taylor, "The French-Canadian Industrial Entrepreneur and His Social Environment," in Marcel Rioux and Yves Martin, eds., French-Canadian Society (Toronto: McClelland and Stewart, 1964), pp. 271-95.

[28] Hughes and Hughes, Where Peoples Meet, pp. 124, 128. Herbert F. Quinn, The Union Nationale (Toronto: University of Toronto Press, 1963), pp. 12, 15. Also: Falardeau, "The Changing Structures of Contemporary French-Canadian Society," p. 117.

[29] Barth, Ethnic Groups and Boundaries, p. 33.

middle class in the Province of Quebec,[30] the composition of the new middle class in Toronto has been ill-defined, with diversity of values and goals among both the permanent residents of the area and the "transients" from Quebec or elsewhere.

An ethnic cleavage within the ranks of the new middle class has been its outstanding characteristic. Over 90 per cent of the permanently resident middle class[31] attended English parishes, and with few exceptions sent their children to English parochial or public schools. They maintained little or no contact with the French parish or other French organizations, and apparently have "passed" into the English-speaking society. This cleavage indicates that less than 10 per cent of the permanently-established French participate regularly in the activities of the Sacré-Coeur and bilingual schools, French voluntary associations and the French mass media.

The non-permanent or "transient" French middle class were mainly from the Province of Quebec, and were of two types. Some were executives who had been transferred to Toronto by their employers to become more intimately acquainted with the English business and industrial world before returning to Quebec. Or they were professionals or graduate students taking further training in the teaching hospitals or universities. They were obliged to spend most of their time within the English-speaking milieu and had little or no time for their French compatriots except on a very casual basis. Thus they remained on the margin of the French population in Toronto.

Others among the transients were more ethnically oriented and their "nationalism" led them to practise a type of "separatism"[32] by avoiding as much as possible fraternization with members of the host society. They confined activities for themselves and their families within existing French organizations, attending the Sacré-Coeur, sending their children to bilingual schools if possible, and becoming involved in French associations, since their career lines were already crystallized within the Province of Quebec and their stay in Toronto was limited. According to several informants, there was a link between the old middle class, the new middle class affiliated with the Sacré-Coeur, and this small group of transients, because some members of each group were declared by such informants to be members of the Jacques Cartier Society. Informants felt that it was the link with this society which has created a small core élite among the upper middle class in Toronto which has been following the authoritarian tactics

---

[30]Guindon, "Social Revolution of Quebec Reconsidered," pp. 704-705.

[31]Fifty-four per cent of the upper middle class owned their houses, 21 per cent rented a house, 5 per cent rented part of a house, 13 per cent rented an apartment, with 7 per cent not known.

[32]The proprietor of the French Book Store described how this "separatism" had excluded from membership in French associations the immigrant French and Toronto residents from French-speaking colonies overseas because although they were French in origin or language they were not French Canadians.

of the Jacques Cartier Society in seeking to promote ethnic solidarity within the French population.[33]

The Lower Middle Class and the Lower Class

It has become increasingly difficult in modern industrial societies to distinguish between the lower middle class of mainly clerical and sales workers, and the upper working class of skilled and semi-skilled workers, because unionization has raised the standard of living and prestige of the latter while lack of collective action has handicapped the former. In Toronto the lower middle class could be distinguished from the upper working class only by occupation as they lived in the same areas, reported the same range of income, and were likewise kinship rather than class oriented,[34] probably because 70 per cent of the French had relatives in Toronto.

The significance of the lower middle class and the working class for this study is that together they constitute 80 per cent of the French population and therefore have played the major roles in setting the patterns of participational identification prevalent within the French minority. Their degree of participation in English parishes and parochial or public schools was slightly lower than that of the upper middle class by some 5 to 10 per cent, but it was still well over 80 per cent. The difference may have resulted from the proximity of many in these strata to the French parish and its bilingual school.

Participation within English social structures, however, has been tempered by continuing identification with the French lenguage and culture through kinship networks. Well over 70 per cent of the lower class, just under 70 per cent of the lower middle class, and 50 per cent of the upper middle class had relatives in Toronto and in most cases they were visited regularly. This deterrent to loss of ethnic identity has influenced members of the upper middle class less, however, because they not only have fewer relatives in Toronto but are more class and less kinship conscious than the lower class.

Class Identification Across Ethnic Boundaries

Several factors must be taken into consideration in accounting for the high degree of participation in the English institutional structures. The heterogeneity of the French population and its dispersed residential pattern have both tended to minimize interaction among the French and maximize their exposure to the English language and culture. But it is the quest for economic security which has

---

[33]See Roger Cyr, *La Patente* (Montreal: Les Editions du Jour, 1964). Reference to the Jacques Cartier Society has been included because it was referred to again and again by middle-class respondents who resented the fact that the policies and programme of the Society were imposed undemocratically and authoritatively from somewhere outside and "above" its members within the French population of Toronto.

[34]The Royal Commission on Bilingualism and Biculturalism, *Preliminary Report* (Ottawa: Queen's Printer, 1965), p. 116; Léopold Lamontagne, "Ontario: The Two Races," in Mason Wade, ed., *Canadian Dualism* (Toronto: University of Toronto Press, 1960), pp. 359-60.

been the major factor in promoting accommodation to the host English-speaking society. To the lower middle class and the working and lower class "it means stable employment, a year-round job, the right not to live in constant fear of unemployment."[35] Many in these strata were prepared before they came to Toronto to pay the ethnic price tag of steady employment. To be confronted daily with the problems of economic survival (food, shelter, clothing) which leave little energy or leisure for concerns beyond the immediate family and its needs is the typical pattern among low-income groups. The concerns of ethnic identity such as language and culture have little or no economic value in Toronto, so they are exercised only in the sphere of kinship relations which are relegated to leisure time activities. Consequently the largest segment of the French population, the lower middle and lower classes, have been no more ethnic conscious than class conscious in the major concerns of everyday life.[36]

Economic security has also been a factor in the identification of so many of the upper middle class with the English-speaking host society. A successful career within the English commercial world demands accommodation to the English value system at whatever cost to mother tongue and French culture. Neither the old middle class, with professional and entrepreneurial independence of status and income, or the transients with their occupational and social roots in Quebec, experienced in Toronto the same pressures to conform to the host society as executives employed by English business and industrial organizations. For them there were no other avenues of occupational and social mobility.

The adoption by French executives of English middle class models was softened, of course, because many of them already possessed, or soon acquired after their arrival, the interests, aspirations and values typical of their English-speaking employers. Once the transition had been made, the only way the advantages of an achieved position could be perpetuated was to identify more completely with the society which had made such statuses possible.[37] Consequently, identification with the host society was the inevitable product of participation.

But economic security for the upper middle class was much more closely related to social status or class position than it was among the lower middle class or working class. This concern for social status was revealed through interviews with a number of high-ranking French executives, proprietors and professionals, aimed at discovering why so many of the most competent members of the French population had identified with the host society.[38] It was evident

[35]Guindon, "Social Revolution of Quebec Reconsidered," p. 709.

[36]Jacques Dofny and Marcel Rioux, "Social Class in French Canada," in Marcel Rioux and Yves Martin, eds., *French-Canadian Society* (Toronto: McClelland and Stewart, 1964), pp. 310-11.

[37]Occupational mobility was possible within the bilingual division of the Ontario Department of Education for the French, but although it operated only within the French population it was only a department of the English-speaking Department of Education.

[38]Interviews were conducted with the Presidents of one of the largest milk-product firms in Canada, a furniture and appliance establishment, a manufacturing company, a children's

throughout that for these "independents" social status was inseparable from occupational status.

The lower-class character of the French parish, its bilingual school, and the immediate neighbourhood, was unacceptable to people in positions which required wide associations in both the business and social world with English-speaking persons of comparable status or class. Several mentioned their resentment at the somewhat dictatorial pressure brought to bear upon them by the clergy at the French parish to persuade them to settle in the parish neighbourhood when they first arrived in Toronto, as if considerations of social status were of no importance. Only in English parishes did they find residence, neighbours and parishioners on the status level of the upper middle class.

Some of these independents said they did not feel at ease at the Sacré-Coeur because they were viewed with ambivalence and suspicion by ethnically-oriented parishioners who assumed that economic success had been purchased by capitulation to the English culture and betrayal of their own. This atmosphere of criticism and even hostility created barriers to religious and social interaction within the parish and other French organizations.

Some of the independents also objected to ethnic separatism in the form of exclusively French organizations. The Vice-President of a nation-wide firm deliberately avoided the French parish and French associations because he felt they would negatively bias his attempt to get to know and understand English Canadians. A French lawyer disapproved of what he called "creeping off into a corner like immigrants" when English Canadians were his fellow countrymen, Canadians just as he was himself. Some of these men mentioned what they considered to be the undemocratic methods of the small clique associated with the Jacques Cartier Society as a major reason why they had disassociated themselves from organized French associations in Toronto.

The "independents" also made it clear that they had not lost touch completely with French culture. Some were sceptical of the value of espousing the cause of French nationalism within the Toronto milieu, but they had no intention of repudiating ethnic ties with French Canada. To this observer, the independents appeared caught between two systems of values, one which functions at work, and the other when with family, relatives and friends. Ambivalence of attitude was unavoidable. One may choose one of these worlds, but it has been difficult if not impossible to have them both together.[39] In the multiethnic community ethnic identity is only one of a number of values such as social class by which human beings identify with one another.[40] The inner role conflicts

---

amusement supply service; the Vice-President of the largest soft-drink manufacturer in Canada; the General Manager of a restaurant chain, the Manager of the French division of a mail-order division of a department store chain, a prominent French lawyer, university professors, and others of comparable status.

[39]Daniel Lerner, *The Passing of Traditional Society* (Glencoe, Ill.: The Free Press of Glencoe, 1958), p. 406.

[40]Shibutani and Kwan, *Ethnic Stratification*, p. 577.

could only be resolved by some kind of opportunism, adaptation to the exigencies of an essentially ambiguous situation.

For instance, a French official in the bilingual school division of the Ontario Department of Education was a confident, aggressive and competent leader within the French middle class, but he was criticized severely by one of his peers because he was obviously ill at ease conversing in French in the presence of his English-speaking superiors in the Department of Education. Such ambivalence reveals in a subtle way the key reference group in the situation.

> The minority leader must be acceptable to his own people, but his position depends ultimately on his acceptance by the majority. . . . In making the demands of both groups palatable to each other, the minority leader therefore must pay more homage to the majority since it is the group that "runs things" in society.[41]

An Unstable Situation

The patterns of stratification within the French population have been an unstable mixture of old and newer structures. The old middle class symbolizes the traditional, pre-industrial class structure of French Canada, while the new middle class and the industrial working class represent adaptation of the French labour force to the urban-industrial system prevalent in English-speaking Toronto.

This instability has been a product of the incorporation of almost all of the middle and lower classes into the status system of the host industrial society from which economic security has been derived. A mediating position has been adopted by the small minority from all strata who have affiliated with French institutional structures such as the parish. They have accepted minority status but have sought to reduce their minority disabilities by "encapsulating all cultural differentiae in [such] sectors of non-articulation,"[42] while participating in the larger system of the industrial society in other sectors of activity. A still smaller faction within the French population, mainly upper middle class, has chosen to emphasize ethnic identity, seeking through existing French organizations to promote French nationalism and to maintain linguistic and cultural "separatism" to the degree possible within the majority English-speaking society.

[41] Leventman, "Minority Group Leadership," pp. 604-05.

[42] Barth, *Ethnic Groups and Boundaries*, p. 33.

Chapter V

The Magnet of
Economic Security

The major point of articulation of the French population with the host English-speaking society has been employment in the Toronto work world. It is an occupation which gives access to a living, a level of comfort, prestige and life chances.[1] In the present chapter the evidence suggests that job security, relative occupational mobility, and the virtual disappearance of ethnic job discrimination for the French have created a climate so favourable to economic absorption within the host industrial society that most of the French population have made the necessary accommodations.

Paradoxically, the very factors which tend to weaken ethnic identity have been favourable to the entry of the French into the Toronto labour force. The diversity of cultural background of the migrants has contributed differential experience to job opportunities. The slow, gradual pace of French settlement has posed no threat to English-speaking members of the Toronto labour force which would stimulate opposition, organized or otherwise, to employment of the French. The dispersed pattern of residence has spread employment chances over a wide range of industries. The low occupational status of the majority of the French migrants has enabled them to supply the demand where the need has usually been greatest, in the manual sector of the labour force.

In order to take advantage of the abundant opportunities for employment at all levels of the occupational ladder, many of the French came to Toronto prepared to accept as a condition of economic success the English-speaking value system. The majority spoke English well before migrating to Toronto.[2] Most of them had come from mixed communities which included both French and English residents. They were thus aware to some degree of the linguistic and cultural costs of economic absorption[3] within a community where French-speaking work organizations were almost non-existent.

[1]Edward Gross, *Work and Society* (New York: The Thomas Y. Crowell Company, 1958), p. 605.

[2]All respondents were asked the question: "When did you learn to speak English well?" Only fourteen said they did not speak English well. Another forty learned English after coming to Toronto. The remainder already spoke English well, twenty-seven having grown up in Toronto or a similar English environment, 105 learned it at school, forty at home, twenty-eight at work, and twenty-three through neighbours, with three miscellaneous answers.

[3]Charles Price, "The Study of Assimilation," in J. A. Jackson, *Sociological Studies 2: Migration* (Cambridge: Cambridge University Press, 1969), p. 221. Price writes that Milton F. Gordon's theory of assimilation which has been discussed in the Introduction to the present study is deficient at several points, two of which are relevant here: "First, it makes no place for economic absorption; yet this cannot be wholly included in acculturation; second, though Gordon refers to uneven assimilation, he does not explain how this

Entry into the Toronto work world has shaped both the careers and the identifications of the French in two different ways. On the one hand, ethnic status has tended to immobilize them within the occupational system. Industry in Toronto, as elsewhere, is a great mixer of peoples,[4] but once an ethnic job structure has been established it is almost impossible to eradicate,[5] as the record of ethnic segregation and discrimination in industry testifies.[6] This is probably why the generally low occupational status of the French in North America has changed little during the first half of the present century.[7] On the other hand, the necessity in an expanding economy of an adequate labour force has tended to push employment lower in the rank-order of discrimination and to open up mobility chances in the occupational system to ethnic workers.[8] In Toronto, industrial expansion has been accompanied by a gradual change in ethnic relations as heavy immigration has continued.[9] Hughes has pointed out[10] that the differences between peoples of Northern European ancestry, such as the French and the English, are small, consisting chiefly of language, religion, and superficial cultural traits. This contrasts with Eastern and Southern European immigrants whose differences in culture are somewhat greater, and especially with non-Europeans such as Asiatics and Africans with their physical visibility. Consequently, in recent years cultural differences between the French and the English have diminished, except on the level of the ideology of nationalism in which most of the Toronto French have scant interest. The result has been the incorporation of the French within the Toronto work world with few disabilities.

Security of Employment

Complete job security, of course, is virtually an impossibility for any ethnic minority, but among the respondents in Toronto there was no unemployment. Many of the French were quite candid about the ease with which jobs could be procured and said that they had never been out of work. This viewpoint clashed with the impression given by priests of centrally-located city parishes and other informants that movement from job to job was quite prevalent among the French-speaking in Toronto. Many in the Don area, particularly Acadians, were said to be looked after by the Welfare Department of the city. In order to assess the validity of these contradictory viewpoints and establish the level of stability

theory compares peoples who are acculturated in different ways or who suffer different kinds of discrimination."

[4]Everett C. Hughes, "Ethnic Relations in Industry and Society," in Sigmund Nosow and William H. Form, eds., *Man, Work, and Society* (New York: Basic Books Inc., 1962), p. 556.

[5]Miller and Form, *Industrial Sociology*, p. 519.

[6]Hughes, "Ethnic Relations," p. 557.

[7]Rosen, "Race, Ethnicity," pp. 151-72; Porter, *Vertical Mosaic*, pp. 85-90.

[8]Gross, *Work and Society* p. 632.

[9]Miller and Form, *Industrial Sociology*, p. 525.

[10]Hughes, "Ethnic Relations," p. 556.

of employment among the French respondents in Toronto, Table 9 relates horizontal occupational mobility, that is, movement from job to job on the same general occupational level, to the length of time respondents have lived in Toronto.

Table 9

Length of Time Living in Toronto and Job Mobility
for Male and Female Respondents Who were
Gainfully Employed

	Length of Time Living in Toronto				
No. of Jobs	Under 5 Years	5 to 10 Years	10 to 20 Years	Over 20 Years	Totals
One	12	4	15	10	41
Two	3	5	16	7	31
Three	1	2	6	5	14
Four	--	--	5	5	10
Five	--	--	3	1	4
Six	--	--	--	1	1
Seven	--	--	1	--	1
Eight or more	--	--	1	--	1
Totals	16	11	47	29	103
Not relevant	35	33	39	42	149
					252

Little movement occurred among those who had been in Toronto less than five years. Of those resident from five to ten years, 45 per cent had a second job, and 18 per cent a third job, and that is all. Most of the existing horizontal occupational mobility took place among those who had spent from ten to twenty years in Toronto. During this time an occasional individual had as many as nine different jobs.

Ethnic Discrimination

Judging from the comments of members of the French-speaking labour force who have lived in Toronto over ten years, decrease in movement from job to job may be explainable in terms of a decrease in ethnic job discrimination over the last decade or so. There was substantial agreement that conditions previous to the past decade were much more difficult in terms of unpleasant situations and ethnic discrimination than they have been in the 1960s, and resulted in greater horizontal occupational mobility. The French-speaking now find a ready acceptance in Toronto as far as employment is concerned, a viewpoint which is substantiated by the present occupational status of the French-speaking labour force.

In order to verify the allegations of a decrease in job discrimination an attempt was made to secure a response indirectly[11] by asking the following double-barrelled question: "In your estimation who gets the best jobs, and who gets the worst jobs, among these different groups?" Both before and after the question the following list of ethnic groups were read in this order: Italians, Germans, English, Polish, French, Ukrainians, Jews, Hungarians.[12]

There was no overt indication from over one-half of the respondents that they were conscious of job discrimination. Between 30 and 40 per cent answered, "I don't know," or "I cannot say." Another 20 per cent replied, in essence, that the kind of work one gets does not depend upon what ethnic group one belongs to but upon the ability, education and training of the individual for the job. In the opinion of another 25 per cent, the English got the best jobs, while 10 per cent assigned this to the Germans, and a few to the Jews. The Italians got the worst jobs, in the opinion of 35 per cent, but only three individuals mentioned the French as getting the worst jobs. Apparently the French did not feel, at least strongly, that they were the victims of discrimination in employment.

Two other indirect opportunities were given to respondents to express resentment at what they considered discrimination, or to describe unpleasant experiences among the English-speaking. The question was asked: "Has your experience of living in Toronto influenced your attitude toward English Canadians—for the better, or for the worse, or no change at all?" Seventy-five per cent indicated no change at all, 17 per cent reported a change for the better, and only 2 per cent reported a change for the worse. When the latter were asked why, only one answer reflected a recent unpleasant experience with the English-speaking, and another a complaint about the difficulty of speaking enough French in Toronto. In interviews outside of the sample, older individuals recalled that more than a decade ago such unpleasant experiences were more common.

The other opportunity was given when respondents were asked if there were any other French-speaking employees at their place of work, and if so, was there any opportunity to speak French? In 33 per cent of the cases all other employees were non-French. In 60 per cent of the cases there were other French employees, but in only three-quarters of these firms was there an opportunity to

[11]The indirect approach was suggested by Dr. Oswald Hall of the University of Toronto, Department of Sociology.

[12]The assumption lying behind the questions was that if the respondent was conscious of job discrimination being practised against the French it would appear in the response that the English or another group were getting the best jobs and the French the worst.

speak French, even occasionally. Resentment about the inability to speak French on the job, however, was minimal in terms of alleging discrimination. Some even stated that they preferred to speak English in the job situation.

Taking all of the above into consideration, it seems justified to conclude that little or no ethnic job discrimination has been practised against the French-speaking in the Toronto area recently, apart from individual reactions to personality traits. Several informants suggested as an explanation of the present situation that the heavy immigration from abroad during the post-Second World War period has accustomed the English-speaking population to many languages.

Occupational Mobility

The decrease in ethnic job discrimination may also be considered one of the factors which has encouraged intergenerational occupation mobility in the French labour force in Toronto. It was pointed out previously that the French-speaking population has a predominantly urban background. The occupations of the fathers of the French-speaking spouses of female respondents were not available, but the patterns of fathers' and sons' occupations were so similar to those of the fathers'-in-law and the sons'-in-law occupations that they have been merged in Table 10 in order to show intergenerational mobility for the entire male French-speaking labour force.

Table 10

The Occupational Distributions of Ninety French-Speaking Fathers and Sons and Ninety-Nine Fathers-In-Law and Sons-In-Law of the Toronto Sample

Occupations	Combined Fathers		Sons and Sons-in-law	
	No.	%	No.	%
Professionals and Technicians	5	2.64	13	6.87
Proprietors, Managers, Officials	18	9.52	24	12.69
Clerical and Sales	10	5.29	22	11.64
Skilled (Craftsmen and Foremen)	56	29.62	73	38.62
Semi-skilled (Operators and Kindred)	19	10.05	28	14.81
Service (Protective, Public, Private)	9	4.76	7	3.70
Unskilled	26	13.75	22	11.64
Farmers and Fishermen	46	24.33	--	--
Totals	189	99.96	189	99.98

The absence of farmers and fishermen from the Toronto sample constitutes the main difference between the two generations apart from the differential proportions found in the various categories. The fact that 24 per cent of the fathers were in this category has in itself created the possibility of the intergenerational occupational mobility which is illustrated by Table 10. Both fathers and sons, fathers-in-law and sons-in-law are concentrated in the skilled worker category, indicating the tendency for sons to follow the same occupation or one on the same general level as their fathers,[13] as well as for daughters to marry within their fathers' particular occupational bracket. The much larger proportion of sons in the skilled category and the smaller proportion in the unskilled category illustrates the occupational mobility of sons. In fact, in every occupation which demands training for an urban environment the present generation of French-speaking males in Toronto has shown intergenerational mobility, except in one area. Both fathers and sons are almost totally unrepresented in the category of semi-professional and technician, occupations which are the product of an industrialized economy in which the more advanced level of scientific or financial training required has traditionally been lacking in the educational system of French-Canadian society.

Education and Occupation

The economic disadvantages of French participation in the Toronto labour force emerge only when the two variables so closely related to occupation, education and income are considered. "A man qualifies himself for occupational life by obtaining an education; as a consequence of pursuing his occupation, he obtains income. Occupation, therefore, is the intervening activity linking income to education."[14]

The level of education of the French-speaking labour force as shown in Table 11 has been a major reason for underrepresentation at most of the higher levels of the occupational ladder. Information on education was not available for the French husbands of female respondents, but 70 per cent of the ninety employed male respondents had had only Grade 10 education or less. Over half of this group had only a primary school education ending at Grade 8, while 10 per cent of them had no more than Grade 5. Of the five individuals who had received no formal education at all, one was a skilled worker, three semi-skilled and one unskilled.

---

[13]Miller and Form, *Industrial Sociology*, p. 570; and Yves De Jocas and Guy Rocher, "Inter-generational Mobility in the Province of Quebec," in Bernard Blishen, *et al.*, eds., *Canadian Society* (2nd ed.; Toronto: Macmillan of Canada, 1964), p. 443: "There is, then, among French Canadians a marked tendency to follow the fathers' occupation. Yet this is not peculiar to the French-speaking Canadians. All studies in other countries have indicated a similar tendency."

[14]Otis Dudley Duncan, "A Socio-economic Index for all Occupations," in Albert J. Reiss, Jr., *Occupations and Social Status* (Glencoe: The Free Press, 1961), pp. 116-17. Also quoted in Blishen, "A Socio-economic Index," p. 50.

Table 11

Amount of Education in the Various Occupational Categories of Employed Male Respondents

Occupation	No Formal Education	Grades				Vocational			Complete University	University Graduate Study	Totals
		1-5	6-8	9-10	11-13	Commercial	Technical	Post-High School			
Professionals, Semi-Professionals and Technicians	—	—	—	—	—	—	—	—	2	2	4
Proprietors, Managers, Officials	—	—	3	3	1	1	—	1	—	—	9
Clerical and Sales	—	—	3	1	1	2	—	1	—	1	9
Skilled (Craftsmen & Foremen)	1	6	17	9	2	—	1	2	—	—	38
Semi-skilled (Operators, etc.)	3	1	6	5	—	—	—	—	—	—	15
Service (Protective, Public & Private)	—	—	1	1	—	—	—	—	—	—	2
Unskilled	1	2	7	2	—	—	—	—	—	—	12
Totals	5	9	37	21	4	3	1	4	2	3	89
Not gainfully employed											18
Not Ascertainable											1
Total Male respondents											108

Yet in spite of this generally low educational level the French-speaking labour force in Toronto has climbed the occupation ladder. Most of them were aware of their own deficiencies in education because when they were asked what level of education their children should receive, the majority of answers specified not only complete high school but preferably some or complete university. Judging from the comments of a number of informants regarding their acquisition of a skilled trade in spite of their lack of education, on-the-job training such as the apprenticeship system has been largely responsible for overcoming educational handicaps. It seems evident that those who migrated to Toronto were the more independent and aggressive types in their home communities and have utilized native skill and enterprise harnessed to industrial training opportunities to good advantage. How long those with only Grade 10 education, which includes 83 per cent of those from Northern Ontario, 74 per cent from Southern Ontario, 71 per cent from Quebec, 79 per cent from New Brunswick, and all from the other Atlantic Provinces, can maintain their present occupational level in a day of rapid change in the world of industry and technology is a valid question.

Even those in executive positions were not well qualified by formal education. Most of them had received from a Grade 6 to a Grade 10 education. In the Toronto sample two non-high school executives had training beyond the primary level, eight others had complete high school, and a few had taken special training beyond high school. Only in the professional category do we find a university education.[15] The picture was very different, however, with a group of thirty-five selected members of the French-speaking population who were members of the middle-class élite and were interviewed over and above the representative Toronto sample in order to determine some of the characteristics of the middle-class leadership in Toronto. Twenty-two out of the thirty-five had whole or part university training and several had done graduate study. But it cannot be denied that these were exceptions to the general educational level of the French-speaking population.

Income and Occupation

The third variable in the triad of social status is income, as shown in Table 12. It has been by far the most difficult to secure in terms of reliable, accurate information. The French-speaking housewife has the reputation of handling the household finances and doing it well, and in the majority of cases it was the wife who was asked to supply information regarding total family income, that is, not only wages and salaries of members of the household, but also income from rents, investments, interest, pensions, etc. Just how successfully this was accomplished is a debatable point because of the very considerable disparity between the average income level of the total population in Toronto and that of the French-speaking population.

[15]Brazeau, "Quebec's Emerging Middle Class," p. 325. This general picture accords well with that presented by Jacques Brazeau who found the educational level of the French in Quebec to be considerably below the general average for the English in Ontario.

Table 12

Family Income of the 252 Respondents in the
Toronto Sample

·Income Level in Dollars	Number of Families	Percentage	Cumulative
Less than $999 per year	5	2.18	2.18
$1,000-$3,999 (low)	56	24.45	26.63
$4,000-$6,999 (below average)	98	42.79	69.42
$7,000-$9,999 (average)	50	21.83	91.25
$10,000 and Over (high)	20	8.73	99.98
Number Reporting Income	229	99.98	
Refused	12		
Don't Know, Not Ascertainable	11		
Total	252		

According to the Dominion Bureau of Statistics,[16] income in Toronto increased on the average one-third between the census year of 1961 and the Toronto survey of the French-speaking in 1965 when the figures in Table 12 were obtained. This would place the average family income from all sources for the total population of Metropolitan Toronto at $8,723 per year. The average family income from all sources for the French-speaking population, according to the Toronto sample, is $5,460 per year. The difference is $3,363, or 37.4 per cent below the metropolitan average. Forty-five per cent of the French-speaking population reside within the city of Toronto, however, where the average family income from all sources is around $1,300 less than the metropolitan average, $7,459. But even this reduced amount is much higher than the average for family income from all sources of the French-speaking. In fact, the average French family income from all sources is even lower than the metropolitan family average for wages and salaries alone at $7,775, or that of the city at $6,629.[17]

Part of the disparity in income may be due to the fact that the average family income for those receiving over $10,000 a year was arbitrarily assumed to be $12,000, when it may have been very much higher. But even this does not give an adequate explanation of the gap between the average for Metropolitan Tor-

[16]Private correspondence with Walter Duffett, Dominion Statistician, dated January 3 and 10, 1967, in which the estimated rise in family income from all sources was given.

[17]Census of Canada, 1961, Bulletin CT-15, Table 2, 1.32.

onto and that of the French-speaking population of 37.4 per cent.[18] Income
level appears to reflect deficiencies in education and skills to a much greater
degree than occupational level.

The most obvious reason for this disadvantaged position of the French-
speaking as far as income is concerned is that 70 per cent were employed in
manual occupations, which in turn reflected a low level of education. But this
cannot be the whole answer because many skilled workers have high incomes.
Furthermore, the disparity is accentuated when the number of wage-earners
contributing to family income from all sources is taken into consideration.

When one considers that 36.5 per cent of the families had multiple wage-
earners and yet average family income from all sources was low, it can only be
concluded that a considerable number of French families are extremely disadvantaged in Toronto as far as income is concerned. Forty-three per cent are
found in the below average income bracket, and another 24 per cent in the very
low income bracket, a total of 67 per cent below average family income from all
sources. Only 22 per cent are in the average income range and another 9 per cent
with high incomes.

John Porter has suggested that disparities of income can be related to religion
as well as to ethnicity, to the Catholic affiliation of the French-speaking as well
as to their national origin.[19] Porter examined the census tracts of Halifax,
Ottawa-Hull, Windsor and Winnipeg, all of which have substantial Catholic populations within city boundaries. He discovered that there is a relation between
income and religion, at least at the top and bottom of the income scale, when
income is taken as an objective class indicator.[20] His assumption was that since
census tracts are normatively made up of small groups and consequently are
fairly homogeneous with respect to income, religion, etc., that "if there is a
consistent pattern of higher income groups having fewer Catholics and lower
income groups having more Catholics it seems valid to assume that there is a
relationship between income and religion."[21]

Porter did not use Toronto in his observations and based his finding upon the
1951 census.[22] A look at Toronto using total family income from wages and
salaries in 1961,[23] to locate the twenty census tracts of lowest median income
and the twenty census tracts of highest median income, shows the same pattern

---

[18]The disparity between the average income of the total population of Toronto and the
sample of the French in 1965 is undeniable, but owing to the difficulty of securing accurate
estimates of income from interviewees caution is necessary regarding the size of the disparity reported here. Cf. Oswald Hall, "The Canadian Division of Labour Revisited," in
Richard J. Ossenberg, *Canadian Society* (Scarborough, Ontario: Prentice-Hall of Canada,
1971), p. 97.

[19]Porter, *The Vertical Mosaic* pp. 98-103.

[20]Ibid., p. 100.

[21]Ibid., p. 103.

[22]Ibid., p. 101.

[23]*Census of Canada, 1961,* Bulletin CT-15, Table 2.

which Porter discovered in the other four cities. Catholics were much more heavily represented in the lowest than in the highest income brackets.

The attitude of the Roman Catholic has always been very different to that of the Protestant or Jew relative to economic success. As Quinn has pointed out:

> The most important principle of the philosophy of life which the Church in Quebec always held up as an ideal was the primacy of spiritual over material values. . . . Man's activities in this world were to be subordinated to the goal of everlasting happiness in the next. The possession of divine grace and the Christian virtues was more important than success in worldly affairs and the higher income which went with it.[24]

Lacking the motivation and drive of the Protestant ethic, the French-speaking Catholics have been content with less than their non-Catholic fellow-workers and neighbours even though the influence of the English-speaking economic environment could not but have an effect over a period of time. Few in Toronto had grown up in an almost exclusively French environment, consequently the force of the Catholic philosophy has been weakened but it certainly has not been lost.

Just as both occupation and education have been influenced by the region from which French-speaking migrants to Toronto have come, so income also differs according to whether the migrants come from Quebec, Ontario or the Maritimes. The average family income from all sources of those who came from Quebec is $6,470, which is $1,000 more than Franco-Ontarians, whose average family income is $5,450 per year. Acadians were nearly equal to Quebeckers with $6,360 per year. Thus the Acadians, who have repeatedly been alleged to occupy an economic status much lower than those who grew up in either Ontario or Quebec, show an income almost on a par with those from Quebec, and certainly far ahead, by $900, of the average family income of Franco-Ontarians. This fact contradicts the stereotype prevalent in Toronto of the Acadians as having an inferior status economically to the other segments of the French-speaking population, and reveals that it is the Franco-Ontarians who have brought the average family income of the French-speaking population so low.

Table 13 below, which gives the analysis of the relative income of those from Ontario, Quebec, and the Maritimes, shows that Quebeckers have the highest percentage of families whose incomes are in excess of the average family incomes of the French-speaking in Toronto, constituting 13 per cent of incomes over $10,000 per year in comparison with 11 per cent for Acadians and 4 per cent for Franco-Ontarians. Quebeckers also have 27 per cent of incomes in the $7,000 to $9,999 range, in which the general metropolitan average family income from all sources is found, in contrast to 20 per cent for Acadians and 19 per cent for Franco-Ontarians. Quebec is underrepresented in the lower income brackets while the Acadians and Franco-Ontarians are overrepresented. Franco-Ontarians begin to dominate the percentages only in the lower ranges of income which reveals why the average income of Franco-Ontarians is so far below that of Quebeckers and Acadians.

[24]Quinn, *Union Nationale*, p. 12.

Table 13

Family Income from all Sources of Respondents in the
Toronto Sample Who Grew up in Ontario, Quebec and the
Maritime Provinces

	Ontario		Quebec		Maritimes		
Income $	No.	Cumu- lative %	No.	Cumu- lative %	No.	Cumu- lative %	Totals
Up to $999	2	2.19	2	3.63	--	--	4
1,000-3,999	24	28.56	9	19.99	24	22.95	47
4,000-6,999	44	76.91	22	59.99	28	68.85	95
7,000-9,999	17	95.59	15	87.26	12	88.52	44
10,000 and over	4	99.98	7	99.98	7	99.99	18
Totals	91		55		61		

The Socio-Economic Effects of Participation

The single socio-economic index formulated by Bernard Blishen on the basis
of the 1951 census to include the three variables of occupation, education and
income has been revised on the basis of the 1961 census with the added dimension of the index of occupational prestige formulated by Pineo and Porter.[25]
Occupations range on the index from a high of 76.69 to a low of 25.36.

When the French labour force in Toronto is located on the revised Blishen
index, three points relevant to participation of the French in Toronto work
world emerge. First, the two top occupational categories, which encompass the
upper middle class, consisting of professionals, proprietors, managers and officials, are quite sharply distinguished on the index from clerical and sales occupations, the so-called lower middle class, and from the range of manual occupations.[26] Second, the clerical and sales occupations are scattered throughout

[25]Blishen, "A Socio-economic Index," pp. 41-53; Peter C. Pineo and John Porter,
"Occupational Prestige in Canada," *Canadian Review of Sociology and Anthropology*, IV,
No. 1 (February, 1967), 24-40.

[26]The guide used in the Toronto study for the classification of occupations was the
Dictionary of Occupational Titles compiled by the United States Department of Labor,
which does not always accord with the ratings of Pineo and Porter. For instance, the
American volume gives managerial status to a railway conductor because he is in charge of a
train, while Pineo and Porter give this position only skilled worker status. Foremen in the
American *Dictionary* are classed among the skilled, while Pineo and Porter give a foreman in
a factory managerial status. In the U.S. guide a firefighter is included under Protective
Service while in Pineo and Porter it is included under semi-skilled. Taxicab driver in the U.S.
guide is semi-skilled while in Pineo and Porter it is unskilled. They also include a farm owner
and operator as unskilled.

most of the range of skilled and semi-skilled occupations, showing why the lower middle class is indistinguishable from the working class among the French in Toronto. Third, only a few of the French are in occupations which are located in the lower third of the Blishen socio-economic index.

The significance of the socio-economic distribution of the French labour force as noted above is that the French labour force in Toronto compares very favourably with the total labour force in Canada. The latter is concentrated in the lower third of the socio-economic index while the Toronto French are located in the middle third rather than the lower third. The occupational mobility revealed by the concentration of French white-collar workers at the executive level, and of manual workers at the skilled level, has given the Toronto French this favourable position in comparison with the labour force in most of the provinces of Canada.[27] The anomaly is that such a position has been accompanied by the disadvantaged position in income of many of the French families.

To sum up the foregoing, the way in which a man makes a living and the kind of living he makes have important consequences for how the man sees himself and is seen by others. These, in turn, shape his relationship both within his own ethnic group and with the larger society around him. The economic absorption of the French within the occupational structure of the Toronto work world has given the French migrant a living, comparable or better than he has known before, a measure of economic security despite a disparity in average income, and an opportunity to improve his social status through occupational mobility. The process has been reciprocal, however, for employment has identified his life chances with the majority rather than the minority society and made it expedient for his future that ethnic values be adjusted to the economic goals current in the host industrial community. The work world has therefore been the major formative influence in the accommodation of the French to the English-speaking society.

[27]Blishen, "A Socio-economic Index," p. 51.

Chapter VI

Religious Values and Ethnic Nationalism

The tangible impact of the particular line of development which the French parish of the Sacré-Coeur has followed is reflected in the extent to which the French population of Metropolitan Toronto has been participating in the various parish activities.

According to the parish priest, in 1965 about 350 families regularly attended services at the Sacré-Coeur. They were the parishioners who contributed regularly to the parish and wanted a receipt for income tax purposes, so they deposited their offerings in a signed envelope. But this number was an approximation because it was possible for families to attend regularly without using the envelope system. Since it was an ethnic parish anyone who was of French origin or spoke the French language could attend the Sacré-Coeur, but they also had the option of attending the English-speaking territorial parish within their own residential neighbourhood. Consequently many French-speaking people who did not attend mass at the Sacré-Coeur went there on special occasions: weddings, christenings, confessions. For instance, in 1964 there were ninety-nine weddings and ninety-one christenings performed, a number higher than would normally be expected from the size of the membership.

The best estimate of the scope of participation in the parish by the French population given by the parish priest was the average attendance at the various services. About 1,500 attended one of the five Sunday masses: the church was two-thirds to three-quarters full at the 7:00 A.M., 8:00 A.M., and 9:00 A.M. masses, full at the 10:30 A.M. mass, and overcrowded at the 12:00 o'clock mass.

The Parishioners

When interviewed the parish priest found it difficult to talk about his parishioners except to say that about half of them resided in the immediate area, that the majority of them were Acadians, and that the parish served as a "social service agency." A participant observer has commented that:

> The Sacré-Coeur appears as a lower class parish. The mothers often show up with curlers, the fathers look uncomfortable in old navy-blue suits. The children are dressed in hand-me-downs, which are usually too long or too short and dirty. The French one hears is poor grammatically and it is punctuated by many English words. And if most of the adults speak French, an overwhelming majority of the children speak English.[1]

There were among the parishioners, of course, some representatives of the middle class. A few prominent French-Canadian families have chosen the Sacré-

[1] Lee, "Evolution of an Ethnic Parish," pp. 37-38.

Coeur as their parish, and were the families which throughout the years sponsored various associations, organized groups both within and without the parish,
and patronized many activities.

The respondents in the representative sample were asked a series of questions
about attendance or non-attendance at the Sacré-Coeur and their responses are
recorded in Tables 14 to 18. Two limitations of the tables should be kept in
mind, however. It is not possible to generalize and draw valid conclusions when
the number of respondents attending the French parish is so small, only 35 out
of the 252 respondents, as indicated in Table 14. But a comparison of the
thirty-five respondents with the rest, especially the 195 respondents who regularly attended English parishes, can offer at least meaningful explanatory information in terms of a number of variables.

Table 14

Church Attendance

Where Attend	Number	Percentage
Attend English Catholic Churches	195	77.38
Attend Sacré-Coeur	35	13.89
Attend non-Catholic Churches	9	3.57
Do not attend religious services	12	4.76
Refused to answer	1	.40
Total	252	100.00

It should be noted also that the thirty-five respondents attending the
Sacré-Coeur represent 13.89 per cent of the total number of respondents. In
contrast, the 1,500 worshippers who attend the French parish on a typical
Sunday represent only 4 per cent of the total adult French population in Metropolitan Toronto. The sample therefore contains an overrepresentation of parishioners of the French parish, largely because the sample was drawn from areas
of concentration of the French of which three were located close to the French
parish. Since the French population was quite evenly dispersed throughout the
entire metropolitan area, the five tables present a picture which is biased in the
direction of higher attendance at the Sacré-Coeur than is actually the case.

Table 15 makes it clear that distance from place of residence to the Sacré-
Coeur was the chief obstacle to attendance there. But to others a variety of
reasons were important. Some 30 per cent of respondents had non-French
spouses[2] and in most of these cases English was the common denominator in

[2] Almost three-quarters of these cross-cultural mariages involve spouses of British ancestry (49 per cent English, Scottish, or Welsh; 24 per cent Irish), and the rest were of varied

language which influenced them to attend English parishes. In spite of the fact that all respondents interviewed were of French origin some declared: "Our name is French, but we are not, and we no longer speak the French language," or "We no longer claim to be French." Many of the Franco-Ontarians and Acadians had already become accustomed to attending English parishes before migrating to Toronto and were not interested in the existence or the location of a French parish.

Table 15

Reasons for Not Attending the French Parish

Reasons	Number	Percentage
It is too far	121	62.05
Part of the family doesn't speak French	16	8.21
We are not French	17	8.72
Didn't know it existed	6	3.08
Other[a]	35	17.95
Total	195	100.01

[a]Includes miscellaneous, no reason, and not ascertainable.

Distance, however, does not explain why a large proportion of respondents living in nearby concentration areas such as the Don, Riverdale and Parkdale did not attend the French parish, as Table 16 demonstrates. The history of controversy at the French parish may be a partial explanation as an ethnic parish may be a partial explanation as an ethnic parish builds its own reputation, drawing parishioners to it or repelling them. Some respondents were quite frank: "We don't want to get too involved at Sacred Heart; we want to keep out of the way of gossipers." One woman stated flatly that she was not going back there to be "torn to pieces."

It was evident from responses that "location in a distinct area results in transfer to the parish of the prestige evaluations assigned to the area and its residents."[3] A middle-class respondent commented: "The district around Sacred Heart is too slummy and anywhere else means travelling a distance." There is little doubt that the character of the district in which the Sacré-Coeur was located was responsible for underrepresentation of the middle class among the parishioners. Constituting 30 per cent of the French population in Toronto, the

ethnic stocks: German, Italian, Jewish, Ukrainian, American, Dutch, Indian, Macedonian, Norwegian, and Spanish.

[3]Fosselman, "The Parish in Urban Communities," p. 149.

middle class represent less than one-half of this proportion among the thirty-five respondents attending the French parish.

Table 16

Areas of Residence and Attendance at the Sacré-Coeur

	Attend		Do Not Attend		
Area	Number	Percentage	Number	Percentage	Total
Riverdale	9	15.52	49	84.48	58
Don	18	45.00	22	55.00	40
Parkdale	6	15.38	33	84.62	39
Lakeshore	--	--	30	100.00	30
Scarborough	--	--	38	100.00	38
Spot Sampling	2	4.26	45	95.54	47
All Areas	35	13.89	217	86.11	252

Even among the thirty-five respondents attending the Sacré-Coeur the parish played a very minor part in the choice of their present area of residence in comparison with economic factors, as shown in Table 17. The proximity of a bilingual school, or even an English-speaking Catholic school, appears more important than the location of the French parish. Why was this seeming indifference to the ethnic appeal of the French parish so widespread, even permeating its own parishioners?

Table 17

Reason for Choosing Area of Residence

Reasons	Number	Percentage
Close to work	4	11.43
"All I can afford"	12	34.28
Near French parish	2	5.72
Near bilingual school	8	22.86
Other[a]	9	25.71
All reasons	35	100.00

[a]Near relatives and friends; near English parochial school; liked area: because of neighbours, shopping, transportation.

Religion and Language

An attempt to discover the root cause of indifference to the Sacré-Coeur among the French population took the form of asking respondents to give their reasons for agreeing, or disagreeing, with two statements read to them by the interviewers. Both statements reflected the ideological viewpoint that the French language and the Catholic religion form a cultural unity for French Canadians and therefore the French language must be retained at all costs by them.[4]

Ninety per cent of the respondents disagreed with the first statement that: "Those who lose their French language will also lose their Catholic faith." Some typical reasons were: "The Catholic faith is the same in English as it is in French." "You don't have to be French to be Catholic," "I lost my religion but still have my French." "Language and religion are not necessarily connected."

The few who agreed with the statement blamed "the influence of a large city in making the French forget both their religion and their language," or "the desire of some of the French is to become like the English, to act as if they were English." Some cited cases of French Canadians who abandoned all contact with the French parish or French organizations after becoming successful in business, mentioning some who had even anglicized their French names because the English had found them hard to pronounce.

Seventy-two per cent disagreed with the second statement: "The French who attend English parishes have lost interest in the French language." The phrase "interest in the French language" apparently was equated with "loss of the French language," for typical answers were: "We go to an English parish, but have not lost our French, for we speak it in the house, with friends. . . ." "Most people go to the English parish only once a week, so it doesn't affect their French." "It doesn't show lack of interest in the French language to speak the language of the majority in a parish." "Attending English parishes is a matter of convenience because there aren't enough French parishes."

Only a few of those who agreed with the second statement gave any reasons. Those who did intimated that opportunities to speak French were drastically limited in Toronto. One claimed that "people are either too shy, or too ashamed of being French, so they try to be like the English." "If people value French only in a sentimental way they won't try to put it to practical use." "Other organizations besides the French parish try to preserve the French language in Toronto." "Children do not value the French language here and do not want to speak it."

It is clear from the responses that the majority of the respondents did not feel that the French language and their religious faith were indissolubly linked together. For them the nexus between Catholicism and the French language has been broken. Religious identification with the Catholic Church takes precedence over ethnic identification with French culture. The reorientation of values which

---

[4]Theriault, "Franco-Americans of New England," pp. 402-03; George F. G. Stanley, "French and English in Western Canada," in Mason Wade, ed., *Canadian Dualism* (Toronto: University of Toronto Press, 1960), p. 332.

has taken place within the Toronto milieu tends to divorce ethnicity from religion. Ethnic loyalties have been virtually displaced by considerations of social status or class, a by-product of socio-economic differentiation within the urban environment.

Religion and Class

In Table 18, which explores the relationship between the level of family income from all sources and attendance at the French parish, low incomes tend to be overrepresented among those affiliated with the Sacré-Coeur in comparison with the incomes of those who attend English parishes. The Don, Riverdale, and Parkdale areas provided opportunities for lower-income families to secure housing within the scope of their financial resources, or close to places of employment. Consequently they are in a position to attend the French parish if they wish to because of its proximity. The same economic factors have operated to spread many of the higher-income working class and the middle class among the English parishes across the city and suburbs.

Table 18

A Comparison of Family Income and Attendance at the Sacré-Coeur French Parish

Income Per Year $	Attend French Parish		Do Not Attend French Parish		Totals	
	No.	%	No.	%	No.	%
Less than $999	--	--	5	2.5	5	2.2
1,000-3,999	13	42.0	43	21.6	56	24.4
4,000-6,999	11	35.5	87	43.9	98	42.8
7,000-9,999	5	16.1	45	22.8	50	21.8
Over 10,000	2	6.4	18	9.0	20	8.7
Totals	31	100.0	198	99.8	229	99.9
Not Ascertainable	3		8		11	
Refused	1		11		12	
	35		217		252	

Consciousness of class has also played an important role in shaping patterns of parish affiliation and participation. Ninety-one per cent of middle class respondents attended English parishes. Only a few of the middle class continued to use ethnic values rather than class values as criteria for determing place of residence, friendships, memberships in organizations, as well as parish affiliation.

Thus within the French-speaking population there has been a clash of competing systems of values: the traditional value system which links the ethnic to the religious, as symbolized by parishioners of the French parish, the Sacré -Coeur and the emergent value system which links the economic to the religious, as symbolized by the middle class who attend English parishes.

The Changing Role of the Sacré-Coeur

Throughout the social development of French-Canadian society the Catholic parish system has been the major source of social integration linking together religion, education and the family into a cohesive institutional triad which has cemented together every aspect of the French-Canadian life. In Toronto, however, under the pressures of minority status, diversity of cultural background or ecological dispersion, and socio-economic differentiation resulting from industrialization, to which daily exposure to the English language and culture has been added, this triple alliance tends to disintegrate.

Within the multi-ethnic community the traditional territorial parish has become an ethnic or national parish which caters only to that segment of the population which is both Catholic and French. The school, in a bilingual form, exists only on the sufferance of the English-speaking Catholic majority, which may be constituted of numerous ethnic groups all needing education for their children in the linguistic common denominator, which is English. The traditional extended French-Canadian family becomes progressively smaller and more mobile as it begins the transition to the nuclear family of parents with two to four children which is characteristic of an urban-industrial milieu.

The major result of these developments in Toronto is that the focus of social organization has passed from the French parish, which increasingly has been performing only religious duties, to other social organizations of middle class origin which have been moving in and taking over the ethnic role of the Sacré-Coeur.

Two increasingly important lines of development are responsible for shifting the focus of ethnic identification away from the parish. First, many non-parish French organizations exist which have appeared quite recently on the Toronto scene: the "Club Richelieu" which groups French-speaking professionals, proprietors and executives; the "Club Rouillé" which organizes dances and other social events for the younger crowd; "France-Canada" which promotes interaction between French Canadians and other French-speaking peoples; "L'Alliance Canadienne" which promotes goodwill between French and English Canadians by organizing conferences and lectures; the "R.T.F." (radio-television-française) whose aim was to secure a French radio station for Southern Ontario and now is to get a French television station; the "Ciné Club" which imports French films for showing to its members; "L'Alliance Française" which promotes French cultural programmes and a French library; and finally, a committee which groups two representatives from all the French associations in Toronto with the intention of building "une maison française à Toronto."

Since these associations cater more specifically to the cultural and social needs of the French-speaking community, the Sacré-Coeur has lost its central position. Its diffused communal role has been replaced by a more specialized religious role. The shift in this direction has received strong impetus from the decrease in religiousness among the urban French population, decreasing the importance of the Church and of the parish in French communities in general.

Second, the decrease in importance of the French parish has been related to the growth in importance of the bilingual schools. They have begun to replace the French parish in some measure as the main socializing agent, and seemingly perform the same functions in a more efficient way. The first bilingual school, the Sacré-Coeur, was an extension of the parish. The second, Sainte Madeleine, founded in Scarborough independently of the parish, has been acting as a stronger magnet than the Sacré-Coeur. While the first migrants to Toronto settled around the parish, many of the recent ones have been concentrating around the new bilingual school.

Chapter VII

Between Two Cultures:
The Bilingual Schools

From the standpoint of the Roman Catholic Church no system of instruction can be called education unless it is based upon religious principles, which in this case consists of the doctrine and social philosophy of Roman Catholicism. The Church therefore assumes responsibility for education within parish boundaries and refuses to delegate such responsibility to any educational authority, governmental or otherwise, which does not recognize the Catholic philosophy of education. So deeply is this educational ideology imbedded in the tradition of the Church that the cost of such education, in whole or in part, is underwritten by the Church if necessary. The parochial school, therefore, is an integral part of the parish system, a vital connecting link between religion and the family for successive generations of children.

If a child has been instructed and nurtured in parochial schools from his earliest school days, the Church assumes that his whole pattern of thinking, his system of values, his way of life, can be expected to conform in the main to Catholic ideals. Through control of education the Church believes that the Catholic family will adhere to the practice of the Christian virtues rather than the pursuit of material prosperity with its implicit denial of Catholic goals for living. Thus, ideally, all levels of education must be permeated with the basic value system of Catholicism, from learning the "three R's" in primary school, through the classical colleges or secondary schools, to the highest seats of learning, the universities.[1]

Within French minority populations such as that of Metropolitan Toronto, however, the implementation of Catholic educational goals is rendered more difficult by two characteristics of ethnic parishes. The dimension of language and culture must be added to that of religion, and the boundaries of an ethnic parish may encompass an entire metropolitan area rather than a limited geographical district within the city. In its bilingual form, the parochial school must weld religion to the minority culture within an educational context throughout its constituency, providing both a religious orientation and a sense of ethnic identity for the children of the migrants. Church and school, as allies, provide the "twin fortresses" of faith and language, the essentials for the survival of the French culture within a French minority population.[2]

In Metropolitan Toronto, however, the Catholic ideals for parochial schools find their approximate realization only in the English-speaking Catholic or sepa-

[1]Quinn, *Union Nationale*, p. 13; Theriault, "Franco-Americans of New England," p. 402; Stanley, "French and English in Western Canada," pp. 332, 344.

[2]Stanley, "French and English in Western Canada," p. 332.

rate school system of the Province of Ontario because the French-speaking do not control bilingual schools. French-speaking Catholics constituted only 13 per cent of all Catholics within the Diocese of Toronto in 1961, so control of bilingual schools has been invested in the English-speaking majority on the Separate School Boards of Education. In essence, the bilingual schools have been confronted with the same problem as the French parish, that of combining the religious and the ethnic within the same institution without possessing autonomy in either administration or planning.

Enrollment of French Children in Toronto Schools

In Table 19 the enrollment and type of school attended in 1965 is shown for all school-age children among the families of the 252 respondents interviewed. Families with children numbered 213, reporting 876 children, 421 boys and 455 girls, an average of just over four children per family, of which 388 (44%) were children of school age in 1965. Since 85 per cent of these children were enrolled in primary schools, most of the families were young. Just over one-third of the school-age children of respondents were enrolled in bilingual schools. Here again the Toronto sample has a built-in bias due to choice of most respondents from areas of concentration of the French population adjacent to the existing bilingual schools. The total number enrolled in all bilingual schools in Metropolitan Toronto in 1965, including the ninety students in the private high school, De Charbonnel, was 1,095 students. There were 21,909 children of French origin below the age of fifteen years in Metropolitan Toronto in 1961,[3] and presumably a larger number in 1965. When the total number of children was adjusted for those not of school age, less than 15 per cent of the children in French families were receiving a bilingual education at either the primary or secondary level in 1965.

Out of 213 families of respondents with children, 77 per cent (174) sent their children to English-speaking schools, with 16.2 per cent attending public schools and the remainder Catholic parochial schools. Of interest are the characteristics of the forty-nine families, who sent their children to bilingual schools. Twenty-two of these families were originally from Quebec, fourteen from Ontario, divided equally between north and south, and thirteen were Acadian families, all but one from New Brunswick. An analysis of family income and place of residence of these forty-nine families is given in Table 20, which indicates that, in spite of its short history, Ste. Madeleine bilingual school has drawn a larger enrollment of the children of respondents than the Sacré-Coeur. It also indicates that higher incomes prevail among families sending their children to Ste. Madeleine, and lower incomes among families sending their children to the Sacré-Coeur. Thus the establishment of Ste. Madeleine school has served to accentuate the class differences existing among the French population which

[3]Census of Canada, 1961, from which data relating to the French population of Metropolitan Toronto had been prepared by the Dominion Bureau of Statistics for the Royal Commission on Bilingualism and Biculturalism.

tended to be obscured previously because so few of the middle class sent their children to the Sacré-Coeur school.

Table 19

The Various Types of Schools Available for the Education of Children in the Toronto Area, and the Number of Children from the Toronto Sample Who Attend Such Schools

	Children	
Type of School	No.	%
Primary: Grades 1 to 8		
Bilingual Catholic (Separate) School	114	34.8
English Catholic (Separate) School	159	48.4
English Public (Non-sectarian) School	53	16.2
Private School	2	.6
Primary School Totals	328	100.0
Secondary: Grades 9 to 12		
Bilingual Catholic (Private) School (De Charbonnel)	3	5.0
English Public (Non-sectarian) High School	27	45.0
English Private High School (usually Catholic)	5	8.3
Vocational School (Commercial-Technical)	20	33.3
Other (Miscellaneous)	3	5.0
Post-Secondary: Various		
University	2	3.3
Totals	60	99.9
Total	388	

Distance from place of residence to a bilingual school, whether it has been the primary schools, the Sacré-Coeur or Ste. Madeleine, or the private high school, De Charbonnel, has affected the attendance of French children at bilingual schools because it has entailed considerable hardship for students outside of the immediate neighbourhood in which the school was located. Prior to 1961, when the bilingual school at the Sacré-Coeur was the only one in the city and suburbs, the distribution of the population on the basis of socio-economic status entailed long hours of travel for over one-half of the enrollment. According to the parish

Table 20

A Comparison of Family Income and Place of Residence of the Forty-Nine Families Who Sent Children to Bilingual Schools, From the Toronto Sample

Income Per Year $	City Areas				Suburban Areas		
	River-dale No.	Don No.	Park-dale No.	Totals No.	Scar-borough No.	Other No.	Totals No.
Less than $999	--	--	--	--	--	--	--
1,000-3,999	1	5	--	6	--	--	--
4,000-6,999	5	3	1	9	5	2	7
7,000-9,000	1	--	2[a]	3	5	9	14
Over 10,000	1	--	--	1	3	3	6
Totals	8	8	3	19	13	14	27
Not Ascertainable		2	21	1			28

[a]Only one family in the spot sampling was located within the city on the fringe of Parkdale so it has been included in the Parkdale area.

priest and the principal, 56 per cent of the students lived beyond the district, for whom travel from all over the city and suburbs shortened the time available for homework and play, and exhausted the energies of the children.

But distance was not the only condition in Toronto unfavourable to the growth of the bilingual school system. There was the domination of Separate School Boards of Education by English-speaking Catholics; the policy of clerical leadership at the French parish for several decades of opposition to expansion of the bilingual school system beyond the Sacré-Coeur; Toronto also lacked concentrations of French families due to the dispersed pattern of settlement; socio-economic differentiation injected class divisions into education; and finally, the problem of maintaining an adequate level of academic proficiency within a two-language school system which seeks to combine education, the Catholic religion and French culture within a single curriculum. The discussion below illustrates how these various elements in combination have served to hinder the development of the bilingual system in a way which parallels the slow growth of the French parish.

A. Separate School Boards of Education

The major concern of Catholic Boards of Education in Toronto has been the provision of separate school facilities for the large numbers of Catholic immigrant children from Europe which have been augmenting the growing Catholic population. In 1964 alone, a member of the Metropolitan Board reported, additions had been made to fifty-three separate schools in order to accommodate the enlarged enrollments mainly due to immigration. Because of this, most members of Separate School Boards of Education viewed bilingual classes and schools for the French as granting special privileges to one particular ethnic group which were seldom demanded by other ethnic groups.[4] The fact that nearly all of the French-speaking population of Toronto were native Canadians who claimed linguistic rights as one of the founding races has had little influence on the Boards of Education.

Bilingual schools required channelling into a specifically French system capital funds which to Board members could be used more profitably for English-language facilities for large and more concentrated immigrant groups to whom linguistic privileges were secondary and cultural integration into Canadian society a primary concern. Prior to the enactment in the early 1960s of the Ontario Corporate Tax Adjustment by the Government of Ontario which placed the Catholic separate schools in a better position, the chronic shortage of capital and operating funds within the Catholic school system reinforced this viewpoint.

French representation on Separate School Boards of Education must also bear some responsibility for the fact that there was one bilingual primary school for a few hundred French-speaking children in 1889, and there was still one bilingual school in 1961 for almost twenty-two thousand children of French origin under the age of fifteen years. The policy of clerical leadership at the French parish over a period of four decades was to maintain only one centre of both French worship and bilingual education in Toronto. Neither the clerical nor the lay representatives of the French community on Boards of Education contended for expansion of the bilingual school system, in spite of the growth of the French population. In fact, a determined effort was made by clerical leadership to prevent the establishment of a second bilingual primary school in the suburb of Scarborough in 1962.

Working-class families therefore had a virtual monopoly of the means of preserving the language and culture of French Canada insofar as this could be accomplished through the French parish and its bilingual school. Yet those who enjoyed these privileges belonged to the class which has shown the least concern in Toronto for matters of language and culture, of ethnic identity. Few middle-class families sent their children to the downtown bilingual school, and even of

---

[4]The gist of an interview with Director Roger Charbonneau of l'Association canadienne-française d'Education d'Ontario, at the headquarters of the Association in Ottawa in November, 1964, and interviews with three French members of the Metropolitan Separate School Board of Education. Lamontagne, "Ontario: The Two Races," p. 370.

those who did, a number did not return to the Sacré-Coeur on Sundays. They preferred to attend English parishes because they believed the bilingual school to be a more important means of linguistic and cultural survival than the French parish with its various associations.

A number of middle-class families, unhappy with the lower-class neighbourhood in which the Ecole du Sacré-Coeur was situated, reluctant to permit their children to travel the long distances from their homes to the downtown school, and impatient with the lack of progress through representation on Boards of Education took matters into their own hands. They circulated a petition in the suburb of Scarborough requesting the Catholic School Board of the municipality to begin bilingual classes in primary schools. In spite of opposition from the Sacré-Coeur such classes began in September, 1961. Shortage of classroom space the following year, however, led to their cancellation. Only a sit-down strike organized by French parents,[5] who sent their children to the Sacré-Coeur by taxicab for the remainder of the school year, led to the re-establishment of classes the following year and the opening of a new bilingual school, Ste. Madeleine, in September, 1965. The new primary school began with an enrollment of nearly 400 children, mainly from middle-class families in contrast to the lower-class downtown school.

Further expansion of the bilingual school system on the pattern of Ste. Madeleine was curtailed, however, by the lack of concentration of the French population in sufficient numbers to warrant, at least in the eyes of Separate School Boards, the establishment of more bilingual schools. Bilingual classes begun in St. Robert primary school in Downsview, a northwest suburb, were cancelled after a year because of movement of French families from the district due to the occupational mobility of the French labour force formerly resident in the area. Bilingual classes in a west-end primary school were announced but never begun because of lack of sufficient enrollment, a situation attributed by respondents to bad planning. Thus only two bilingual primary schools, twenty miles apart, were operative in 1965. Over one-half of the enrollments in each school came from outside the immediate area, entailing in the eyes of many French parents, an unjustifiable expenditure of travel time and physical energy by the children.

B. Social Class and Bilingual Education

As long as the Sacré-Coeur was the only bilingual primary school in Toronto class divisions within the student body were inevitable. Children from the immediate area, according to the principal, came from lower-class homes, of which the majority were Acadian in background. Many of the Acadian families had to rely on welfare for a time after arriving in Toronto as their limited educational background was a handicap in securing employment. Their children tended to be

---

[5]The sit-down strike was recorded in picture and in print in *The Globe and Mail* (Toronto) of Thursday, September 15, 1962.

slow to learn and harder to handle than other children in the estimation of the principal and teachers. They tended to stick together and show hostility to other children. When they did poorly at school, the parents blamed the teaching staff, who in return felt that it was the Acadian children who gave the school a poor reputation as an educational institution. A clash of class values was evident in the situation.

The situation was created, remarked the principal, because parents from Quebec and Ontario who had a better educational background moved out of the district more rapidly than the Acadians. It was the former whose children came from a distance to continue their bilingual education. Few of these were middle-class parents, who preferred to send their children to English parochial schools in their area of residence. When Ste. Madeleine primary school in a middle-class area opened its doors, quite a number of the middle class began to move into the northern area of Scarborough. Thus the already complex relationship of education, religion and culture within bilingual schools was further complicated by the factor of social class. The status factor has determined for many of the middle class the relationship between the bilingual school and the kind of parish attended. If the school, such as Ste. Madeleine, conformed to middle-class values but the parish, such as the Sacré-Coeur, did not, then an English parish was preferable. Class values have separated the role of the French parish from the role of the parochial bilingual school at the very point where traditionally they have been allies in the preservation of the French language and culture.

The dominance of class values over ethnic values is evident in the case of the French-Canadian sales manager of a large pharmaceutical firm who was transferred from Quebec to Toronto. The clergy at the Sacré-Coeur urged him to settle within the parish district and send his children to the parish school. After examining the area the executive would not even consider settling in a run-down neighbourhood and secured housing in the Don Mills area of upper and middle-class homes not far from his office. He discovered at the same time that bilingual classes were about to begin in Scarborough, which was the solution to continuing the education of his younger children in French. But his decision on residence had been made before he had heard about the bilingual school, so it was based upon class values, the type of residential area rather than proximity to a bilingual school.

C. Academic Proficiency and Bilingual Education

Considerations of class were also evident in the repeated criticisms by middle-class respondents of what they considered to be the low academic level of existing bilingual facilities. Were such criticisms based upon their own educational experience, or upon their aspirations for their children? Table 21 records the educational background of the 252 respondents. The level of parental education is low throughout, with almost one-half having received only a primary school education, one-third of them having Grade 5 or less. Four per cent had received no formal education at all. Regional variations in educational background are significant. Of those with only a primary school education, 67 per cent were from New Brunswick, 51 per cent from Northern Ontario, and only 40 per cent from Southern Ontario and Quebec. By Grade 10, 83 per cent of the Acadians and 76 per cent from Northern Ontario had completed their education in contrast to 65 per cent from Southern Ontario and 55 per cent from Quebec. Only 21 per cent of the 252 respondents had received an education beyond the Grade 10 level. The criticisms may have emerged from the desire for a better education for their children than they themselves possessed.

Table 21

The Amount of Education and the Type of Schools in Which It Was Received, for Respondents in the Toronto Sample Who Were Asked the Question: "How Much Education Did You Have the Opportunity to Get Yourself?"

Type of School	No.	%
Elementary School—Grades 1 to 5	31	12.30
—Grades 6 to 8	87	34.50
Secondary (High) School—Grades 9 and 10	51	20.20
—Grades 11, 12 and 13 (Grade 12 in Quebec)	26	10.30
Vocational School—Commercial	13	5.25
—Technical	3	1.20
Supplementary Education (Post-High School): —Some University (but not complete); nursing; night school courses; employer-sponsored (and provided) courses; Teacher's College	16	6.30
Complete University	3	1.20
Graduate Work at University	3	1.20
Not Ascertainable	7	2.80
Refused	1	.40
No schooling whatever of a formal type	10	4.00
Not asked	1	.40
	252	100.05

There was a growing awareness that standards of education had advanced considerably since the respondents received their own. Table 22 indicates how much education the 252 respondents felt that a young man needs today. Few believed that less than Grade 12 was sufficient, and not many were satisfied with that level in the Ontario schools. A much larger proportion felt that Grade 13 was sufficient, but the largest group of responses came from those who were convinced that some university, or complete university or even more, should be the objective. A third of the parents, however, did not voice a definite reply to the question.

Table 22

How Much Education Respondents Felt Most Young Men Should Have Today

Education	No.	%
Less than Grade 12	9	3.57
Grade 12	18	7.14
Grade 13	53	21.03
Some University	31	12.30
Complete University or more	57	22.61
Did not know, uncertain, not ascertainable, miscellaneous	84	33.26
	252	99.91

One-third of the respondents, therefore, largely middle class in status, were conscious of and concerned about educational standards up to and including university. They were the ones most aware that advancement in the English-speaking world was difficult without the proper kind of education. So they were concerned about the educational equipment which was provided for children of French-speaking families and critical of that which might handicap them in this essential requirement for life in an industrial society. For most of this group the solution had been to send their offspring to English-speaking primary and secondary schools.

Another third of the respondents did not set their sights so high. They knew that primary school was no longer sufficient in the world of today, but they were satisfied with complete high school. Here again it meant English-speaking high schools, except for the few children who attended the private school, De Charbonnel. The remaining third of the respondents lacked awareness of what education their children required, or did not care, and in this sense were typical of working-class families such as resided in the district around the Sacré-Coeur. They made few demands on either their children or the educational system, seemingly content with the nearest school, whether it was French or English-speaking.

The most severe criticisms of the Sacré-Coeur school came from the immigrant French who measured its performance by European standards and spoke of the "impossibly poor French" taught there. They either refused to send their children there, or removed them after a period of time. A few sent their children to two private French schools which used European models and operated under non-French auspices. Most of the immigrant French sent their children to English-speaking schools where they were exposed to the English culture, relying upon informal and formal associations among themselves to ensure the survival of their language and culture.

It has been the ethnic rather than the religious nature of bilingual schools which has generated the problems which have hindered academic proficiency. In Southern Ontario it has been difficult to secure bilingual teachers as well qualified as the teachers in the English-speaking separate schools. If they have been brought in from elsewhere, Quebec for instance, their training as teachers may not meet the requirements of the Ontario system or their English may be deficient. A recent principal of the Ecole du Sacré-Coeur resigned her position after a year because many of the parents of pupils were unable to converse with her in French over the telephone and her English was inadequate. Even her successor, also from Quebec, admitted that her own English had been used very little prior to her arrival in Toronto and was only barely adequate at the time of the interview.

The children themselves rarely shared the concern of their parents for competency in the French language. As the principal of the downtown bilingual school remarked, French may be used in the classrooms, but only English was heard on the playground. One recent arrival from Quebec who knew very little English was virtually ostracized by the other students. The symbol of status in the peer group was English, not French, and this fact has tended to undercut the motivation among the children to apply themselves to the French language. Most of the primary school children had never experienced life in a French-speaking community, so they attributed to the language little of the value ascribed to it by the older generation. Since so many of the children in bilingual schools attended English parishes where the religious language, apart from ritual Latin, was English, the traditional religious studies and observances carried on in French in bilingual schools seemed out of touch with reality.

D. The Bilingual High School

The scope of the problem of establishing and maintaining bilingual schools with adequate academic standards can be illustrated in the founding of the private bilingual high school, De Charbonnel, by the French-speaking middle class in 1963. A bilingual high school was originally established in the early fifties in a large residence on St. George Street, not far from the campus of the University of Toronto, under the name La Ville Marguerite Bourgeoys. Its accommodation was so limited that agitation arose for much larger quarters.

Property was obtained in the Don Mills area not far from the present site of Ste. Madeleine primary bilingual school, an area of upper and middle-class homes in northeast Metropolitan Toronto. The name, De Charbonnel, was chosen in honour of an early French-Canadian bishop of the Diocese of Toronto. Men's and Women's auxiliaries named "les clubs de Charbonnel" were organized to gather funds.[6] But considerable controversy about the site and other arrangements marred the negotiations and eventually the site was changed from the Don Mills area to Lawrence Avenue East near Bayview Avenue. It was far more central than the Don Mills location but still quite remote from any sizable concentration of the French-speaking population.

The school was opened under the sponsorship of Cardinal McGuigan, who was represented by Archbishop Pocock at the dedication ceremonies in September of 1963. But controversy over the way the school should be administered still continued. So in January, 1964, the administration and staffing was entrusted to Les Soeurs de la Congregation de Notre-Dame with headquarters in Montreal.

The enrollment in the first year was seventy-six to eighty students, rising to ninety in the second year, 1964-65. The majority of the students had been born in Ontario, with a few from Quebec, and four or five Acadians. Most of the students had taken their primary school training at the Ecole du Sacré-Coeur. Parents of students were largely from the middle class, the children of professionals, business proprietors and executives. But there was also a proportion from homes where the father was from a clerical, skilled or semi-skilled occupation, as on a number of the registration cards the father's occupation is given as foreman in a factory, painter, carpenter, electrician, machinist, upholsterer, railway-checker, factory operator, draftsman, railway clerk, school janitor, etc. Thus the class composition was mixed, spreading from the upper and lower middle class through the skilled section of the working class whose children could commute easily by bus from areas of working-class homes west of Yonge Street and south of Eglinton Avenue.

On the whole, the response to the establishment of the bilingual high school was considerably below the expectations of those who had toiled to organize and provide financial assistance to the school. But there were doubts in the minds of many parents regarding the ultimate usefulness of such a school, based on three factors.

First of all, the circular advertising the school during its first year declared that its Grade 12 certificate (it did not offer Grade 13) was adequate for en-

---

[6]Public funds were not available in the Province of Ontario to separate schools beyond and including Grade 10. Consequently a high school education beyond Grade 10 had to be subsidized by private funds.

trance to bilingual teachers' colleges at Ottawa and Laurentian Universities, and to schools of nursing. But the raising of standards to Grade 13 at such institutions made the De Charbonnel certificate terminal. Considerable doubt was raised in the minds of parents about the ultimate usefulness of a course which leads nowhere, particularly since the introduction in Ontario of the Robarts Plan of three streams within the high schools placed general high school education in Ontario on a plane which a private school like De Charbonnel could not duplicate.

A second factor, decisive to many parents with sons, was the female character of the school. The only male teacher was one who handled the recreational programme for boys, and he left in June, 1965. With an otherwise completely female staff of teaching sisters, all but 10 per cent of the student enrollment was also female. Parents reported that their boys refused to attend the school under such circumstances. The only alternative was to send boys to private Catholic high schools, of which there are several in the Toronto area, or to public high schools; but in each case the teaching was in English.

The third factor which parents questioned was the financial structure of the school. In the first year of operation the fees charged per student were $150, which rose to $200 in the second year, with every indication of further increases as the cost of living rose. Members of the "clubs de Charbonnel" were expected to contribute a dollar a month to the support of the school, as well as to organize suppers, dances, and other events for the purpose of raising funds. Wealthy families were expected to give bursaries for needy students. For parents not resident in north-central Metropolitan Toronto the cost of travel had to be added to that of fees. When all these factors are combined, the resultant picture has not proved favourable to parents and there seems little cause for a change in their attitude to this type of bilingual school in the future.

E. Ethnic Identity and Bilingual Education

A bilingual education proves expensive not only in terms of buildings, teachers, transportation, but in certain human costs as well. It may well be that to attribute the loss of the French language and culture in the Toronto area to lack of the traditional matrix of French-Canadian family and community life, the comprehensive national parish and parochial school system, is too superficial a judgment. The human need for social identification, for discovering a personal identity within the cultural milieu in which one lives, may be a much more important reason for the French who live in Toronto to seek an accommodation to the English-speaking environment in Toronto.

The plant superintendent of a firm in Scarborough, who was the leader in the campaign for a bilingual school there, declared that it is the children, not the parents, who pay the highest costs and have the most difficult time because of lack of identification with any one communal group. When his son was attending the Sacré-Coeur bilingual school, he was going to the nearest English Catholic parish in Scarborough, and in neither case could he identify with the community or neighbourhood where he lived. He was pulled three ways at the same time with results quite noticeable to his parents.

An executive of the French-language radio station, CJBC, found it hard to answer his seven-year-old's question: "Why do we have to go to a bilingual school?" followed by an oft-repeated request to let him go to the local English separate school where his playmates in the neighbourhood were enrolled. If he stayed in Toronto, he said in the interview, he would much rather send his child to the English Catholic school than see his·personality split and divided by not knowing where he really belonged. He asked for a transfer back to Montreal after three years in Toronto and went back in 1965.

A family which has resided in Toronto for eight years since migrating from Quebec sought to preserve the French language for their four children by speaking it in the home at all times. They felt it was too far from the western suburb of Etobicoke to send their children all the way to the Sacré-Coeur, even though they knew this action exposed them to the criticism of part of the French community.

But their five-year-old boy had trouble understanding the commands given to him in French by his mother. She attributed his lack of response to disobedience. While reprimanding the child following one of these episodes, her seven-year-old interrupted her with the comment, "It's only your silly French." This family returned to Quebec in 1965. The father did not have as good prospects of advancement in Quebec as he had had in Toronto, but the decision was made, he said, for the good of the family.

A solution to the problem of a blurred sense of ethnic identity which involves return to a home community or province has been neither feasible nor desirable among the majority of the French in Toronto. When respondents were asked where they would most like to live outside of the Province of Ontario, over 60 per cent wished to remain where they were, in Toronto. For all but the most recent migrants social roots have gone deep enough within the community to require a local solution. Most parents in Toronto have solved this dilemma by choosing to make a religious rather than an ethnic identification, sending their children to English parochial and public schools.

In summary, the dimensions of a bilingual education in Toronto have embraced many factors which have hindered its growth. On the one hand there has been the restrictive policy of French clerical leadership and the opposition of Separate School Boards of Education based upon lack of density of the French population and pyramiding demands for English parochial schools. On the other hand there are the costs of a bilingual education in three dimensions: the physical costs to the children of long hours of travel; the academic costs of trying to combine education, religion and culture in one school system, all within the influence of the surrounding majority society; and finally, most important of all, the human costs of the incompatible demands of two cultures with the child caught in between.

Chapter VIII

French as
Mother Tongue

"The French family has been and is even now the major instrument of cultural continuity of the French-Canadians," wrote Philippe Garigue,[1] as he ascribed to the family the key role in the interlocking triad of church, school and home, as means of perpetuating the faith and culture of French Canada. French nationalism, with its vision of one nation, one religion, and one homeland, has recognized the strategic place of the family in the integration of French-Canadian society by the rallying cry, "la langue, la paroisse, la famille," and has exalted its reproductive role in the slogan "la revanche des berceux." It has been the conviction of French nationalists that: "Survival needed both numbers and a well-integrated society. The most efficient sociological instrument for achieving those aims is the family."[2]

Basic to such sentiments has been the claim that French-Canadian society possesses a familial character which has left its imprint upon all the major institutions of the society, religious, educational, economic, and political. Traditionally the French family has been the centre of cultural and social activities for an extended yet cohesive circle of kinship relations whose life beyond the family has usually been bounded by the parish system of the Church. Thus the strength of the French-Canadian family, especially in a rural milieu, has been its integration with the parish system to supply an almost total environment for members of the families in every sphere of living. But this strength has become its weakness in an urban-industrial environment such as Toronto, where the all-inclusive community, characteristic of the parish ideal, does not exist. Occupational, social and residential mobility has isolated the ethnic parish from the majority of the French-speaking population, and dissipated the influence of the French parish system.

Thus the traditional ideal of the French family has little environmental and institutional support in Metropolitan Toronto even though a substantial minority of the French population has originated in a rural setting. The extended kinship pattern still influences the form of the French-Canadian family within the urban-industrial community, but the trend is in the direction of the prevailing North American pattern of the small, nuclear family of parents and children. Relative isolation from intimate kinship and parish relations has exposed French-speaking families to the acculturating influence of English-speaking neighbours and fellow workers, stimulated fraternization of children with non-French playmates, and subjected students to the English cultural atmosphere

---

[1] Philippe Garigue, "The French-Canadian Family," in Mason Wade, ed., *Canadian Dualism* (Toronto: University of Toronto Press, 1960), p. 199.

[2] Ibid.

and curricula of both the English Catholic and the public primary and secondary schools.

Increased exposure of minority families to a majority culture is a critical factor because the family is the primary agency through which the cultural heritage is learned, reinforced, and transmitted to subsequent generations. By means of the mother tongue as the medium of communication within the family circle, the awareness of shared traditions, beliefs and values crystallizes into the unique perspective and style of life which is characteristic of a particular culture. The substitution of another language introduces another perspective, a different set of cultural definitions, another viewpoint from which to interpret the social and material world. Because language is such an essential element of culture, the predominant use of English and disuse of French involves the cumulative loss of French culture through the gradual erosion of the beliefs and values characteristic of French Canada, and their gradual replacement by an English cultural orientation.

It is in the agency of primary socialization, the family, that these consequences become evident, through changes in family interaction patterns, both within and outside the family circle. Ideally, family behaviour patterns reflect the influence of religious and educational institutions in mediating the traditions, beliefs and values of both Roman Catholicism and French culture. Similarly, the cultural behaviour patterns of families within French minority populations reflect either continuity with French culture through maintenance of the linguistic and cultural patterns of the minority group, or they show discontinuity through the adoption of the linguistic and cultural patterns of the majority English-speaking population. The pattern which is followed by most of the members of the minority population supplies a criterion for assessing the effectiveness of ethnic social structures such as the French parish system in developing and maintaining the French language and culture within such populations.

In this chapter, it is assumed that changes in linguistic patterns such as use of the French language by families of French origin in the varied circumstances of life in Toronto reflect changes in cultural patterns in the direction of closer conformity to those of the majority society. It is recognized, as E. C. Hughes has pointed out, that reliance upon statistics of French as mother tongue can be misleading if equated with loss by the French of a sense of ethnic identity.[3] But maintenance or loss of the French language is used here as only one of the indices developed in this study which indicate whether the trend within the French population is in the direction of the maintenance or the dissolution of ethnic identity.[4]

[3]Hughes and Hughes, *Where Peoples Meet,* p. 157. From his extensive experience of research in French-Canadian society, E. C. Hughes warns against underestimating the tenacity of the French in retaining their language and culture in spite of statistical evidence that it seems to be on the wane. This suggestion has been kept in mind in the final chapters of the study.

[4]In succeeding chapters other indices of French integration are examined, such as memberships in French-speaking or bilingual voluntary associations; and the French patron-

Of prime importance is the fact that 78 per cent of the migrants to Toronto claimed to speak English well before they arrived in the city. Out of 252 respondents only fourteen said that they could not speak English well, and an additional forty had learned it after coming to Toronto. The French parish of the Sacré-Coeur would have its greatest attraction for the newcomer who could not speak English well. But this was true of few among the French migrants. Many newcomers made no effort whatever to affiliate with either the French parish or bilingual schools, but simply settled into the local English Catholic parish. A recent arrival from Quebec complained, rather bitterly, that when he spoke to many of the French in Toronto in the French language, they answered him in English. At times they insisted on speaking English, especially when English Canadians, such as their employers or friends, were around. His impression was that they did not feel comfortable speaking the French language except when alone with other French people, and even then seemed self-conscious about inadequacies in their grasp of that language.

The unstable state of the French language in Toronto is illustrated in the tables interspersed in the text of the following pages. The tables cover a span of three generations: First, the parental generation of the respondent, who was asked the question: "When you were a child (aged five to fifteen) what language was spoken most of the time in your family home?" Second, the adult generation of the respondent himself, who was asked the question: "Now that you are living in Toronto what language do you speak most of the time in the following places (situations): around the house, with relatives, with church groups, at work, and socially with friends?" Third, the generation of the children of respondents, about whom the respondent was asked the following question: "What language do your children speak most of the time in the following places: with adults around the house, with each other in and out of the house, at school, with playmates, with (older) relatives?"

It has not been possible to include in most of the tables a breakdown of linguistic use according to province or place of origin, but this is noted in the text when significant. For instance, French was spoken most of the time in the first or parental generation of 94 per cent of respondents from New Brunswick, 92 per cent from Quebec, and 78 per cent from Ontario, the last-named figure bringing the general average for all respondents to 85 per cent. It is necessary also to note that due to choice of the Toronto sample from areas of French concentration, the statistics in the tables show a greater use of French than in all probability is prevalent throughout the total French population.[5]

age of the mass media, namely, French and English-language newspapers, magazines, books, radio and films. The changed orientation of the majority of the French to the economic goals of the English industrial system, and the association of the majority of the French population with English Catholic parishes, has already been discussed.

[5]Since 14 per cent of the families in the Toronto sample attend the French parish of the Sacré-Coeur, while only 4 per cent of the French-speaking population attended the French parish on any particular Sunday, with the core congregation even smaller, and since

Table 23 demonstrates the progressive disuse of the French language from the
first or parental generation, through the second or adult generation, to the third

Table 23

**Comparative Percentages of the French and English
Languages Spoken in Various Circumstances by the
Toronto Sample of the Population of French Origin**

| | Language | | | Number |
| | French | English | Both | of Cases |
Circumstances	%	%	%	
Language spoken most of the time:				
When a child (aged 5-15)in your family home	85	7	8	252
Now in Toronto:				
Around the house	40	50	10	252
With relatives[a]	57	28	15	230
With church groups[a]	18	77	5	217
At work[a]	4	86	10	133
Out socially with friends	23	48	29	247
By your children:				
With adults around the house	28	62	10	175
With (older) relatives[a]	37	56	7	159
With each other in and out of the house[a]	11	78	11	158
At school[a]	11	68	21	153
With Playmates[a]	2	89	9	164

[a]Note: All cases of No Answer, Not Asked, and Not Relevant (no relatives in Toronto, do
not attend church, not gainfully employed, children too young to speak a language, only
one child in the family, children too young or too old for school, Children too young for
playmates) were deducted from the gross number of cases before percentages were computed.

35 per cent of the children in the Toronto sample attended bilingual schools, while less than
15 per cent of the French children of school age in the metropolitan area attended such
schools, it seems reasonable to assume that the use of French would be higher among
respondents' families in the sample than throughout the entire French population.

or child generation. The least drop in the use of French was when respondents or their children were talking with relatives. In fact, the language used in communicating with relatives is the outstanding example in the present study of the retention of the French language, exceeding the use of French in the homes of respondents. At the time of the study, 70 per cent of the respondents had relatives living in Toronto who were visited at least once a week by most respondents, once a month by others, with only a few admitting they seldom visited their relatives. The presence of such relatives appears to be the strongest social mechanism operative in the Toronto situation to promote the retention of the French language in a viable form. In spite of the disruptive effects of the urban-industrial system, the traditionally extended French family has continued to promote a sense of ethnic identity in terms of the French language among a majority of the French population.

The most drastic drop in the general use of the French language for the adult generation occurs at work where English is spoken most of the time. The questions asked about language at work were answered in terms of the language spoken most of the time during working hours. French was not eliminated entirely from the work situation, as can be seen in Table 24, because it was available on occasion to nearly half of the workers to whom the question was applicable. But French was eliminated as a working language in 80 per cent of the work situations of respondents. There can be little doubt that the linguistic habits practised throughout the day at the place of employment by one or both of the parents would carry over into home life and influence the patterns of family communication.

The impact of the Toronto situation does not reach its maximum, however, until the third generation, the children of respondents. As with their parents, use of the French language by children was most prevalent with older relatives. But among themselves the children rarely used any other language but English. With the exception of three families from Quebec, children rarely used French at school, and certainly English was the channel of communication with playmates, even in the schoolyard of bilingual schools. Many of these children had never lived in a community where French was spoken almost exclusively. Like most children, they were conformists. The language of the peer group was almost exclusively English and thus became the language of the in-group. French, even when spoken by their parents, just did not fit into the context of a child's world in Toronto.

This trend can be illustrated by the small group of respondents who grew up in the Toronto area, some of whom had children of school age. As indicated in Table 25, the differences between the three generations for this group is far more dramatic than for any other group of respondents. French has almost disappeared from this group of children. French is spoken most of the time in the home of only a single family. Equal use of both languages is evident only in the three families who sent their children to bilingual schools. An additional factor influencing the linguistic patterns of this small group of respondents was

Table 24

The Ethnic Origin of Fellow Workers at Place of Employment
For Both Men and Women Among Respondents in the Toronto
Sample Who Are Gainfully Employed, and the Opportunities
to Speak the French Language Where There are Some French
Fellow Workers

	Males		Females		Both	
	No.	%	No.	%	No.	%
Fellow workers all English	13	15	2	13	15	15
Fellow workers English and other nationalities	17	20	4	25	21	21
Some French fellow workers: Opportunity to speak French all the time	8	9	1	6	9	9
Opportunity to speak French sometimes	35	41	5	31	40	39
No opportunities to speak French	13	15	4	25	17	16
Totals[a]	86	100	16	100	102	100

[a]Note: Cases of No Answer, Not Ascertainable, Not Relevant (no longer speak French, work alone, not gainfully employed, students, housewives) were deleted from totals before percentages were computed.

the cross-cultural marriage of French with non-French. Twelve of the twenty-two families in this group represented cross-cultural marriages,[6] while two others represented, in addition, the factor of mixed religious faiths, Catholic marrying Protestant, where the impact on the use of the French language is even greater. Even in the ten families in which both spouses were French, in every case they came from different provinces, introducing the factor of regional differences in cultural background.

The most extensive changes in linguistic habits among all the respondents have taken place in the 30 per cent of the 240 families in the study which represent cross-cultural marriages, among whom the additional variable of mixed religious faiths was also present.[7] Table 26 contrasts the retention of French in

[6]Ten of the twelve non-French spouses were of British origin, the other two of other ethnic origin.

[7]In nearly three-quarters of these cross-cultural marriages the partner was of British

Table 25

Comparative Percentages of the French and English Languages
Spoken in Various Circumstances by the French in the
Sample Who Were Born and Grew Up in Toronto

Circumstances	French %	English %	Both %	Number of Cases
Language spoken most of the time:				
When a child (aged 5-15) in your family home	79	8	13	24
Now in Toronto:				
Around the house	17	62	21	24
With relatives[a]	32	36	32	22
With church groups[a]	10	80	10	20
At work[a]	--	87	13	15
Out socially with friends	5	77	18	22
By your children:				
With adults around the house	5	78	17	18
With (older) relatives[a]	--	88	12	17
With each other in and out of the house[a]	--	94	6	16
At school[a]	--	75	25	16
With playmates[a]	--	100	--	17

The "Language" spanning header sits above French %, English %, and Both %.

[a]Note: All cases of No Answer, Not Asked, and Not Relevant (no relatives in Toronto, do not attend church, not gainfully employed, children too young to speak a language, only one child in the family, children too young or too old for school, children too young for playmates) were deducted from the gross number of cases before percentages were computed.

stock, with one-quarter of them Irish, which underlines the influence of the residential proximity of those of French and British origins in Toronto. It also emphasizes that Canadians of French and British origins are drawn together by aspects of North American culture which they share. Only 28 per cent married into other ethnic groups: German, Italian, Jewish, Ukrainian, American, Dutch, Indian, Macedonian, Norwegian and Spanish.

Table 26

Comparative Percentages of the French and English Languages Spoken in Various Circumstances: (A) By Families in Which Both Spouses Were French, and (B) By Families Where One Spouse is French and One Non-French

| | (A) Both Spouses French | | | | (B) One Spouse French, One Non-French | | | |
| | Language | | | Number of Cases | Language | | | Number of Cases |
Circumstances	French %	English %	Both %		French %	English %	Both %	
Language spoken most of the time:								
Now in Toronto:								
Around the house	52	36	12	160	9	85	6	66
With relatives[a]	64	21	15	147	41	46	13	61
With church groups[a]	27	66	7	136	3	95	2	60
At work[a]	5	89	6	63	2	87	11	55
Out socially with friends	30	39	31	156	4	76	20	66
By your children:								
With adults around the house	36	55	9	114	4	92	4	47
With (older) relatives[a]	47	44	9	103	11	89	--	45
With each other in and out of the house[a]	15	71	14	103	2	93	5	42
At school[a]	15	64	21	100	--	75	25	40
With playmates[a]	3	85	12	105	--	100	--	46

[a]Note: All cases of No Answer, Not Asked, and Not Relevant (no relatives in Toronto, do not attend church, not gainfully employed, children too young to speak a language, only one child in the family, children too young or too old for school, children too young for playmates) were deducted from the gross number of cases before percentages computed.

families where both spouses are French with families where one spouse is French and the other non-French. Mixed cultural marriages tend to create an unfavourable climate for the preservation of the French language and culture, so it is not surprising that the use of French drops below 10 per cent in all circumstances except fraternization with relatives, in which it is presumed that the French spouse has been the person involved.

A significant variable is that 29 per cent of the marriages of respondents were across provincial boundaries in terms of place of origin of the spouses. Background exposure to the English culture varies widely from province to province, leading Mason Wade to comment that

> each of these outlying groups has its own ideology, which is perhaps closer to the prevailing regional one than to that of the French-Canadian of Quebec. It has long been recognized that French-Canadians and Acadians are very different, and frequently do not get along as well with each other as they do with English Canadians . . . there are many other instances of such profound differences among French-speaking Canadians.[8]

The contrast between all-French marriages and cross-cultural marriages is sharpened when the French couple are from Quebec, since Quebeckers have consistently retained the use of French most of the time in various circumstances to a much higher degree than any other regional group among the French in Toronto, as illustrated by Table 27. The question arises, however, as to whether a French mother, in her role as the spouse who is responsible for the home training of the children, maintains the use of French by her children to a greater degree than a French father who has married a non-French wife.[9] The results recorded in Table 28 are not decisive. Loss of French takes place no matter which combination of spouses occurs. It is evident that other factors, such as type of school, playmates, neighbourhood, are operative in the situation.

The climax of the trend to disuse of the French language is reached only when mixed religious faiths are added to cross-cultural marriages. Thirty-nine per cent of the respondents who had contracted cross-cultural marriages had married

---

[8] Mason Wade, "Conclusions," in Mason Wade, ed., *Canadian Dualism* (Toronto: University of Toronto Press, 1960), p. 417.

[9] Among cross-cultural marriages of respondents, there is an imbalance between the number of French husbands who married non-French wives, and the number of French wives who married non-French husbands, because of the method of choosing the universe of French families, from which the sample was drawn, through recognition of French names of families (or husbands) in the Metropolitan Toronto Directory. There were fifty-one French husbands who married non-French wives, and only twenty-one French wives who married non-French husbands. Husbands preferred wives of British origin in forty-one cases out of fifty-one, while wives were more evenly divided on this score, with eleven out of twenty-one marrying husbands of British origin. Of even greater significance is the fact that French husbands married twenty-three Protestant wives, while French wives married only five Protestant husbands.

Table 27

Comparative Percentages of the French and English Languages Spoken in Various Circumstances By Families From Quebec, With: (A) Both Spouses French, and (b) One Spouse French, and One Non-French

Circumstances	(A) Both Spouses French				(B) One Spouse French, One Non-French			
	Language			Number of Cases	Language			Number of Cases
	French %	English %	Both %		French %	English %	Both %	
Language spoken most of the time:								
When a child (aged 5-15) in your family home	92	3	5	60b	–	–	–	–
Now in Toronto:								
Around the house	75	16	9	45	–	86	14	14
With relatives[a]	81	8	11	36	67	25	8	12
With church groups[a]	46	51	3	41	–	100	–	14
At work[a]	20	70	10	45	8	67	25	12
Out socially with friends	42	19	39	43	–	73	27	15
By your children:								
With adults around the house	57	27	16	30	–	100	–	10
With (older) relatives[a]	75	17	8	24	22	78	–	9
With each other in and out of the house[a]	29	53	18	28	–	100	–	9
At school[a]	11	39	50	28	–	44	56	9
With playmates[a]	10	70	20	41	–	100	–	10

[a] All cases of No Answer, Not Asked, and Not Relevant (no relatives in Toronto, do not attend church, not gainfully employed, children too young to speak a language, only one child in family, children too young or too old for school, children too young for playmates) were dedected from the gross number of cases before percentages computed.

[b] Includes all in Toronto sample from Quebec, whether both spouses French or one spouse French.

Table 28

Comparative Percentages of the French and English Languages Spoken in Various Circumstances By the Children in Families Where: (A) the Father French, the Mother Non-French, and (B) the Father Non-French, the Mother French

Circumstances	(A) Father French, Mother Non-French				(B) Father Non-French, Mother French			
	Language			Number of Cases	Language			Number of Cases
	French %	English %	Both %		French %	English %	Both %	
With adults around the house	3	97	--	33	6	72	22	18
With (older) relatives[a]	3	97	--	32	29	65	6	17
With each other in and out of the house[a]	3	97	--	29	--	81	19	16
At school[a]	--	93	7	28	--	50	50	16
With playmates[a]	--	100	--	32	--	100	--	18

[a]Note: All cases of No Answer, Not Asked, Not Relevant (no relatives in Toronto, children too young to speak a language, only one child in family, children too young or too old for school, children too young for playmates) were deducted from the gross number of cases before percentages computed.

Table 29

Comparative Percentages of the French and English Languages
Spoken in Various Circumstances by the Children in Families
Where One Spouse is Catholic and One Spouse is Protestant

| | Language | | | Number of |
Circumstances	French %	English %	Both %	Cases
With adults around the house	--	100	--	18
With (older) relatives[a]	--	100	--	16
With each other in and out of the house[a]	--	--	100	--	16
At School[a]	--	94	6	17
With playmates[a]	--	100	--	18

[a]All cases of No Answer, Not Asked, Not Relevant (no relatives in Toronto, children too young to speak a language, only one child in family, children too young or too old for school, children too young for playmates) were deducted from the gross number of cases before percentages computed.

Protestants. The effects are revealed in Table 29, in which the inference is clear although the numbers are small. English has completely displaced the use of French except in one family whose children attended a bilingual school. It is noteworthy that in the case of these children, both languages were spoken in the bilingual school context, but nowhere else. Thus the French language was reduced to its barest minimum.

The European French-speaking immigrant population in Toronto has used a different approach to the French language problem in an English milieu. To the French-Canadian they appear to have neglected means for maintaining the French language because they disparage the type of French spoken by French-Canadians and instead of sending their children to the Catholic bilingual schools prefer to send them to English-speaking schools where, the French-Canadians claim, they are lost to the French-speaking community within a single generation. The French immigrants seem to have reconciled themselves to a transition to an English-language milieu as far as occupational life is concerned, but they have made vastly more use of voluntary associations, cultural and recreational programmes, drama, music and the cinema in promoting French language and culture. In this sense the immigrant French have adopted a typical North American agency, the voluntary association, and adapted it to the goals and interests of their own culture.

In sum, the Toronto milieu has not only influenced the use of the French language directly through limiting opportunities for its practice, but it also has provided the social setting in which cross-cultural liaisons take place, and mixed-religious-faith marriages become more common. Diversity of ethnic and religious outlook has been imported into the homes of cross-cultural marriages and in the encounter with the dominant cultural emphasis in the community, at work, at church, at school, or out socially, the cultural outlook of the French-speaking person has suffered eclipse and a cumulative deterioration of both the French language and culture has taken place.

On the basis of the criterion of the use of language by families of French origin, the majority of the French population in Toronto has experienced displacement of the French language by English within a period of three generations to the degree that the use of the French language has almost disappeared in the third or child generation. When primary socialization of children reflects the majority rather than the minority culture, it indicates a marked change in the focus of ethnic identity. The effects of cross-cultural and mixed-religious-faith marriages have been even more drastic.

The lack of institutional support normally provided by the French parish and bilingual schools for families of French origin has revealed the inadequacy within the Toronto milieu of the traditional source of ethnic identification in French-Canadian society, the Catholic parish system. Implicit in the loss of the French language has been the weakening of the values and goals of French culture as French families have taken on the colour of the English cultural environment with its inherent stress upon economic goals. The only stronghold of the French language and culture remaining in Toronto appears to be the extended family circle of kinship relations which still survives in spite of the adverse pressures of the English socio-economic system.

Chapter IX

Choosing Associates
and Friends

Surrounded by easily available English parishes and schools while isolated by distance from the only French parish in the metropolitan area, the majority of the French-speaking population has had little or no opportunity for articulation and expression of ethnic identity through the traditional medium, the French parish system. Its members have had to choose between two alternatives: either adopt non-parish patterns of relations that give unity and identity to their minority group, or merge with the English-speaking population.[1]

The situation has posed three questions for this study: first, what functional alternatives to the French parish system exist within the French population; second, how effective have such alternatives been as sources of ethnic identification; and third, to what extent has the French middle class been involved in promoting and maintaining such sources of ethnic identity?

The French middle class has been instrumental in creating at least two alternative channels of ethnic participation. They have organized voluntary associations and promoted expansion of the French mass media of communications. Both voluntary associations (the theme of this chapter) and the mass media (discussed in the following chapter) represent means of identification which are characteristic of the social structure of urban-industrial societies. They serve as connecting links between masses of discrete individuals and families by supplementing the bonds of kinship, neighbourhood, and parish, which have been weakened by social mobility and cultural differentiation.[2]

By accelerating the rate of social, occupational and geographical mobility within modern societies, industrialization, with its attendant urbanization, has introduced divergent cultural patterns, values, and goals. Linguistic pluralism often accompanies these developments. Consequently, industrial cities such as Toronto possess highly differentiated populations with a diversified, specialized labour force. This environment is in direct contrast to traditional French-Canadian society, especially in rural areas, in which common cultural patterns, values, and goals, and French as mother tongue, mutually reinforced each other. The resulting degree of homogeneity within that society made it possible for a single institutional bond, such as the Roman Catholic Church, to become the integrative focus of the society. The heterogeneity of cultural background existing within an industrial society requires multiple bonds to ensure the meshing of

---

[1]Don Martindale, *American Social Structure* (New York: Appleton-Century-Crofts, 1960), p. 428: "An ethnic minority which has lost its original point of integration must find a new one which is an adaptation of elements of an old community to meet the issues presented by the enveloping presence of a new one."

[2]Olsen, *Process of Social Organization*, pp. 161-65.

the complex set of complementary and interdependent differences which exist
between members of its population.[3]

Over 60 per cent of the French-speaking migrants to Toronto have come from
urbanized areas where some form of urbanization has taken place. Another
10 per cent grew up in Toronto, while others have lived in that city for years.
Consequently, the French minority population displays the characteristics associated with urban-industrial populations, namely, cultural heterogeneity of background, class differentiation, and residential dispersion according to socio-
economic status. Many of its members have experienced a reorientation of values
and goals in which economic values have displaced ethnic values, again typical of
industrialized populations.

The complex network of voluntary associations which link people together in
a web of like interests is one of the strongest of the multiple bonds which help
integrate industrial societies. Voluntary associations have become so much a part
of urban life in North America that

> the key to city life is the multiplicity of group ties; each may have strong
> influence on the individual, but each is limited to a specific area of behav-
> ior and is balanced by others . . . the individual interacts with many
> groups . . . he is a group member whose involvement in collective life is
> very great but whose involvement in any one group is limited.[4]

This segmentation of urban life, however, means that the degree of consensus
and consequently of cohesion among the members of any ethnic group may vary
widely. The generic term "group" implies as a minimum an awareness by the
individuals involved of "some common identity or shared fate."[5] At this level
communal structure may consist of no more than an informal

[3]Emile Durkheim, *The Division of Labour in Society* (New York: The Free Press,
1933). In this classic volume the writer introduced the concepts of "mechanical solidarity"
to describe the integration of primitive and traditional rural-peasant societies, and "organic
solidarity" to describe the interdependence which integrates industrial societies, terms
which have been replaced in contemporary sociological writings by "normative or consen-
sual" integration, and "functional or symbiotic" integration, although the new concepts are
admitted to lack precise definition; cf. Robert Cooley Angell, "Social Integration," *Encyclopaedia of the Social Sciences*, VII (1968), 380-86. The terms "unibonded" and "multi-
bonded" were used in P. A. Sorokin, *Social Mobility* (New York: Harper, 1927). The
increasing differentiation within ethnic groups in Canada, including the French, has been
noted recently in Frank G. Vallee, Mildred Schwartz, and Frank Darknell, "Ethnic Assimilation and Differentiation in Canada," in Bernard Blishen, *et al.*, eds., *Canadian Society* (3rd
ed.; Toronto: Macmillan of Canada, 1968), p. 596.

[4]Joseph Kahl, "Some Social Concomitants of Industrialization and Urbanization," in
William A. Faunce, ed., *Readings in Industrial Sociology* (New York: Appleton-Century-
Crofts, 1967), p. 34.

[5]J. Milton Yinger, "Social Forces Involved in Group Identification and Withdrawal,"
Daedalus, No. 91 (1960). "'Group' is a generic term that includes collectivities of widely
varying degrees of cohesiveness. The term implies as a minimum an awareness by the

network of interpersonal relations: members of a certain group seek each other's companionship; friendship groups and cliques are formed. But beyond this informal network, no formal organization may exist. The immigrant who is a member of such a group will establish all his institutional affiliations in the native (majority) community since his ethnic group has little or no organization of its own.[6]

The term "structural assimilation" has often been applied to this process whereby the minority group coalesces with the majority population in terms of social structure.[7] Any higher level of social cohesion or integration within the minority population demands persistent and repetitious social interaction among its membership, reaching its highest level when the minority group is characterized by social structure. The group has then "developed a more formal structure and contains organizations of various sorts: religious, educational, political, recreational, national, and even professional."[8]

These institutionalized channels of communication create cohesion by facilitating persistent and repetitious interaction within an ethnic group. The same social processes which create cohesion, however, can also dissolve it. Absence of social structure can facilitate social interaction with the majority rather than the minority population, with consequent disintegration of ethnic solidarity. Maintenance of a sense of collective identity by the French population rests, therefore, upon the extent to which its members participate in the communication channels provided by the social structure of the minority rather than the majority group.

There is evidence to show that a positive correlation exists between the presence of formal organization and participation within ethnic boundaries. The ethnic migrant

> who is a member of an institutionalized ethnic community is more likely to have . . . a higher proportion of in-group relations than the one who belongs to a less institutionalized one. . . . He is three times more likely to have acquired associates within his own group than if he is part of a group with a more informal social organization.[9]

individuals involved of some common identity and shared fate. The members of more cohesive groups will, in addition, engage in social interaction. And if this interaction is persistent and repetitive, the group is characterized by social structure. We can avoid errors of interpretation if we keep these levels of cohesiveness in mind in the study of minority groups. Even the simple awareness of a common identity may be an influence on minority-group members. But it is the meaning of 'group' in the fuller sense, involving social interaction and social structure, that is of greatest importance" (p. 247).

[6] Breton, "Institutional Completeness of Ethnic Communities," p. 78.

[7] Gordon, *Assimilation in American Life*, Chapter III.

[8] Breton, "Institutional Completeness of Ethnic Communities," p. 78.

[9] Ibid., pp. 89, 91.

Accommodation between the minority and majority culture therefore takes place on the more superficial level of acculturation or "cultural assimilation." The formal social structure of the minority group provides the communication channels for primary interaction. Contacts with the majority group are restricted to impersonal, secondary relationships in the course of daily life.[10]

It is necessary, in assessing the Toronto situation, to establish the position of the French population relative to the extremes of "structural assimilation" and "cultural assimilation." The starting point, therefore, is to determine the ethnic role played by the formal social structure existing within the French population.

A. Formal Associations

French Canadians traditionally show little interest in joining associations.[11] The Catholic parish system seeks to satisfy every social as well as religious need of its membership. According to the philosophy of the Catholic Church, the French Catholic is a member of his church from baptism and does not need to join anything beyond the associations which the parish provides. This viewpoint has even penetrated the trade union movement in the Province of Quebec. Trade unions have been organized, in which the initial impetus came from clerical leadership, in order that French-Canadian workers might be represented by Catholic unions. This obviates joining international unions which are religiously neutral, or espouse social philosophies which are anti-religious in character.

Lack of interest in joining organizations is also characteristic of working-class populations. When the Catholic faith and working-class status coalesce, as they do for the majority of the labour force in French-Canadian populations, voluntary associations play a very small part in the scheme of living. In Toronto, 58 per cent of the respondents did not belong to any organizations, and another 9 per cent belonged to trade or labour unions where little choice can be exercised regarding membership. Respondents were asked to name the organizations to which they belonged, and indicate whether each organization was French, English, or bilingual; how often they attended; and whether they held office or not. Table 30 indicates the distribution of such memberships among 107 respondents out of 252.

Only 42.5 per cent of the respondents participated in formal organizations. Even more significant is the affiliation of respondents in the ratio of five English-speaking organizations to one French-speaking organization. This ratio is cut in half, of course, if bilingual organizations are included with French organizations. Actual participation of the French population in strictly French-speaking organizations, however, may be even lower than Table 30 indicates. The Toronto sample of the French population has consistently shown higher

[10]Gordon, *Assimilation in American Life,* p. 235.

[11]Lamontagne, "Ontario: The Two Races," pp. 359-60.

rates of participation in the French parish and bilingual schools than the total French population, and this may be true of voluntary associations as well. A levelling factor in the ratio between memberships in English and French organizations is that twenty-three of the English organizations were trade unions, in which memberships are often compulsory for employees. An additional point of interest is that just twenty-three respondents were involved in organizations sufficiently to occupy executive positions, seventeen with one position and six with more than one.

Table 30

Memberships of Respondents in French, English and Bilingual Formal Organizations

Type of Organization	Respondents		Memberships	
	No.	%	No.	%
French	14	5.6	27	16.0
English	76	30.2	124	73.4
Bilingual	17	6.7	18	10.6
None	145	57.5		
Totals	252	100.0	169	100.0

Within English-speaking populations, the middle class has become the stratum which is primarily involved in voluntary associations. But the French in Toronto have not followed the English model in this respect. Only 40 per cent of the French-speaking middle class have memberships in voluntary organizations. Of these, the professionals have the highest percentage, 54, the proprietors, managers and officials 39 per cent, and the clerical and sales 32 per cent. In this respect, then, the middle class in Toronto still follows the traditional patterns of French-Canadian society even though the major source of integration of that society, the parish system, functions for only a tiny segment of the French-speaking population of Toronto.

Only six of the total of seventy-four French and English organizations named by respondents were French. Just four of these were French Canadian in leadership and membership. This does not exhaust the number of French associations in Toronto, of course, as others exist to which respondents did not belong. But almost all other French associations are found among the immigrant French, with very few French Canadians within the memberships.

La Fédération des Femmes Canadiennes Françaises

Only one of the four French-Canadian associations was connected with the parish, the Fédération des Femmes Canadiennes Françaises. It had grown over a period of seven or eight years from a small struggling group of twenty-five women to a membership of around sixty, mainly because of the influx of the new middle class into Metropolitan Toronto of recent years. But this accretion also placed a strain on the internal structure of the group as the main body of women had been Acadians from the lower working class of the immediate area. The newcomers were middle class from outside the area and tended to monopolize the executive positions and run the association to suit themselves. There is some doubt that the association will long survive its internal divisions. At best its small membership reflects a minimal influence upon the parish itself, let alone the larger French-speaking population beyond. The fact that no other parish association was mentioned also underlines the minimal influence of parish organizations throughout this larger population.

Club Richelieu

The most important and influential of French-Canadian voluntary associations was the Toronto branch of an international French-Canadian service club, the Club Richelieu. During the attempt to establish a west-end national French parish during the early fifties, a number of the French-speaking middle class, professionals and businessmen, became involved in the planning. Although the project was unsuccessful due to the intransigence of the parish priest at the Sacré-Coeur, the taste of independent action by the middle class evolved into the founding of the Club Richelieu in 1953. This professional and executive type of fraternal organization had a membership of fifty in 1965. It held a supper meeting monthly in the Swiss Chalet on Bloor Street, of which one of its members was the manager.

The first major project undertaken by the Club Richelieu was that of promoting bilingual education in Toronto by subsidizing transportation to bilingual schools of children whose parents were unable to afford the daily cost. Until 1960 the project was responsible for the increased enrollment at the Sacré-Coeur and its consequent enlargement to twenty-one rooms completed in 1962. Since then it has also assisted in the same way with the Scarborough bilingual school, Ste. Madeleine. Its members have played a responsible role in the organization and financing of the private bilingual high school, De Charbonnel. The Club also sponsored four candidates who ran for election to the Metropolitan Separate School Board. Two of them were elected.

The second major project undertaken by the Club involved leadership and co-operation in founding the Association de la Radio et de la Télévision françaises du sud de l'Ontario. Fraternization takes place from time to time with other branches in Windsor, Sudbury and Eastern Ontario, and for the fall of 1967 the Toronto branch assumed responsibility for hosting an international convention of the Clubs Richelieu in the Royal York Hotel in Toronto. A member of the Toronto branch, Mr. George Paradis, was elected president of the Associated Clubs Richelieu of North America, and was made responsible for the organization of the convention. When Premier Lesage of Quebec visited Toronto, the Club Richelieu organized a special reception for him.

For its members, the Club Richelieu serves an integrating function among the French-speaking middle class, especially those interested in the French parish and bilingual schools, although only part of its membership is affiliated with either the parish or the schools. In common with most minority ethnic associations its main function tends to be social,[12] rather than the larger community projects with which most service clubs are occupied.

One-third of the membership of the Club, as well as some ex-members, were interviewed in order to discover the exact role which the Club plays among the French-speaking in Toronto. A former president of the Club, a professional, was critical of its preoccupation with bilingual schools at the primary level when advanced education in the French language was completely lacking in Toronto. He envisaged also a much wider leadership role for the Club among the French-speaking population and was disappointed that its vision was so often limited to social trivialities. Several who had been members of the Club resigned because of what they claimed to be non-democratic procedures and interference by l'Ordre de Jacques Cartier of which the ruling clique in the Club were alleged to be members. The name of one of this clique appeared in a recent publication which was an exposure of the activities and organization of l'Ordre de Jacques Cartier.[13]

The independents among the French middle class were rather caustic in their comments about the Club Richelieu. "Kid stuff" was the comment of one who admired the Club Richelieu in Montreal but dropped out of the one in Toronto. "It makes little contribution to the French cause or to anything else," was the remark of another successful French-speaking businessman. "I disagree with their whole point of view," declared a lawyer, "they act like an immigrant group. I am not a member of an immigrant group because I am in my own country. I cannot accept the ethnic angle simply because I speak French." In his opinion the Club Richelieu had no overall objectives for the French-speaking population in Toronto and that was precisely what was needed. He may have put his finger on the reason why so few of the over four-thousand of the middle class in the French-speaking population had joined the Club in over a decade of existence. "There are so few who are interested," lamented a past president, as he half apologized for the small membership.

L'Alliance Canadienne

The third French-Canadian association mentioned by the respondents was the Alliance Canadienne, which was organized in Toronto in the same year as the Club Richelieu, in 1953, by Madame St. Hilaire from Quebec. The goal of the organization is to foster better relationships between the French and the English by bringing them together in a common organization to which both are invited.

[12]Shibutani and Kwan, *Ethnic Stratification*, p. 214.

[13]Cyr, *La Patente*, p. 41. An exposure of the activities of l'Ordre de Jacques-Cartier.

Its programme seeks to deal with aspects of culture of common interest to both groups. With the head office in Quebec City, branches have been established at Montreal, Ottawa and Sudbury, and new groups were being organized at Hamilton and the Lakehead. But according to a professor in the French Department of Victoria University in Toronto, none of them had been going well, particularly Toronto.

The president of the Toronto branch admitted that attendance had fallen off. She blamed the separatist movement in Quebec with resulting alarmist publicity in the Toronto papers for the fact that two-thirds of the Association's English members had ceased to attend. The university professor mentioned above, who occupied the president's chair for two years, felt that the problem had deeper roots, namely, there was much talk but little action. With an admirable objective he felt that there was too little planning. When he was president he was able to call upon his colleagues in the University of Toronto French and English Departments for talks on the French novel, French-Canadian poetry, French-English Canadian relations. During these two years the Alliance Canadienne had the highest attendance in its history.

To an observer there appears to be lack of trust between the French-speaking and the English-speaking members who held executive positions. The professor, himself not French, claimed that in spite of visiting back and forth with French-Canadian families and making every effort to cultivate friendships, he still felt like an outsider, that the French Canadians in Toronto were a group apart. When the English were in charge of the programme the French were restive. Yet when they had their turn the programme was mostly in French, an unequal sharing of the two languages. Speakers were often irrelevant to the purpose of the organization. On the other hand, the French-speaking felt that the professor was a difficult man to get along with as he did not consult with others sufficiently in the planning. It is true that the meetings which this observer attended were predominantly in French. This may have been because only two or three of the twelve to fifteen people who attended the meetings were English Canadians. Internal jealousies and animosities, similar to those which have been common at the French parish, seem to have been the cause of lack of popularity of the organization. Certainly most of those who attended were from the small group associated with the French parish.

A factor of importance in the decline of the Alliance Canadienne has been lack of funds with which to remunerate special speakers. The national president, Col. Ross of Quebec City, has tried without success to secure funds from the provincial governments of Quebec and Ontario, and was seeking federal financial help as well. Speakers who would serve without remuneration were hard to secure. As a result programmes did not prove attractive to either the French or the English.

The highlight of 1965, during the Toronto study, was the national convention of the Alliance Canadienne, for which the Toronto branch was the host. Sessions were held at the University of Toronto. Delegates came from the Province of

Quebec and other parts of Ontario. But the Toronto delegation, in spite of its prominent position as the host group, was very small except for the final banquet when a member of the Parent Commission on Education in the Province of Quebec addressed a large audience on that subject. Local department stores assisted in the financing of the convention, the provincial governments having supplied no funds. The proceedings were very largely in French, with an occasional explanation in English. This procedure was not liked by the English-speaking Canadians present. Little cognizance was taken of the objectives of the organization either in the programme of the convention or the planning for the future. It was really a major social event for the French-speaking representatives, with little attempt at fraternization between the two major ethnic groups.

L'Association canadienne-française d'Education d'Ontario

The Association sponsors a number of French-speaking organizations throughout Ontario. In Toronto only two were mentioned by respondents, apart from professional organizations of bilingual teachers. One was the Club Rouillé the youth wing of the Fédération des Clubs sociaux franco-ontariens, which held dances weekly and organized other functions of a social nature for the younger set among the French-speaking in Toronto. It was largely middle class in its orientation with its clientele from Ontario and Quebec. Acadians claimed that they were not made welcome at the functions. The other organization mentioned was the Parent-Teacher or Home and School Association connected with the bilingual schools. A number of informants claimed that far more activity resulted from these associations at the bilingual schools and the Clubs de Charbonnel than was initiated by the French parish. A number of small social clubs had also been spawned among the parents of the bilingual students in these schools. But again, these organizations were distributed only among the small group of parents who were associated with the French parish and bilingual schools and consequently did not touch the French-speaking population at large.

L'Assomption Society

The only regional association among the French Canadians was the Acadian organization, l'Assomption Society, which published the New Brunswick newspaper L'Evangeline, and carried on a three-fold programme in its various branches, embracing religious, social and economic activities. The economic programme involved credit unions and life insurance. However, the Society was far from involving the Acadian population at large. It had around 300 in its membership out of the 7,500 Acadians resident in Toronto in 1961. Acadians complained that until recently the social aspect was neglected. There were many attempts to include Franco-Ontarians and Quebeckers in their functions but in spite of invitations very few turned up. The Acadians claimed that it was very difficult to cross the barriers which had been set up by differences in background between themselves and other French Canadians in Toronto. They found it easier to fraternize with Franco-Ontarians than those from Quebec, although in neither case did they find much in common.

It appears evident from the above that voluntary associations have not prolif-
erated among the French-speaking population, even the middle class, as they
have among the English-speaking population of North America. In the industrial
milieu of Toronto the French Canadians are still in the process of transition
from a parish orientation to a secondary group orientation, and this has been
reached by only a small portion of the middle class.

B. Immigrant French Associations

The immigrant French, who have not been oriented to the parish system of
the Sacré-Coeur and the bilingual schools, have been making far greater use of
voluntary associations as a way of preserving the French language and culture
and stimulating primary social interaction among the members of their own
group. There were some thirty immigrant French associations in Toronto. Most
of them were small, consisting of supper and dancing or recreational clubs. Three
of them play an important part among the French-speaking population in Toronto even though French-Canadian participation in each of them is minimal; the
Alliance français, the Alliance France-Canada, and the Ciné Club.

Alliance Française

The Alliance français, founded in France in 1883, established a branch in
Toronto in 1902, and has similar branches scattered among French-speaking
groups around the world. Most of the branches operate a three pronged programme, cultural, social, and educational. Cultural activities include lectures in
French, concerts, films, and plays. Social events of various types are arranged.
The educational aspect consists of schools for teaching French, for which certifi-
cates of graduation are granted through the Paris headquarters.[14] In Toronto,
the three functions have become fragmented between the three French associations listed in the paragraph above, each of which is run independently of the
others.

The Alliance française du Canada majors in cultural activity, organizing a
series of six lectures each year for its 200 active members, using visitors from
either Europe or Quebec as speakers in the fields of literature, the arts and
music. The lecture is usually followed by a French film, finishing off with coffee
and biscuits. This procedure allows those present to enjoy an hour of chatting in
French, an opportunity to meet each other, and perhaps be introduced to the
speaker of the evening. The programme is supplemented each year by a concert,
often using French-Canadian artists, and a drama night, when a French play is
usually presented. Talent from Quebec has usually been utilized, although the

[14]Victor E. Graham, *How to Learn French in Canada* (Toronto: University of Toronto
Press, 1965), p. 13. This book is a handbook for English Canadians which lists all the
sources of contact with the French language available in Canada. A description is given of
the various French clubs in the section quoted.

University of Toronto students of the Department of French put on the play in 1965. A minor facet of the programme consists of trips to explore Ontario and ski weekends in the winter.

The president of the Toronto branch of the Alliance française was a French Canadian who grew up in Toronto. He studied and married in Europe, then became a professor of French at Victoria University. "The unfortunate part about this excellent French programme," he observed, "is that very few French-Canadians attend." "L'Alliance tends to be rather intellectual, and a bit snobbish," he added. The difference in the pronunciation of French by European and French Canadians has caused arguments and unpleasantness. A small group of French Canadians who seek to make their presence felt socially in all French-speaking organizations attends. But the programme has little appeal to the average French Canadian. He appears to feel more at home with English Canadians, with whom he shares a larger bundle of cultural patterns than he does with the European French, from whose culture he has been separated for a long period of time.

Alliance France-Canada

The second immigrant French association, the Alliance France-Canada, was founded by M. Henri Hulot in November, 1948, and placed under the honourary presidency of the French Consul General in Toronto. It had dual aims:

> one, to renew, encourage and maintain a French atmosphere for French citizens in Toronto, which was accomplished by a varied programme of social and cultural activities which included dinner-dances and buffets, picnics, gala evenings, lectures, films, symposia, garden-parties, children's Christmas Tree, cocktail parties, receptions, artistic and theatre evenings and shows put on by members, and chartered flights to France; the other aim, a closer relationship between the immigrant French and Canadians, was neglected for a number of years until in 1953 the French consul reminded the members of their dual aims and, as a result, under the Secretary, a French-Canadian, various sections under the leadership of committees were set up such as social, cultural, linguistic, sports, youth and university, assistance, travel.[15]

The linguistic section resulted in the establishment of evening classes for the teaching of French which in other countries have been organized by the Alliance français. These were particularly aimed at the English-speaking population who wished a conversational knowledge of French. A broad programme such as this attracted some 460 active members during the 1965-66 season. French Canadians, however, were again conspicuously absent, although the association has made efforts to attract them.

[15]Quoted from a newsletter issued by l'Alliance France-Canada in which a brief resumé of the history of the organization was included.

Ciné Club

Finally, the Ciné Club, also sponsored by the immigrant French, has a membership of close to 1,000, making it the largest French-speaking organization in Toronto. But less than 10 per cent of its membership were French Canadians; only eighty were enrolled in 1965, some of whom were among the middle-class respondents in the Toronto study. The president at that time, M. Jaubert, was concerned about this fact and in the fall of 1965 visited the French parish and some of the French-Canadian organizations mentioned above, seeking a larger representation. But only a few more responded. The Ciné Club even planned children's programmes of films in addition to the adult programme with the French Canadians in mind, but with what success is not known at the time of writing.

Participation of French-Canadians in French-speaking organizations sponsored by the immigrant French is thus almost non-existent. Few of the French-speaking population in Toronto have been "joiners." Those who do join organizations have been attracted to English associations rather than to French. An attempt was made through questioning to discover what value respondents saw in either French organizations or English organizations. Replies showed little evidence of clear-cut motivation to join French organizations, or of any goal to be accomplished in terms of the French community. Reasons given were largely personal in nature, such as wishing to keep their own language and culture, wanting to meet new French friends, showing an interest in their children through bilingual Home and School Associations. Motives for joining English associations were of a social nature except for Home and School Associations in English parochial schools. They wished to meet different people and make friends, to participate in English parish life, and in particular, to relax and enjoy life in Toronto. There was certainly very little consciousness of an ethnic identity to be nurtured and strengthened by participation in French-speaking voluntary associations.

The participation of the French population in formal associations, which has just been summarized, indicates a minimal influence of French associations on that population. Only a small minority of the French-speaking population have even been associated with voluntary associations. Those who have joined organizations have forged a closer relationship with the majority culture through memberships in English organizations than they have with the French culture through French organizations. Consequently, formal associations have not provided a viable alternative to the traditional source of ethnic integration, the French parish system, for the vast majority of the French population of Toronto. Only among the immigrant French has there been an attempt to utilize in a realistic way the voluntary association as a means of ethnic integration and preservation of an awareness of ethnic identity.

C. Informal Associations

When formal social structure does not provide an adequate means of integration within an ethnic group, informal networks of interpersonal relations may develop which maintain a sense of ethnic identity among the members of the minority group. Therefore, the respondents in the study were queried regarding their friendships: first, with others of French origin; second, with those of English (British) background; and third, with those of other ethnic groups (New Canadians). The purpose was to discover, if possible, who their friends were, and the closeness or intimacy of such friendships, using a descending scale of valuation from intimacy to casual acquaintance, as is shown in Table 31. Each respondent was asked, "Are there any among the French you know in Toronto whom you would consider—an intimate friend with whom one can share confidence; or a good friend with whom one can say what one thinks; or merely a friend who calls one by the first name; or a casual acquaintance." Ten per cent of the respondents claimed to have no friends on any of these levels among people of French origin. It is always possible that the questions may have been misunderstood as two of the twenty-six respondents who gave this answer attended the French parish regularly, and three others went there occasionally. But quite a number who attend mass at the Sacré-Coeur leave immediately after the service without social interaction with other worshippers. A French-Canadian executive from Montreal stated that he and his wife had attended services at the Sacré-Coeur parish for over a year before getting beyond the level of chance acquaintance with other worshippers. They resented the fact that anyone could attend for that length of time without getting involved with others.

Other explanations may be just as valid, however. The twenty-six grew up in widely scattered places, twelve in Southern Ontario, three in Northern Ontario, five in Quebec, four in the Maritimes, and two in Western Canada, so they represent widely varying backgrounds, largely in English-speaking environments. In spite of the bonds of a common language and culture there is anything but a common outlook shared by those of French origin from different parts of Canada. Instead they tend to gravitate to their own regional segment of the population. Or, as may be the case of this group, they represent the end product of exposure to the all-pervading English culture, such complete assimilation that all activities and friendships are among the English Canadians. On the other hand, all but four of the twenty-six had relatives in Toronto, and eleven of them visited back and forth every week, so French friends may have proved expendable.

When the same questions were asked about friendships among the English Canadians, more of the respondents had intimate friends among them (56%) than they had among those of French origin (46%). When this is broken down into the three major groupings, however, it becomes apparent that it is the Franco-Ontarians (64%) who have the most intimate friends among the English-speaking. It is less for those from Quebec (52%) and the Maritimes (47%), but

Table 31

Toronto Sample—Frequency Distribution of Friendships by Ethnicity of Friends, By Intimacy or Closeness of Relationship

Alternatives presented from (a) to (e)	With French—Are there any among the French you know in Toronto whom you consider		With English—Are there any among the English you know in Toronto whom you consider		The main question asked With other than French or English—Are there any among the New Canadians, of other national (ethnic) background than French or English whom you consider	
	No.	%	No.	%	No.	%
(a) Intimate friend (a close friend with whom you can talk over confidential or personal matters)?	116	46	140	56	46	18
(b) Close friend (a good friend to whom you can say what you really think)?	52	21	55	22	40	16
(c) Merely friend (someone who calls you by your first name)?	46	18	31	12	52	21
(d) Acquaintance (someone you know just to speak to)?	11	4	17	7	17	6
(e) No friendships (none at all)?	26	10	9	4	96	38
Total	252		252		251	

still in every case higher than the level of intimate friends among the French-speaking, which testifies to the prevalence of primary group or face-to-face relations between the French and the English in the Toronto setting. Only 4 per cent had no friends or acquaintances among the English in comparison to 10 per cent among the French.

When the same questions were asked about friendships among those who were neither French nor English, the proportion drops considerably. The French-speaking by preference live in areas where British stock predominates. Few had intimate friends among the ethnic groups often called New Canadians. There were 38 per cent who did not know any New Canadians on even a casual acquaintance basis. Although no attempt was made to secure information on the sex of those making certain responses, these respondents may well be French housewives with restricted contacts outside of the home. Some housewives have had little opportunity for even casual contacts with New Canadians, or in some cases, even with English Canadians. It did not seem to matter where the respondents grew up; only 21 per cent of Franco-Ontarians, 15 per cent of Quebeckers, and 18 per cent of Acadians had made intimate friends among New Canadians.

When respondents were asked how they had come to make friends with English Canadians, only 4 per cent said they had made no friends with them. Ten per cent had never had this problem because they had grown up in an English environment. Of the remainder, some had met them through neighbours (29%), others at their place of employment (28%), and the rest at social functions (20%) and in miscellaneous circumstances (8%). The fact that the majority of the migrants could speak English well before arriving in Toronto had simplified the making of English friends.

An important factor in the ease with which friends have been made with English Canadians in Toronto has been the virtual disappearance of job or social discrimination against those of French origin, as was mentioned in Chapter V on the Toronto work world. Only when the older respondents reminisced about early days in Toronto were such unpleasant experiences as being told to "speak white," or "go home where you belong" rather common. One prominent member of the French middle class confessed that he was almost afraid to speak French in public when he came to Toronto from Gaspé some thirteen years ago. He said that the climate began to change several years ago when immigration from Europe was so heavy. Hearing other languages became a commonplace experience on the streets, on public transport, in the stores and other places where people congregated in numbers. "Since then there is no difficulty," he asserted. In fact most of those interviewed had never at any time experienced anything unpleasant or discriminatory in their relationships with the English-speaking. One railway worker declared that when others tried to bait him as a French Canadian to "get his goat," and he retaliated in kind, there was no trouble or rancour but merely humourous banter.

Franco-Ontarians, however, expressed the opinion that Quebeckers and Acadians often came to Toronto with a derogatory stereotype of the English Canadian which was a result of previous lack of contact between the two groups. This made them critical of everything in the English system. This critical attitude began to dissipate when they found that most English-speaking Torontonians were oblivious of any issues between the French and the English, or just plain indifferent. In this somewhat neutral atmosphere, as the respondents in the Toronto sample testified when they were asked the question about unpleasant experiences, attitudes to English Canadians changed for the better.

The proprietor of the French Book Store had seen a marked change since he visited Toronto for the first time in the early fifties. A long-time resident of Toronto, one of the old middle class who had been resident in Toronto for over forty years, confirmed the view that the present ethnic climate is a late development. Toronto used to be a very difficult place for French Canadians to settle, he claimed, which is why the French population grew so slowly. At one time if a French family stayed in Toronto more than three years it was a feat of endurance, he stated. *The Toronto Telegram* in particular came in for a scathing denunciation as having been a journalistic enemy of both Roman Catholics and French Canadians until recent years. In this respect, therefore, the ethnic climate has favoured the formation of close relationships on the informal level between the French-speaking and the English-speaking populations of Metropolitan Toronto.

The conditions of settlement and distribution of the population of French origin in Toronto, therefore, have laid the foundations for close and continuous social relationships with members of the majority English-speaking population. The realities of life in an English-speaking metropolis involve residing among and working alongside of English-speaking people. Members of the French-speaking population come to know them as persons, not merely as ethnic stereotypes. A few of the French-speaking minority group have maintained the rigid reserve founded on ethnic stereotypes and impersonal characterizations of English-speaking people while living in Toronto. One executive in particular, in spite of all that others of the French middle class in Toronto could do to make him feel at home, insisted on maintaining the same stance and attitude of suspicion of and antagonism to English culture with which he had come to Toronto from Quebec. Lacking close friends among both the French and the English-speaking populations, even after three years in Toronto, he applied for a transfer back to Montreal. As was pointed out by some of his compatriots, he was in charge of programming for radio station CJBC during that time and could have done much to alleviate tensions and foster harmony between the two major ethnic groups in the city.

Differences tend to disappear when fraternization takes place between two language groups. The more personalized knowledge French-speaking persons have of English-speaking persons in a common environment, the greater the sense of identification in neighbourhood, employment, English parish and elsewhere. As the social distance between members of the two ethnic groups decreases, however, acculturation into the majority culture increases. Those of

French identity tend to become more like the English-speaking people around them through the gradual displacement of their own cultural values and goals. The lack of supporting and reinforcing social structures among the majority of the French-speaking population has accelerated this process for it leads to constant exposure to and almost unconscious adoption of the values and goals of the majority group. This process has certainly been made easier by the tacit acceptance by many of the French-speaking population of the idea that success in Toronto is contingent upon the adoption of the English language and culture.

In majority-minority relationships, change in identification tends to be in the one direction, from the minority to the majority group, seldom the reverse. Integration with the majority culture is thus the end product of a cumulative process in which the similarities rather than the differences between the two groups come to the fore. In Metropolitan Toronto, it is only in the militant segment of the French-speaking population which is affiliated with the French parish and the bilingual schools that incompatibility of interests has caused antagonism between the French and English. Variations in acculturation among members of this group, however, have resulted in considerable ambivalence and the formation of factions. Some seek isolation from the majority wherever possible, while others repudiate such extreme policies.

Little in the way of a practical solution to the problem of acculturation and eventual identification with the English-speaking culture has emerged even among the militants in the French-speaking population. The adjustments which have taken place have been the result of unplanned accommodations to the realities of life in another culture. Without a radical change in the pattern of settlement in the direction of a French residential enclave, something which to date the migrants have avoided, relationships with the English-speaking cannot be avoided. They have become part of the network of social interaction of which daily life consists. As a result, economic and communal identification have become more important than ethnic identification.[16]

There seems little reason to doubt that this acculturation process, begun on the level of informal associations at work, in the neighbourhood and in English parishes, has resulted in the "structural assimilation" of the majority of the population of French origin in Toronto. Even more seriously for the maintenance of a sense of ethnic identity, however, is the apparent absence of viable informal networks of interpersonal relationships within the greater part of the French population. Such networks represent the lowest level of integration to which the generic term "group" can be applied. When informal relationships with members of the majority group predominate over informal relationships with members of the minority group, a French population is in danger of losing any viable sense of ethnic identity.

---

[16]Shibutani and Kwan, *Ethnic Stratification,* Part V, pp. 469-570, to which recourse has been made for the foregoing.

D. Kinship Networks

A strong, traditional barrier to loss of ethnic identity exists, however, in the French extended family circle. Long a part of the social structure of French society in Quebec, the Maritimes, and Northern Ontario, it has been perpetuated to some degree in the Toronto milieu. Most of the respondents (70%) had relatives in the metropolitan area. Almost half of these respondents visited their relatives at least once a week. Another 15 per cent visited their kinfolk once a month. Only 10 per cent stated that they seldom saw their relatives. The presence of so many relatives would have some influence on the necessity of making friends, or joining associations, among either the French or the non-French people of Toronto.

The bonds of kinship, however, offer a precarious basis for the integration of a mobile, scattered population such as the French minority in Metropolitan Toronto. Within an urban-industrial society, strong family loyalties tend to segment the ethnic group in terms of kinship circles which may rarely intersect. Only in small, homogeneous communities does kinship provide the overall cohesion which binds all members of the ethnic group together. Social, occupational and geographic mobility gradually weaken rather than strengthen the ties of kinship. The end result is the comparatively isolated nuclear family which is so characteristic of North American industrial society.

The complete lack of participation in formal organizations by over half of the French population, and the paucity of interaction within voluntary associations by the remainder, either at the formal or the informal level, have created few channels of communication which could serve an alternative means of ethnic identification within the French population. The voluntary associations which do exist are mainly among the middle class associated with the French parish and bilingual schools and do not reach the vast majority of the middle class, the ones who attend English parishes and have been content to "pass" into the English cultural system. Even fewer channels of associational interaction exist within the largest segment of the French population, the working class, who have shown the least concern for matters of culture and ethnic identity. There remains within the scope of the present study only the French mass media of communications as an alternative means of ethnic identification for members of the French population.

Chapter X

Use of the
Communications Media

Modern society exhibits two somewhat paradoxical aspects. On the one hand it consists of a network of organized groups which range all the way from the informally constituted group of friends, neighbours or fellow workers, through increasing associational complexity to the highly formalized organizations such as the Church, the trade union, the business corporation or the state. On the other hand, the increasing complexity of modern society with its social and occupational mobility and large urban populations has divorced individuals from their local cultural and communal groups and created detached aggregates or masses of people who are linked together, if at all, by the mass media of communication. In fact, the mass media constitute the form of communication which is typical of a society in which many secondary groupings thrive. In such a society it is mainly through the ties created by the various forms of mass communication that the members of secondary groups in modern society are bound together into a functioning whole. Described in these general terms, therefore, mass communication refers to "the relatively simultaneous exposure of a large, scattered and heterogeneous audience to stimuli transmitted by impersonal means from an organized source for whom the audience members are anonymous."[1]

Within the English-speaking culture, therefore, the network of interrelated voluntary associations supplemented by the English-speaking mass media provide the integration which in French-Canadian society is supplied through the comprehensive structure of the Catholic parish system. The French parish system in Toronto, however, no longer functions as the integrative centre of a Catholic population of French origin. The few sparsely-attended non-parish, or even parish, associations have had little impact as forces of integration and ethnic consciousness upon the majority of the population of French origin. Thus the failure of social interaction at the level of the parish and other voluntary associations has thrown the burden of maintaining consciousness of ethnic identity upon the remaining channel of communication which is available to the entire population of French origin, the mass media of communications.

There is a certain parallelism between the characteristics of the French-speaking population in Metropolitan Toronto and the characteristics of the mass audience of the mass media. In both, the audience is scattered over an entire area with an absence of the compact groups familiar to communal life. Both are heterogeneous in cultural background, isolated from regular contact between the members, anonymous in the sense that both represent an aggregate of individuals

---

[1]Lundberg, et al., "Mass Communications," Sociology (4th ed.; New York: Harper & Row, 1968), pp. 449-51.

or families rather than an integrated group, and unattached because individual taste and judgment, as exercised in self-selection rather than group behaviour, determines to a very large degree what is read, heard and seen, or any combination of these three.

In a wider sense, then, than either the parish or educational system permits, individual or family preferences may be expressed through the mass media, by means of the choice of French or English newspapers, magazines, books, films and radio or television programmes. The measure of anonymity afforded by the private home allows self-selection of the preferred media according to personal tastes. The advent of a French-language radio station, CJBC, just seven months before the interviewing of the Toronto respondents, added a dimension to the mass media which is significant for the French language and culture. The mounting frequency with which French films have been advertised and shown is not only evidence of the increasingly cosmopolitan character of Toronto but a further opportunity for contact with French language and culture. In this chapter it becomes evident to what extent the French population of Toronto has been making use of the French mass media.

A. The French-Language Newspaper

Among the larger ethnic groups in Toronto, the local newspaper, printed in their own language, has been a potent factor in maintaining the consciousness of ethnic identity. Between the late 1930s and the late 1950s the number of languages in which they were printed doubled to twenty-six while the number of such newspapers increased threefold. But five attempts to establish a French-language newspaper in the Toronto area have all been abortive. In the middle 1950s the first of the five, *L'Alliance*, was founded by Jacques Dusseault and lasted a year before his translations firm began to take up too much of his time. He admitted that it was very difficult to satisfy the wide variety of viewpoints found among the French-speaking in Toronto, his paper being criticized from opposite points of view at the same time. The second attempt was named *Le Bulletin* and soon expired. The third, entitled *Toronto-Presse*, lasted for only two months. The fourth newspaper, *Les Nouvelles Françaises*, lasted the longest, for the period of between two and three years while its editor, Professor Michel Sanouillet, remained as a visiting professor from France at the University of Toronto. Publication ceased shortly after Professor Sanouillet returned to Europe. Finally, *L'Alouette*, the fifth attempt, ceased publication in 1964 for lack of a reading public and sufficient financial backing. The editor, who was also the proprietor of the French Book Store in Toronto, complained that closure was the result of the withdrawal of a subsidy granted by the Department of Cultural Affairs of the Province of Quebec because he would not tolerate any interference from Quebec with the editorial policy of his paper. In an interview on the French-language radio station CJBC, as well as in an article printed in

La Patrie on October 7, 1964, the editor, Marc Foisy, blamed authoritarian influences such as l'Ordre de Jacques Cartier for his dilemma.

None of the editors of the five newspapers mentioned above had much, if any, experience in newspaper publishing prior to essaying their Toronto publication. Nor were capital funds to defray costs of publication easy to obtain. *L'Alouette*, for instance, was only published sporadically because of lack of capital to absorb the losses which are inevitable with a new publication. Furthermore, the same price was charged for four and six-page editions as the Toronto daily papers charged for their voluminous editions in the English language. The editor also found that it was difficult, if not impossible, to satisfy the variety of viewpoints existing within the broad spectrum of regional differences existing within the population of French origin in Metropolitan Toronto.

The French Book Store on Gerrard Street West, in the heart of the Toronto downtown shopping area, close to potential customers among the French-speaking in the central areas of French concentration, sold very few of the French dailies from Ottawa, Northern Ontario or Quebec. In the experience of the proprietor, few French-language magazines were read widely in Toronto, nor were French books in demand except those used as textbooks for French in Toronto schools and colleges. In his judgment, echoed by other informants, the main reason for this state of affairs was the low level of education of the majority of the French population in the Toronto area. Some of his customers, however, complained that the handling of book orders by the French Book Store was so inefficient that they were forced to order directly from Quebec, or from France, or place orders with one of the established English book stores. Consequently, lack of education was not the only deterrent to circulation of French-language publications in Toronto.

The Toronto study tends to confirm these general observations as can be seen in Table 32. In the Toronto sample 85 per cent read English-language newspapers, *The Daily Star* and *The Telegram*, and to a lesser degree, *The Globe and Mail*. Only 23 per cent read French newspapers, and some of this number only

Table 32

Regular Reading of French and English Newspapers, Magazines and Books by Respondents in the Toronto Study

Do you read regularly?	French		English	
	No.	%	No.	%
Newspapers	59	23	214	85
Magazines	62	25	158	63
Books	62	25	120	48

read them occasionally. Seven newspapers were mentioned by name, of which the Ottawa paper *Le Droit* appeared to be the favourite. *Le Devoir* was read by a few, but criticized by others as projecting a viewpoint not readily understood by many of the French residents of Toronto. *Le Soleil, La Patrie, Le Matin,* and *Le Petit Journal* were also mentioned. More numerous were the local weeklies, with an occasional daily, which informants received from their former home districts, such as the Acadian paper *L'Evangeline.* These twelve publications plus a farm paper and two Catholic publications complete the catalogue of the French press read by members of the Toronto sample. Several who did read French newspapers expressed satisfaction at the reserved way in which the French press treated "separatist" incidents in comparison with the treatment accorded the same incidents by the Toronto English-language press.

B. French Magazines

The proportion of the sample who read French-language magazines, 25 per cent, parallels newspaper readership, leaving English magazines as the staple reading matter of the majority of the population of French origin. Along with a few Catholic publications of a more regional nature, the popular magazine titles were *La Revue Populaire, Nous Deux, Le Samedi, La Ferme, La Voix Nationale,* and the French editions of *Maclean's, Chatelaine* and *Reader's Digest.* Continental French magazines such as *Paris Match, Femmes Aujourd'hui, Elle, Constellation,* and *Ici Paris* had some circulation.

C. French Books

The limited educational background of the majority of the sample is reflected in the fact that many did not read books at all, either in French or in English. The 25 per cent who did read French-language books in part confessed that they read few of them a year. One problem was the procurement of French books. Few were available for purchase apart from those required for French courses in the schools, either in the French Book Store or elsewhere. Apart from the University of Toronto libraries, which were not accessible to non-students, the only sizeable library of French literature was the collection belonging to l'Alliance Français, which had accumulated over the years through accessions from the headquarters of that organization in Paris. Consisting of well over a thousand volumes, it was stored in the Parkdale Branch Public Library, which administered the use of the books through a member of the library staff who was also a member of l'Alliance Français. But very few of those of French origin in Toronto were even aware of the existence of the library, according to Professor Rathé of Victoria University, the president of l'Alliance.

D. French Radio

The preliminary work on the Toronto study began around the time of the transfer of radio station CJBC from the English to the French language on October 1, 1964. According to the French-language Programme Director, who had already been with the CBC in Toronto for two years preparing for the transition, the transfer had been planned some years earlier when the Dominion network of the CBC had been disbanded, leaving Toronto as the only city in Canada with two English-language CBC radio stations. It therefore seemed wise to aim at the transfer of one of them eventually to the French language. But in the interim CJBC had built up a large English listening audience by means of quality programming. Opposition to any change was strong among the large listening audience of CJBC. The actual transfer took place a month before it was originally scheduled in order to circumvent delay by means of legal strategems under consideration by the English-speaking opposition to the change.

A French-speaking population of some 165,000 resided within range of CJBC broadcasts at the time of the transfer, scattered in varying-sized groups from Belleville on the east to London on the west and Parry Sound on the north. Interest in French-language radio among these groups crystallized in 1956 when l'Association de la Radio et de la Télévision française du sud de l'Ontario, or A.R.T.F. as it is popularly called, was formed, with its first president the principal of a Catholic high school in Welland. At the time of the Toronto study the proprietor of the French Book Store was president of the A.R.T.F., followed in 1966 by Lucien L'Allier, a French-Canadian businessman prominent on the executive of l'Alliance France-Canada, a largely immigrant French organization. The new organization began presenting briefs to the federal government requesting the establishment of a French radio station from its inception until the transfer was consummated in October, 1964.

It is an indication, however, of the weakness of middle-class leadership in Toronto and its environs, either clergy or laity, that such an organization did not emerge in Toronto until the mid-1950s. In Western Canada as early as 1939 there had been agitation for French-language radio stations in order to combat what was considered by the French to be the insidious threat to the French language and culture of English-speaking radio coming into the home, the one-time inviolate citadel of the French language for those of French origin. In 1941, an association known as Radio-ouest-française, with representatives from the three prairie provinces, was formed, and by 1946, French-language radio stations were operating in the west. The aggressive leadership of the clergy as well as the middle-class laity has been credited with stimulating the birth of this movement. But such leadership was obviously lacking in Toronto until the advent of the new middle class of professionals and executives in the mid-1950s.

Action in Toronto, therefore, had to await the formation of the Club Richelieu by the new middle class in 1953, which eventually precipitated the formation of the A.R.T.F. which finally was successful in securing the transfer

of CJBC to the French language. But the negotiations were not without diffi-
culties. One member of the executive, a university professor, resigned in protest
against what he considered authoritarian and undemocratic procedures by the
A.R.T.F., actions which he attributed to the influence of l'Ordre de Jacques
Cartier. In another incident a number of the middle class of French origin in
Toronto refused to attend the Gala held at the Lord Simcoe Hotel at the end of
October, 1964, the original date of the transfer of CJBC to the French language,
because the French-Canadian soloist who had been invited to sing had refused to
sing for the Queen on her visit to Quebec not long before, an action which they
considered an affront to the British connection. It was an incident which revealed the wide variation among the middle class in the value placed upon the
British crown.

During the first few months that radio station CJBC operated in the French
language, listener surveys and the volume of mail received showed that far more
English-speaking persons than French-speaking persons were in the station audience. Two factors may have been operative here: first, the reluctance of former
English-speaking listeners of CJBC to change their listener habits, as well as the
novelty of listening to French programmes, and secondly, the slowness of the
French-speaking population to take advantage of the French-language programme opportunities. It must not be forgotten that in the census of 1961 only
42.3 per cent of the population of French origin in Toronto claimed French as
mother tongue, a factor which narrowed the potential listener audience among
the population of French origin. The influence of these factors is obvious in the
responses to questions regarding CJBC asked of respondents in the Toronto
study, summarized in Table 33 below.

Over half of the population of French origin in Toronto listened exclusively
to English-speaking stations or did not bother with radio at all, possibly because
of the competition of television. One hundred and thirteen families out of a
possible 249 listened to station CJBC. Thirty-four per cent of this number
listened only occasionally, and another 15 per cent less than one hour daily.
Even when the 12 per cent who could not estimate their listening time are
included with those who listened to CJBC from one to four hours and over, the
confirmed and devoted listening audience among the French population of Toronto, acquired over a period of eight months since the station began French
broadcasts, was approximately 12 per cent of the total French population.
Among this regular listening audience, however, some had already begun to form
patterns of listening, as 35 per cent named a favourite programme and another
19 per cent named a second favourite programme.

Research in the field of the mass media has revealed that radio audiences do
not readily change their tastes either in stations or in programmes, but prefer
that for which they have already developed a liking.[2] This appears to be the case

[2]P. F. Lazarsfeld, "Audience Research," in Bernard Berelson and Maurice Janowitz,
eds., *Reader in Public Opinion and Communications* (New York: The Free Press of Glencoe,
1950 and 1953), pp. 337-46.

Table 33

Patterns of Radio Listening Among Those of French
Origin in Toronto

Listening Habits[a]	CJBC Only		Both French and English		English Only		None	
	No.	%	No.	%	No.	%	No.	%
Regularly	30	12	83	33	106	42	30	12

	No.	%
CJBC Occasionally	38	34
Less than one hour daily	17	15
One to four hours daily	23	20
Over four hours daily	22	19
Don't know	13	12
Totals	113	100.0

[a]Three respondents were not asked the questions re radio.

with the population of French origin in Toronto. Over a year after the Toronto survey in 1965 fan mail from French listeners was just beginning to reach parity with the mail from English-speaking listeners. A member of the French parish who turned his car radio to CJBC while driving his children to the bilingual school in the mornings discovered that they did not like listening to French over the radio. But he persevered and over a period of time the children developed an appreciation and a liking for CJBC programmes. Some of the Franco-Ontarians, however, were quick to criticize the amount of content in CJBC programmes which was piped in from the Quebec network, claiming that their interests and outlook were often quite different from those given expression on the Quebec network. In answer to such criticisms, a beginning was made late in 1965 to originate programmes in Ontario.

An article by Dennis Braithewaite in *The Globe and Mail* of Toronto for September 1, 1966, underlines the results of recent surveys which indicate a continuing small listener audience for CJBC.

The most recent audience survey for Toronto's radio stations by McDonald Research Ltd., a leading firm in the survey field, tallies the listeners of 11 AM and FM stations in half-hour (and sometimes quarter-hour) periods of the day, from 6 a.m. to midnight. Surveys usually list only the numbers of homes tuned to a particular station; this one counts the individual men, women, teenagers and children that are listening. Teenagers and children hardly register at all on the CJBC chart which is hardly surprising, so we can forget them. The adult audience is the significant one. Well, what about it? Take the period 5:45 to 6 p.m., a peak period for all radio. At that time, CFRB, the pre-eminent station for adults, has an audience of 236,900; CHUM has 54,400; CHFI, 33,800; CKEY, 26,400; CJBC—600. At no time of the day, according to this survey, has CJBC more than 2,800 listeners (that peak is reached between 11:45 a.m. and noon); in the same period CFRB has 221,900. Now, it must be remembered that CJBC has one of the most powerful signals of any Canadian radio station, a reach, as broadcasters say, that easily encompasses all those areas of Southern Ontario—the Niagara Peninsula in particular—where its potential French-speaking audience lives. Another peak radio period is 8 to 8:15 in the morning. That's when CFRB reaches 327,900, and even the listless CBL collars 60,000. CJBC in that quarter hour has 1,000 listeners. What about the period 9 to 10 p.m., a time when adults might be expected to have the leisure for listening? According to McDonald's chart, CJBC musters a total of 100 men and women! There must be nearly that many people involved in putting the shows on the air.

E. French Films

The fifth medium of communication of the French culture in Toronto is the French-language film. French films, however, touch only a small fraction of the French-speaking population in the metropolitan area. Almost half (46%) of this population did not attend moving-picture theatres and thus saw no films at all. Only 7 per cent saw films regularly, and another 47 per cent sometimes, but of these two groups together, 72 per cent, almost three-quarters, have never seen a French film in Toronto. Even of the 28 per cent who have seen French films, few have seen them regularly. In terms of the total French-speaking population of Toronto, only 14 per cent have seen French films and most of these very seldom. Few in the Toronto study were even aware of the existence of the French Ciné Club. Nearly all of the Ciné Club membership are European immigrants or English Canadians with a command of the French language. Thus the Ciné Club reaches about 2 per cent of the adult French-speaking population of Metropolitan Toronto. Participation in the mass media through French-language films represents the lowest rate of use of any of the French mass media in Toronto.

F. Television

The one mass medium which had no counterpart in Toronto among the French-language mass media at the time of the research was television.[3] Ninety-

[3]Since 1966 there have been French-language programmes on television, Channel 6, on Sunday mornings. Channels 6 and 9, in Toronto, and 11, in Hamilton, have programmes in languages other than English on Sunday mornings.

eight per cent of the Toronto respondents possessed television sets in their homes, one reason for the percentage of the French-speaking who no longer listen to radio. As the latest arrival in the mass communications network, television tends consistently to outdo the other media in audience participation because it combines both visual and auditory stimuli and acquires a position in the home which makes the people reflected on its screen almost members of the viewer's family, in large part because its dramatic content so closely simulates primary interaction.[4]

It has been estimated that the average North American child aged three to sixteen years spends as much time viewing television as he does in school,[5] which illustrates the potent influence this predominantly-English medium can have on the children in a French-speaking family, as well as on the adults. Since the average family has its television set on for just over six hours per day, according to audience research,[6] such exposure to a glamourized and exciting English cultural milieu with its constantly-changing context cannot but hasten the acculturation of French-speaking families, especially through its appeal to the young. There seems little doubt that it is through television that the English-language mass media has its greatest impact upon those of French origin in Toronto.

The respondents in the Toronto study were asked if they were satisfied with English-language television, and 69 per cent replied in the affirmative, 22 per cent in the negative, with 9 per cent having no opinion. The question: Would you like some French television on the CBC station in Toronto? elicited the following response: 65 per cent yes, 24 per cent no, and 15 per cent no opinion. An additional question was asked to discover whether the respondents had any knowledge of the size of the French population in Toronto, namely: Do you think there are enough French in Toronto for a television station? Fifty-six per cent said yes, 21 per cent said no, and 23 per cent had no opinion. Actually very few of them had any conception of the size of the population of French origin in Toronto. They would have justified a French-language television station in Toronto on the basis of a much smaller French population than actually exists. One argument in substantiation of this point of view was that since Quebec City had an English-language television station for a small English-speaking population the CBC was obligated to provide one for the French-speaking in Toronto. Apparently they were not aware that the television station in Quebec City to which they referred was a private station, financed by the English-speaking community. Those who argued against a French-language television station in Toronto were from the middle class who knew the enormous costs of television programmes and questioned whether there would be sufficient income from French advertisers to make the plan commercially feasible.

[4]Lundberg, et al., Sociology, p. 448.

[5]Ibid., p. 445.

[6]Ibid., p. 470.

G. Patterns of Mass Media Use

On the basis of separate consideration of the five mass media discussed above, newspapers, magazines, books, radio and films, the majority of the French-speaking population make no use whatever of the French mass media in Toronto. Whether this springs from the limited educational background of most of the French-speaking population, or from the "all or none" tendency which pervades the mass media field, in which participation tends to be in all the mass media or in none at all, it is difficult to conclude. But the convergence in reading, listening and watching which are evident in the percentages which have been quoted all point to a focussing of behaviour patterns in the channels of the English mass media, at variance with the French ethnic inheritance. Conformity to English patterns appears to confirm the tendencies already obvious in the preceding chapters regarding the general drift toward identification with the English cultural system. The mass media tends to accelerate conformity to the environment in which it is dominant, breaking down the group loyalties and ethnic patterns of French culture.

The five mass media have been assessed only individually, however, and when they are considered in relation to each other, patterns of use emerge, since few of the families who use the French mass media use all five of them. Thirty different patterns of use of the mass media are possible, of which twenty-seven are actually used by 145 families out of the 252 in the Toronto study, which represents 57.5 per cent of the total French-speaking population. The optimum use of the French mass media would be for the 145 families to use all five media which would represent a potential of 725 usages. But the 145 families reported only 331 uses of the five media, which represents 45.6 per cent of the potential use, an average use of 2.3 of the mass media per family. This raises the question of which patterns of use are most prevalent. Only ten of the twenty-seven mass media use patterns occurred with sufficient frequency to be considered significant, and are shown in Table 34. They involved only 105 families out of the 145 families who use the French mass media, and represent 42 per cent of the total French-speaking population.

In view of the short period of time in which the French-language radio station CJBC was broadcasting, it is rather surprising to find that radio has the highest rate of use of any of the mass media. French-language radio-represents 24 per cent of the 331 uses made of the five mass media by the 145 families. French magazines and books represent 19 per cent each, French newspapers 18 per cent, and films only 10 per cent. There is a tendency for families to use the single French medium of radio and omit the others. In fact, radio is the only medium which is represented in nine of the ten significant patterns. If it were deleted, as it would have been if the Toronto study had been carried out in the spring of 1964 before French-language radio station CJBC was transferred from English to French, it may be conjectured that the rate of use of the other four French-language mass media would be very low indeed. Even as it is, with radio the leading French mass medium, its regular listener audience of over an hour a day is only 12 per cent of the French-speaking population of Metropolitan Toronto.

Table 34

The Ten Most Significant Patterns of French Mass Media Usage Among the 145 Toronto Families of French Origin Who Report 331 Usages of One or More of the French Mass Media

	Patterns of Usage of the French Mass Media					Participation by Families		
Pattern No.	News-papers	Books	Maga-zines	Radio	Films	No.	%	Rank Order
1.	X					9	6.2	4
4.	X	X	X	X		10	6.9	2
5.	X	X	X	X	X	7	4.8	9
9.	X		X	X		8	5.5	5
10.	X		X	X	X	4	2.8	10
12.	X			X		10	6.9	2
16.		X	X	X		8	5.5	5
17.		X	X	X	X	8	5.5	5
19.		X		X		8	5.5	5
25.				X		33	22.7	1
Totals						105	72.3	

One would expect that affiliation with the French parish or bilingual schools, or both, would influence the use of the French mass media positively in contrast to those of French origin who attended English parishes. When the 64 families which were so affiliated were contrasted with the 81 families which attended English parishes the differences were not significant. There was only a tendency for the former to make multiple use of the French mass media while the latter concentrated on one or two of the French mass media.

The question of whether use of the French mass media is class-oriented also arises, as audience research shows that the upper middle class and the working class tend to use the mass media, with the possible exception of television, to a far less degree than the lower middle class. Since the majority of the middle class were resident in the suburbs the use of the French mass media by families resident within existing city boundaries was contrasted with the use by families of French origin residing in the suburbs. The differences, however, did not prove significant, indicating the absence statistically of class-orientation.

The statistical evidence presented above indicates that the French-speaking population has adjusted to the omnipresent English mass media in Toronto and has maintained that orientation in spite of the existence of French mass media facilities. The extra effort required to procure French-language newspapers, magazines and books, the sporadic nature of the showing of French-language films, and the late arrival of the French-language radio station CJBC on the media scene have encouraged the French-speaking population to embrace the English-language mass media rather than the French. Furthermore, the working-class status of 70 per cent of that population, their generally low level of education, their preoccupation with the mere business of living, coupled with the substantial loss of French as mother tongue, have all combined to relegate the French mass media to a very minor role.

Participation in the English mass media is also more directly related to the social milieu in which the French-speaking live and work in Toronto. This correspondence tends to reinforce the influence of the English media, while the French mass media, with its different cultural emphasis, tends to conflict with the values and goals of the English-speaking social and economic world. Thus repetitive use of the English mass media orients the French-speaking population to the English culture and disorients it for the French culture. It has been an illusion that provision of a medium automatically ensures an audience for it. Middle-class French leadership may assume that all that the French-speaking population wants is provision of French-language facilities, without ever asking the question: Does that population really want or will they use such facilities? The statistics would appear to prove that the majority of the population neither want nor will they use such facilities.

Audience research has shown that people tend to listen or read what they have previously liked rather than form new tastes. Thus the mass media functions as a strong advocate of the status quo. Most of the French-speaking population have lived in Toronto for a number of years, their tastes have been formed and are not likely to change. In other words, every radio programme, book or magazine tends to select its own audience of those already conditioned to like the material, and repulses those who do not like it. As Lazarsfeld points out,[7] this circular reinforcement of the familiar works to the disadvantage of those who would initiate change, and is probably the greatest obstacle to what the new French middle class seeks to accomplish within the Toronto population. The content of the mass media is forced to conform to attitudes and patterns of behaviour already sanctioned by the vast majority of the audience, which involves English and not French culture. It is not in the interests of the economic control of the mass media to introduce any issue which would antagonize any part of the mass audience. The result is merely to widen and intensify the sanction of already-accepted views, which are in harmony with the social and economic realities of the English-speaking culture.

[7]Lazarsfeld, "Audience Research," pp. 337f.

Chapter XI

Prospects
for Survival

It has been maintained in this study that social participation is so closely related to group identity that identity tends to be a function of the locus of participation. Social participation within ethnic boundaries creates, sustains and reinforces ethnic identity, while participation outside of ethnic boundaries leads to alternative identifications which weaken and dissolve ethnic identity.

Traditional French-Canadian rural society has been cited as an example of almost total participation within ethnic boundaries which coincided with the parish structure of the Roman Catholic Church. A strong, unitary identification with French culture and the Catholic faith was the result. In contrast, the French minority population of Metropolitan Toronto exemplifies almost total participation outside of ethnic boundaries within the English-speaking host population. Alternative identifications have virtually dissolved ethnic identity among the majority of the population of French origin.

A major finding of the study of the French minority in Toronto has been the uniformity of patterns of participational identification with the English-speaking host society of all but a small minority of the French population. Every aspect of the communal life of members of the French minority, economic, religious, educational, cultural and associational, has been involved in accommodations to the host society. No more than 5 to 15 per cent of the members of the French minority have concentrated participational identification within the existing institutional structures of the French population.

A second finding of the study has been to identify some of the variables which have determined the patterns of participational identification of the French in Toronto. As is true of any multi-ethnic community, such variables have operated against the background and growth of the community, and their interrelationships have been determined to some degree by local conditions and circumstances. This has been evident throughout the study in relation to variables such as the degree of economic absorption of the French; the pattern of residential settlement; socio-economic differentiation of the French population; the institutional completeness of French social structure; the level of homogeneity or heterogeneity of the French migrants; and the extent to which the host society has been open or closed to ethnic penetration.

The influence of three of these determinants has been the product of Toronto's position as an industrial metropolis. The economic absorption of nearly all the French migrants within the occupational structure of the Toronto labour force has resulted from the almost total absence of French-owned and operated businesses or industrial concerns. The sphere of employment reflects the primary motive for migration to Toronto and has been the most influential channel of exposure of the French in Toronto to the values and goals current in the English-speaking industrial society.

The economic motive has also been dominant in the choice by migrants of an area of residence in proximity to employment and has scattered the French population without significant concentrations throughout the entire metropolitan area. As a consequence of this dispersed pattern of settlement the French have become involved in networks of social relations with the non-French rather than the French in the neighbourhood as well as at work.

The process of social stratification which is endemic to industrial societies has accentuated a third variable, socio-economic differentiation. Class differentials such as occupation, education, income, residence, and style of life have tended to emphasize class values rather than ethnic values. The major concern of the lower-class majority within the French population has not been ethnic values but economic survival. Hence they have been indifferent to an ethnic identity which would contribute little to economic security, and might even endanger it.

Class values have played their major role in the participational identification of members of the French middle class. Finding the only traditional focus for French identity in Toronto, the French parish of the Sacré-Coeur, unacceptable because of its lower-class status, over 90 per cent of the middle class have turned to the only viable status alternative, English parishes and parochial or public schools in middle-class residential areas. The cumulative pressures of employment, residence, associations, religion and education, all located within an English-speaking context, has fostered both the passing of most of the middle class into the host society, and the siphoning off from the French minority of potential ethnic leadership.

A fourth determinant has been the degree of institutional completeness within the French minority. In any minority population the degree of completeness is dependent upon the extent to which interaction with the host population remains on the superficial, secondary group level of acculturation, while primary social interaction is confined within the traditional social structures of the minority population. But the opposite process has been dominant in Toronto from the earliest records of French migration. Traditional institutional structures such as the French parish, bilingual schools, voluntary associations and mass media have never provided the organizational means to channel participation of the majority of the French population within ethnic boundaries. This low degree of institutional completeness has left the vast majority of the French population no alternative but to participate within the social structures of the host society, a clear case of structural assimilation of the minority population.

Local conditions and circumstances indigenous to Toronto have played a major role, therefore, in facilitating participation of the French minority outside of ethnic boundaries. But they do not explain why, contrary to the usual experience of ethnic minorities, an alien milieu has not drawn the French together for mutual support. Two considerations are relevant here: the character of the migrant French population and the nature of the host society.

Within a homogeneous ethnic minority internal group pressure tends to maintain social interaction within ethnic boundaries under the penalty of negative sanctions. But the diversity of place of origin and hence of cultural background of the French migrants to Toronto has prevented the development of consensus and fragmented a common ethnicity by regional identifications and loyalties. The wide variation among migrants in the degree of acculturation to English-speaking society which they experienced in their home communities has created further division within the French minority while at the same time it has eased the entry of many of the migrants into the host society upon arrival in Toronto.

Reinforcing the influence of cultural heterogeneity within the French population has been the openness of the host society which has gradually developed over several decades of heavy immigration from abroad. A closed host society, impervious to ethnic penetration, usually exerts the external pressures of ethnic discrimination and rejection upon the members of an ethnic minority. It thus slows accommodation to the host society by forcing social interaction to remain within the ethnic boundaries of the minority population. But multi-ethnic Toronto has become increasingly open to penetration by members of ethnic minorities who have become established within the industrial system, even though the upper levels of the status hierarchy remain closed to those outside of the predominantly British economic élite.

The major impact of the heterogeneity of the French population and the openness of the host English-speaking society has been to remove both internal and external pressures which would tend to confine social interaction within ethnic boundaries. Participation outside of ethnic boundaries has taken the form of alternative identifications which have progressively oriented the members of the French minority towards acceptance of the dominant English-speaking culture. In this context, three alternative identifications have loomed as particularly significant in relation to ethnic identity, namely, religious, community, and class identifications.

A religious identification has replaced the traditional partnership of the French culture and the Roman Catholic Church. The affiliation of the majority of the French population with English parishes and schools has affected ethnic identity in two ways. The French migrants have discovered that religious duties may be performed and vows fulfilled satisfactorily in the English as well as the French language. The consequent divorce of religious worship and education from the French language and culture has severed the bond between French ethnic identity and the Catholic Church. Once this traditional bond has been broken, the role of a French parish and bilingual school as a focus for ethnic identity becomes difficult if not impossible to fulfill, as it has in Toronto.

A community identification has emerged as a result of the dispersed pattern of French settlement, reinforced by involvement in the Toronto work world. Ethnic identification demands differentiation from the larger population, usually successful only within an ethnic enclave, a pattern which has been rejected by the French population in Toronto. Some indications of the progress and strength of the alternative communal identification are the loss of French as mother tongue over a span of three generations, and the increasing use of English and disuse of French throughout the French population; the proportion of cross-cultural and mixed-religions marriages, especially with those of British stock; the predominance of memberships in 'English associations and of friendships with English Canadians; and the almost universal use of the English mass media.

A class identification, strongest among the middle class, has replaced an ethnic identification for two reasons. Socio-economic differentiation has strati-fied the French population and in so diversifying further an already culturally heterogeneous minority has accentuated the differences now dividing the French population. Conversely, within class strata the similarities of shared experience with the English-speaking population in employment, parish, education, resi-dence, association and style of life has generated rapport and consensus across ethnic boundaries, creating a sense of class unity within a context of ethnic disunity.

These emergent religious, communal, and class identifications, seen as alterna-tives to an ethnic identification, reflect the impact of institutional participation as a basic condition for the formation and maintenance of group identity. A strong sense of ethnic identity is likely to be fostered only where primary social interaction amongst the French can be concentrated within ethnic boundaries. In Toronto, however, conditions of employment, residence and acceptance with-in the host community, together with the diversified character of the French migrant population, have promoted participation outside rather than within eth-nic boundaries, with the resultant weakening of ethnic identity for a nominally French population.

Chapter XII

Postscript 1976:
The Trends of a Decade, 1966-1976

No decade of the twentieth century has made Canadians more aware of the French presence in their midst than the ten years just passed. The Quiet Revolution of the early sixties which began to change the social structure of the Province of Quebec, and the rise in intensity of the separatist movement which accompanied it, set the stage for the more dramatic events to follow. The continual unrest within French Canada became a matter of political concern for the Federal Government and led to the establishment of the Royal Commission on Bilingualism and Biculturalism which initiated the most intensive research in the field of ethnic relations ever undertaken in Canada.

The hearings conducted from coast to coast by members of the Royal Commission and the publication of their findings and recommendations in coordination with the findings of numerous supplementary research projects, not only made the French fact more visible on the Canadian scene, but led to definitive legislation. A direct result of the work of the Commission was the adoption of a policy of bilingualism and biculturalism which was followed in 1969 by the Official Languages Act which gave the French language a more comprehensive status both within the federal civil service and throughout the country wherever the concentrations of the French-speaking population warranted such action.

The inclusion of non-French and non-English members on the Commission, however, drew attention to the claims of this segment of the Canadian population. Recognition was eventually given to this substantial (26.7% in 1971)[1] segment of the people of Canada through broadening the policy of biculturalism to one of multiculturalism within a bicultural framework. The French protested that the new policy was an erosion of their position as a charter member within the federal system. But to the advantage of French organizations, the federal government proceeded to initiate a programme of financial grants to ethnic organizations which sought to preserve the essential elements of their ancestral cultures,[2] a programme administered by the Social Action Branch of the Department of the Secretary of State.

The Quebecois drew attention to their province and the French culture during the decade through momentous events such as the celebration of Canada's Centennial at Expo '67, followed almost a decade later by the Olympic Games. Both were extravaganzas which attracted hundreds of thousands of visitors to "La Belle Province" and introduced many of them to the cosmopolitan atmos-

---

[1]*Census of Canada*, 1971.

[2]Jean Burnet, "Ethnicity: Canadian Experience and Policy," *Sociological Focus,* 9, No. 2 (April, 1976), 202-204.

phere of Canada's largest metropolis, French-Canadian Montreal. But even more dramatic in their impact were events such as the separatist violence of the F.L.Q. which led to the imposition of the War Measures Act, the highly controversial visit of General Charles de Gaulle of France to Quebec and his provocative declaration in a speech in Montreal, "Vive le Quebec libre!" Finally, there was the consolidation of several splinter parties of the separatist movement into the Parti Quebecois under the leadership of former Liberal cabinet minister, René Levesque,[3] and the party's final triumph at the provincial polls in the fall of 1976. The rest of Canada began to realize the seriousness with which many of the French Canadians (or "francophones" in recently popular terminology) viewed their situation within Confederation in relation to English Canadians (or the "anglophones").

One may well ask to what extent these events have influenced the situation of francophones in Metropolitan Toronto? Leading members of the French population obviously welcomed the stimulation such events gave to the consciousness of French identity among Toronto francophones. In both conversation and in print one encountered such phrases and comments as: "The climate has certainly changed in Toronto" . . . "the scene has changed enormously" . . . "there has been much greater acceptance of the French during the last ten years, an openness which did not exist before. Negative reactions have decreased and there is much more of a positive reaction to the French" . . . "Interest in the French language has increased enormously."

Such enthusiastic remarks were illustrated by reference to specific areas of change which had taken place during the decade. For instance, many pointed to the new status of French-language schools in Ontario through provincial legislation which has permitted expansion at both elementary and secondary levels. They mentioned increased communication media facilities which had begun with the allocation of radio station CJBC to the French language in 1964, followed by Educational Television in French in 1970, and a French-language station in 1973. The increased use of French films in public theatres and in schools was welcomed. The publishing of a newspaper, the *Courier Sud*, beginning in 1973, was considered an important event, as were also the establishment of two major French book stores and the greater availability of French literature in Toronto libraries.

Frequent mention was made of attempts to coordinate and publicize an increasing number of French cultural, artistic, social and recreational associations, through two umbrella-type organizations, La Maison Française de Toronto, and La Chasse-Galerie. Both served as cultural centres, providing a French milieu in which to maintain and promote the French language and culture. Middle-class francophones made reference to the establishment of a second French parish, St. Louis de France, situated in the Don Mills area of north-east Toronto where a growing middle-class French population was resident.

[3]Ibid., p. 201.

The cumulative effect of these developments, respondents claimed, has been to bring about more change in the French situation in Toronto than in any previous decade. Such optimism was refreshing to hear, but the crucial question to be considered here is whether such changes have resulted in greater social participation within ethnic boundaries for the francophone population of Metropolitan Toronto. An answer to this question involves first an examination of the growth of the French population in terms of possible changes in the pattern of residential settlement which would promote primary social interaction through higher concentrations of francophone families.

A second consideration has been to determine to what extent greater institutional completeness of the francophone minority has been fostered by the expansion of French-language schools, the coordination of a broader spectrum of voluntary associations through the founding of French umbrella-type organizations, and the establishment of a second French parish. Third, in what ways have the multiplied communications facilities reached a more numerous francophone audience in seeking to promote the French language and culture? And finally is the question of the use or disuse of the French language as the vehicle of culture, not only as mother tongue, but as the language spoken most often in the homes of francophones.

Definitive answers to such questions would require a replication of the original study reported in the preceding eleven chapters. But this has not been possible at this time. The data on employment for instance is not available. Stringent limits upon content and details are inevitable in a single concluding chapter. So what follows here is an attempt to portray the trends which have been developing in a fluid, rapidly changing situation. Needless to say, some aspects of what is stated below may be invalidated before what is written is in print.

Patterns of Residential Settlement

Metropolitan Toronto experienced the greatest influx of francophones in its history between the census years of 1961 and 1971. The French population increased by 49.7 per cent, from 61,421 to 91,975, while the total metropolitan population for the same period was not far behind, 43.9 per cent, from 1,826,481 to 2,628,130. Consequently the francophone percentage of the total population increased only marginally, from 3.36 per cent in 1961 to 3.49 per cent in 1971.[4] If the rate of increase of the French population had continued in the first half of the 1970s as it did in the 1960s, the francophone population would now be over 100,000. The graph below illustrates the proportional growth of both the urban core and the fringe areas in the decade and projects that rate of growth to 1976 and beyond.

The only major shift discernable in the settlement pattern appears to be the result of the scarcity of land and high cost of housing close to the city core

---

[4]*Census of Canada*, 1961 and 1971. Bulletins CT-15 and CT-21B. The statistics in this chapter, unless otherwise indicated, are from the Census of Canada, both 1961 and 1971.

which has been driving the metropolitan population outward to the fringes, a movement shared by the francophones. Statistics Canada has recognized this shift by enlarging the urban fringe of the metropolitan area to include many communities outside the area in 1961. On the west, additions include the growing city of Mississauga, and the communities of Brampton, Port Credit, Oakville, Streetsville, Woodbridge, Bolton, Georgetown, Milton and Acton; to the north, Richmond Hill, Aurora, Newmarket, Markham, and Stouffville; to the east, Ajax and Pickering; and sections of townships between the above communities. The 1971 census has also recognized the higher population densities within adjacent fringe areas by enlarging the urban core of metropolitan Toronto.

For the purpose of this chapter and the graph below, however, consistency of area with the 1961 census seemed necessary for valid comparisons of francophone population growth. The basic urban core unit in 1961 was Toronto City and the thirteen suburban municipalities which became the Metropolitan Corporation in the middle sixties, that is, Toronto City and the five Corporation boroughs of York, York East, York North, Etobicoke and Scarborough. The urban core unit adopted here is the Metropolitan Corporation, and all outside Corporation boundaries are considered, as in 1966, the urbanized fringe.[5]

In spite of the growth of the francophone population it is significant that there has been no appreciable change in the residential settlement patterns of the newcomers to Toronto. In both core and fringe areas the francophones have dispersed residentially across the entire metropolitan area as in previous decades with minimal changes in the densities of particular census tracts. For instance, within the Metropolitan Corporation, only 107 out of 347 tracts show densities of the French in excess of 4 per cent, and only eight of these have higher densities than 10 per cent. The highest is a small census tract of only 610 persons of whom 100 are francophones for a density of 16.3 per cent. In the fringe areas residential dispersion has been even greater as the highest densities of the French have been 5.2 per cent in Georgetown, 5 per cent in Port Credit, 4.8 per cent in Pickering Township, 4.2 per cent in Ajax, and 4.1 per cent in Mississauga. All others in both the core and fringe areas were below 4 per cent, so francophones continue to be isolated from primary contact with each other in their communities of residence and consequently exposed to the influence of the surrounding anglophone culture. Good transportation facilities can, of course, minimize residential dispersion, but since these are approximately the same as at the beginning of the decade it is assumed that they have not made a significant difference in interaction among francophones.[6]

[5]*Census of Canada*, 1971, Bulletin CT-21B, which includes a map showing the boundaries of the Metropolitan Corporation, and the fringe areas.

[6]In 1961, francophones resident within the boundaries of the urban core area which became the Metropolitan Corporation, numbered 54,806, while those in the fringe numbered 7,617, just 12.4 per cent of the total. By 1971 the francophone population within the Corporation had increased 31.1 per cent to 71,885, but the fringe had expanded 163.7 per cent to 20,090, or 20.8 per cent of the total.

GROWTH OF THE FRANCOPHONE POPULATION
IN THE TORONTO CORE (Metropolitan Corporation)
AND THE FRINGE AREA

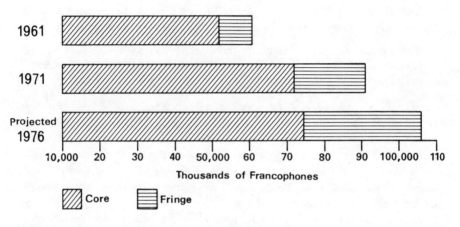

Source: Census of 1961, and of 1971

Education in the French Language

The most comprehensive institutional change during the decade was the result of a new policy for French-language elementary and secondary schools in Ontario. Four aspects are important here: the new legislation; implementation of the new policy in Metropolitan Toronto; educational television in both French and English; and a trend toward French-language non-denominational schools within the public school system. There had already been several decades of effort by Franco-Ontarians through briefs and representations to the provincial government which sought a more equitable tax base for the separate school system. This objective was finally achieved in 1964 when Premier Robarts introduced the Ontario Foundation Tax Plan which did much to close the existing gap in financial support between the public and separate schools throughout the province.[7]

Canada's Centennial year, however, brought the most dramatic recognition of the linguistic rights of the French in Ontario. On August 24, 1967, Premier Robarts assured the Association Canadienne des Educateurs de langue-française at its Twentieth Annual Conference in Ottawa, that the government of Ontario was sympathetic towards the desire of French-speaking citizens of Canada to preserve and foster their language, customs and culture. He went on to say that

[7]Lionel Remillard, *Development of the French Language School System and Its Financing*, Report prepared for E. B. Ridout of the Ontario Institute for Studies in Education, April 14, 1975.

It is a fundamental necessity of 1967 that the Franco-Ontarians be enabled to experience the full benefits of our educational system. Encompassed in this recognition of necessity is the proposal to extend what is now being done to provide, within the public school system of Ontario, secondary schools in which the language of instruction is French.[8]

The same year, the Bériault Committee on French Language Schools in Ontario was formed and formulated recommendations on the premise that

The French-speaking community in Ontario has always looked upon education as one of the most important forces, if not the most important, for its survival as a cultural group.[9]

Legislation was passed in 1968 which gave French-language schools full legal status in the province, provided for French-Language Advisory Committees to assist local school boards, and implemented the necessary changes in administration within the French-language section of the Department of Education.

In 1969, Premier Robarts of Ontario and Premier Lesage of Quebec established the Ontario-Quebec Permanent Commission in which both governments declared their commitment to the question of language rights. In 1970, the Ontario Institute for Studies in Education created a French-language branch in the field of educational research, with its own director, supporting staff and budget.[10] But while the legislation establishing a French-language public secondary school system was welcomed in some communities, it was strongly opposed in others.[11] As a result of unrest in Sturgeon Falls and Cornwall, the Symons Commission on French Language Secondary Education was appointed in 1971. It recommended further checks and balances to ensure the smooth functioning of both French and English public schools, so further legislation was passed in 1972. A Standing Committee on French-language schools was appointed, whose chairman was a francophone with the rank and title of Deputy-Minister of Education. A Linguistic Rights Commission in Education was created. The French-Language Advisory Committees were strengthened.[12]

By 1976, the implementation of this legislation resulted in a total of 24 French-language and 38 bilingual, or mixed English and French, public secondary schools, and 10 French-language public elementary schools added to the

[8]Ontario, *Report of the (Bériault) Committee on French-Language Education in Ontario*, November 28, 1968, p. 3.

[9]Ibid., p. 14.

[10]Remillard, *Development of the French Language School System*, p. 23.

[11]Danièle Juteau Lee and Jean Lapointe, "Conflict Over Schools in a Multi-Ethnic Society: A Case Study," in Richard A. Carlton, Louise A. Colley and Neil J. McKinnon, *Education, Change and Society: A Canadian Reader* (Toronto: Gage Educational Publishing, 1977), p. 162.

[12]Ontario, *The (Symons) Ministerial Commission on French-Language Secondary Education*, February 17, 1972.

already existing 292 French-language separate (Roman Catholic) elementary schools.[13] The chief deterrent to the expansion of the French-language public and separate school systems was the scattering of French-speaking families in both rural and urban areas, requiring the use of expensive transportation in order to secure adequate enrollments.[14] For several decades this dispersed residential pattern had been a major obstacle to the establishment of additional French-language schools in Metropolitan Toronto.

For instance, there were only two French-language elementary schools in 1966, the Sacré-Coeur and Ste. Madeleine, with an enrollment between them of almost one thousand students, and De Charbonnel, a private French-language Roman Catholic secondary school with an enrollment of ninety students. Since French families in the Toronto sample had just over four children per family, it was estimated that approximately 21,000 francophone children of school age lived in the metropolitan area. Thus no more than 5 per cent of the potential enrollment were actually enrolled in French-language schools. The picture changes somewhat when potential enrollment is limited to the 42.3 per cent of the francophones who claimed French as mother tongue as their school age children would number approximately 9,000, of which 11 per cent would be in French-language schools. The major problem was still the dispersed character of the French population.

The scene began to change when metropolitan and borough separate school boards, stimulated by the change in provincial policy toward French-language schools and by the prominence given to the French language by the Royal Commission on Bilingualism and Biculturalism, moderated their previous resistance to expansion of the French-language school system. Three more such elementary schools were built, each strategically located in an area of moderate French population density. In 1968, Ecole George Etienne Cartier was erected on Gainsborough Road in south-east Toronto. In 1969, Ecole Noel Chabanal was located in north-west Toronto in Downsview. In 1974, Ecole St. Jean de Lalande was established in north-east Scarborough in the former village of Agincourt when it became evident that Ecole Ste. Madeleine situated near Victoria Park Avenue and Highway No. 401 could not handle its growing enrollment.

In every case French-language classes began in English separate schools until enrollments justified the erection of the new buildings which each of the schools now occupy. But the only solution was busing, ranging from two buses used by Ecole George Etienne Cartier to ten used by Saint Noel Chabanal which is the only French-language elementary school in the entire west end of Toronto and buses 75 per cent of its enrollment. Many students who formerly spent long hours on public transport travelling to Ecole Sacré-Coeur in downtown Toronto are now enrolled in the new schools. So the Sacré-Coeur enrollment has dropped to only 160 from over 700, rendering its two spacious buildings far too large for

---

[13]Information supplied by the Ontario Department of Education.

[14]Remillard, *Development of the French Language School System*, p. 24.

its needs. An exchange with a neighbouring and expanding English separate school was necessary to provide the smaller quarters required. When the enrollment of the five schools is totalled, however, it exceeds the enrollment of the two elementary schools in 1966 by only a little over three hundred, which reveals that the additional three schools have not yet tapped the potential enrollment of a much larger francophone population.

A new development for Metropolitan Toronto, however, has added to the number of French-language elementary schools. In September, 1975, the Borough of North York established the first French-language public elementary school in Toronto. With an enrollment of 80 students, meeting in an English public school, the name Ecole Jeanne Lajoie has been chosen in anticipation of a building of its own in the future. The following year, the Board of Education of Toronto City, with surplus classrooms available in downtown Sackville Street Public School, established French-language classes there. Launched with some trepidation, the classes have been a success from the beginning, with an enrollment of 260, and 90 more expected in the fall of 1977, and a waiting list of 117. Preference has been given to francophone families, with second choice going to families where the parents speak French and the children have some fluency in the language. The name of a prominent French-Canadian writer has been adopted for the school, Ecole Gabriel Roy.

In spite of the challenging opportunity provided in the legislation of 1968, only the borough of North York has established a French-language secondary school within Metropolitan Toronto. Following the closing of the private secondary school, De Charbonnel, in June 1969, Ecole Etienne Brulé opened in September of the same year. At first in temporary quarters but now in a spacious, new building, the almost 600 students, nearly all francophones, enjoy the same wide range of programmes and facilities as any other secondary school in the province.[15]

When Premier Robarts made it clear in 1967 that Ontario could not afford the luxury of a parallel system of public and separate secondary schools, in view of the financial commitments involved,[16] he began a trend which has been gathering momentum since then. Etienne Brulé and the two public elementary schools in Metropolitan Toronto are a small part of this trend gradually spreading throughout Ontario. A 1975 report on the development of French-language schools in the province states that many francophone parents throughout the province have recently requested French-language elementary schools in the public system.[17]

Over 12 per cent of the francophone population of Ontario are resident in Metropolitan Toronto. But how many of these have been sending their children

---

[15]The principals of all of these schools but one, the secretary of Ecole Jeanne Lajoie in this case, were interviewed. Enrollments are as of January, 1977.

[16]Ontario, *Report of the (Bériault) Committee on French-Language Education in Ontario*, p. 3.

[17]Remillard, *Development of the French Language School System*, p. 26.

to French-language schools within the area? The total enrollment as of January 1977 of the five separate elementary schools was 1,304, plus the two public elementary schools of 341, for an elementary total of 1,644. Add the 600 at Etienne Brulé and the grand total is 2,244. Since all of these schools are within the Metropolitan Corporation, a conservative estimate of the number of francophone children of school age within Corporation boundaries, based upon the 1971 census with allowance for subsequent migration, would place the number at 30,000 or more. The graph below shows actual French-language school enrollment in 1965 and 1976, projected to 1981. Also shown as a point of contrast are three categories of francophone children: children of school age of families where French is spoken most of the time in the home; children of families where French has been claimed as mother tongue; and children of francophone families in totality within the Metropolitan Corporation.

A COMPARISON OF FRANCOPHONE CHILDREN
ENROLLED IN FRENCH-LANGUAGE SCHOOLS
AND THE POTENTIAL ENROLLMENT IN
THREE CATEGORIES

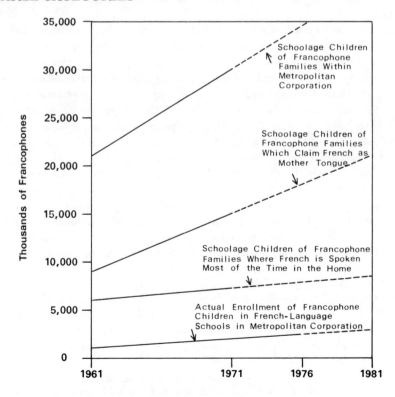

Source: Adapted from Census of 1961, and of 1971

In general terms, the present French-language school system in Toronto has been serving 31 per cent of the francophone children in whose homes French is spoken most of the time; 15 per cent of the children of francophone families who claim French as mother tongue; and 7.5 per cent of all francophone children of school age within the Metropolitan Corporation.

Several factors are relevant to this situation. Toronto possesses only 3 per cent of the French-language schools of the province while hosting over 12 per cent of the provincial population. Secondly, francophone officials in the Department of Education and principals of both elementary and secondary schools complain that it has been difficult to convince francophone parents that an education in the French language in a predominantly English-speaking community will not handicap the future careers of their children. Many francophone parents, especially in working-class families, believe that economic security is dependent upon the English and not the French language and the loss of French culture does not disturb them. Thirdly, it has been much easier to send children to local English schools rather than arrange for their children to travel long distances by bus to French-language schools. In the fringe area outside of the Metropolitan Corporation the difficulties are compounded for the existing or planned French-language schools because of the lower densities of the French population.

The Bériault Committee on French Language Schools in its recommendations in 1967 recognized that such schools would require all the reinforcement possible, so Educational Television in the French language was a major element in its report. In 1970, the Province of Ontario incorporated the Ontario Educational Communications Authority and enlarged its scope to cover three areas, English-language schools, French-language schools, and the general public. At present, a staff of thirty-five produce French-language programmes, supply video tapes to schools throughout the province, and conduct workshops on the most effective use of programmes and equipment. Seventeen per cent of the Authority's programming is now in the French language, and through relay transmitters covers all of Southern Ontario, with plans for Northern Ontario when funds become available.[18] Also supplementary to the French-language schools has been the organization of a French-language section with its own administrator by the metropolitan library board, both to publicize French literature and to make French books more readily available to schools and the francophone public.

The Quest for Cultural Unity

In traditional French-Canadian society the Roman Catholic parish served as an umbrella organization since it sought to coordinate within its boundaries a variety of parish associations which would meet not only the religious but also the social, recreational, and even the economic needs of the parishioners, all within a

[18]Pamphlet published by the Office de la Télécommunication Educative d'Ontario (O.T.E.O.), Division des Media Educatifs Français, supplemented by an interview with the Associate General Manager of the Division.

French cultural environment. But in Toronto the original parish of the Sacré-Coeur, established in 1887, was able to fulfill this integrative role for only two to three decades as the French population grew rapidly and scattered widely among English parishes. From then on, the downtown working-class parish concentrated almost wholly upon its religious and welfare roles with little attention to its ethnic role in spite of the efforts of some of the parishioners to change this focus. Most of the growing number of middle-class francophones affiliated with middle-class anglophone parishes. Consequenty they had no alternative for the maintenance of the French language and culture but to rely upon the organization of ethnic associations which had little or no relationship to the Sacré-Coeur parish apart from the few who attended there. So the initiative for seeking to ensure the survival of the French language and culture passed from the parish to the French associations.

In 1966, eighty years after the founding of the first French parish, and in response to a concentration of middle-class francophones in the Don Mills area of north-east Toronto where their children had access to the French-language elementary school, Ste. Madeleine, a second parish, St. Louis de France, was established on Don Mills Road. Essentially a middle-class parish of some three hundred families, its most active associations were among the women and children. So it appears to serve a religious rather than an ethnic role, although the latter has found expression in the provision of leadership for francophone associations and the expansion of the French-language school system.

With the onus for cultural continuity resting mainly upon francophone associations, there had been discussions among francophone leaders for several years in the early sixties concerning the establishment of a cultural centre which would provide a focus for francophone social and cultural interaction by coordinating the activities of the existing independent associations. It was hoped that such a centre would mobilize kinship, friendship, and religious obligations within the French population in support of an informal authority agency which would bridge the cultural differences resulting from the variety of backgrounds represented among the francophone migrants to Metropolitan Toronto. Long cherished hopes and plans came to fruition on October 24, 1966, when La Maison Française de Toronto became a reality as a Centennial project. Eight founding associations were participants: Alliance Française, Alliance France-Canada, the Association des Françaises Libres (Sec. Ontario), the Association Sépharade (French-speaking Jews from North Africa), the Chambre de Commerce Française au Canada (Sec. Ontario), the Ciné Club Français, the Club Richelieu, and the Fédération des Femmes canadienne Franco-Ontarien (Sec. Sacré-Coeur de Toronto). Also affiliated was l'Association Canadienne-Française de l'Ontario, known as ACFO.[19]

---

[19]Gladys Hitchman, *La Maison Française de Toronto: An Evaluation Study*, Report submitted to the Social Action Branch of the Secretary of State's Department (Toronto, July, 1973). Permission has been given to the author to use a copy of this confidential document and to quote from it. It has been utilized along with interviews with executive

La Maison Française de Toronto, or MFT as it was popularly known and will be referred to here, secured a central location close to both the east-west and north-south subway lines as well as main traffic arteries. The two older semi-detached houses provided room for a secretariat and telephone information service, various types of meetings, French-language classes, basement space for a printing press and accessories and some surplus space rented to professional and commercial interests. Its major drawback was the small size of rooms so that large gatherings could only be held in rented quarters elsewhere. Its major asset was that for the first time a number of francophone associations were linked by a new sense of unity in promoting the French language and culture, with co-ordinated information and publicity services for their variety of activities, pro-vision of a welcome centre for francophone newcomers, and even an employ-ment service.

In spite of the ideal of a unified focus of French cultural life in Toronto, it soon became evident that tensions were inherent in the very structure of MFT from the beginning. Four variations in cultural background and outlook were represented in the member associations: the European French who composed most of the 5.6 per cent of francophones in Toronto born outside of Canada; the French Canadians, an overwhelming majority of the francophone population but divided by regional loyalties, linguistic variations and social class; the Fédération des Femmes, the only working-class association within MFT; and the French-speaking Jews with their variations in religion and life style.

Anglophones have a tendency to group all persons of French ancestry under the single category of "the French." But widely disparate regional and cultural differences in background and experience have so diversified the self-conceptions of francophones in Toronto that they do not see themselves merely as French, but as Quebecois, Acadians, Franco-Ontarians, European French, Franco-Americans, and so on. The French language alone is not able to bridge these differences, and may in the case of linguistic variations intensify them. In an umbrella organization such as MFT this broad spectrum of regional identifica-tions created barriers to social interaction which frustrated efforts to attain cultural solidarity.

Within MFT circumstances tended to accentuate such differences. The major use of the new premises was by the two associations dominated by the European French, partly because of their regular French-language classes, but also because the other member associations had alternative accommodations which they regularly utilized, depending upon MFT for publicity and information services, but only occasionally for the use of the building. As a result, MFT became identified with the European French. Alliance Française was a branch of an organization with headquarters in Paris, France, while Alliance France-Canada in

members of some of the founding associations, the secretary of MFT, publicity distributed by MFT, and visits to the Charles Street East centre and the new Harbour Front centre. The affiliate, Association Française Franco-Ontarien is the successor of L'Association canadienne-française d'Education d'Ontario, which has broadened its scope.

1969 had become a member of the Association Nationale France-Canada (Paris), a federation with close to fifty branches in France and Canada. Close relations between these two organizations and the French consul in Toronto was a constant reminder of the European influence.

French Canadians complained that they did not enjoy the type of programme typical of the European associations in the arts, drama, theatre, and recreation as they were so intellectually oriented that they had popular appeal for only a small élite of the middle class among the French, and the French-speaking Europeans and anglophones who constituted at least one-half of the participants. Barely 10 per cent of the French who attended were French Canadians, and some of these felt they were being patronized and subjected to snobbishness.

Less than a year and a half after MFT opened its doors, the dissatisfaction of French Canadians found expression in the establishment of a second umbrella-type organization, La Chasse-Galerie. Sparked by leadership from Quebec, the new organization had its inauguration in May, 1968, with the avowed objective of providing a cultural milieu in which French Canadians would feel at ease, although a welcome was extended to all francophones. Unlike MFT, La Chasse-Galerie was a service organization without member associations, seeking to serve individuals, groups and associations through a comprehensive programme of workshops in the arts and crafts, theatre, concerts, films, supplemented by an art gallery, a bookshop, a library and a boutique supplying materials for the programmes. Publicity and information was supplied through a full-time secretary, but otherwise the activities of the organization were supervised by volunteer workers. Initially located in North Toronto, substantial grants by the federal and provincial governments enabled La Chasse-Galerie to occupy a multi-room former mansion on Jarvis Street in downtown Toronto, convenient to transportation. The larger premises provided facilities for a youth hostel and coffee house, and a reception centre for francophone newcomers.[20]

But the same cultural diversity which had created divisions within MFT was also present in La Chasse Galerie. As a competent observer has written,

> The Chasse-Galerie appears to appeal mainly to the middle, professional classes, many of which are Quebecois .... The working class people are definitely under-represented .... Franco-Ontarians, as well as European French are also under-represented. But the numbers of Franco-Ontarians

[20]Gladys Hitchman, *The Chasse-Galerie: An Evaluation Study*, Report submitted to the Department of the Secretary of State, Social Action Branch (Toronto, August, 1972). Permission has been given to the author to use a copy of this confidential document and to quote from it. Interviews were held with the founding director, and other leading francophones in Toronto, as well as visiting the centre and using its publicity material. In addition, David Stansfield's booklet, *How to Live French in Toronto* (The Ontario Educational Communications Authority, 1975), describes the activities of both la Chasse-Galerie and MFT, as well as furnishing other material of value to this chapter.

are increasing, as the initial suspicions about the Chasse-Galerie disappear.[21]

Relations with both MFT and the Association Française Franco-Ontarien continued to be quite formal and cool as the latter two organizations not only
resented a duplication of their services but feared a fragmentation of efforts to
consolidate the French presence in Toronto. La Chasse-Galerie conducted some
workshops and other activities in the parish of the Sacré-Coeur, but its regular
programme held little appeal for the working-class francophones. One observer
noted the existence of some hostility between members of the parish and those
of La Chasse-Galerie. The founding director stated in conversation that almost
three-quarters of the participants in La Chasse-Galerie were anglophones who
were interested in learning French or achieving more facility in the language
while participating in the programmes. Since the original objective of the organization was to provide a French-Canadian milieu as a refuge from the all-pervading
anglophone atmosphere of Toronto, one wonders how this could be accomplished
when so many anglophones were participants. They inevitably introduced an anglophone cultural influence and some use of the English language, thus diluting the
original purpose of La Chasse-Galerie.

Neither MFT nor La Chasse-Galerie could have survived without financial
grants of considerable proportions from the federal government, along with
grants from the Province of Ontario, and occasional financial assistance from the
City of Toronto. A small membership fee was also charged by La Chasse-Galerie
for both adults and children, which indicated a membership of around 700 in
1975, when many of the interviews on which this section is based were conducted. At that time both MFT and La Chasse-Galerie were operating successfully in the judgment of a casual observer or participant. But appearances were
deceiving. Unrest among French Canadians associated with MFT focussed on the
word "Française" in the name of the organization as being too indicative of the
European French, so a new title was adopted, "La Maison, Centre Francophone
de Toronto." But an even more critical issue arose when it was discovered that
for some reason, undisclosed, no formal application for a grant had been for-
warded to Ottawa. Consequently, without funds to pay the substantial rental for
the premises of the cultural centre, MFT was faced with the problem of finding
alternative quarters.

In the meantime, discussions had apparently been going on regarding a more
satisfactory umbrella organization than MFT had proved to be for French
Canadians. An emergency meeting was held in April, 1976, initiated mainly by
Franco-Ontarians, to which representatives of some fifteen francophone organizations were invited. A new umbrella-type organization was formed with the
title, "Le Conseil Francophone des Organismes de Toronto Métropolitain."
Application was made to the federal government for an organizational grant, and

---

[21]Hitchman, *The Chasse-Galerie*, pp. 56-57.

permission to occupy space at Habour Front, on the Toronto waterfront, where the federal government had remodelled several former warehouses for the use of ethnic groups in Toronto.[22] MFT was represented at the meetings, and as its contribution to the new organization offered the use of its furniture and equipment which had to be removed from its former cultural centre. The Alliance Française now took over the former premises of MFT for use as a French-language school, a director being appointed by the headquarters in Paris with the French Government being responsible for his salary.

At the time of writing the situation was still rather fluid, but a spacious office had been allocated to the new umbrella organization and its member associations, and several events had been held in the fall of 1976 when several hundred francophones took advantage of the spacious accommodations provided by the federal government. Present plans call for occupation of the second and third floors of an older, renovated office building at the foot of Spadina Avenue on the waterfront. The new cultural centre is not centrally located as it was formerly in terms of public transportation, although easily accessible by car via expressway.

La Chasse-Galerie also encountered a crisis in 1976 which closed its doors in October of that year. Substantial grants had been received for its operations from both the federal and provincial governments. But as sometimes happens when volunteer staff is responsible for an extensive programme, adequate financial control of expenditures was not practised. Some leeway had been permitted in terms of expenditures in excess of grants in previous years by the granting agencies, but when substantial debts were incurred in 1976 the government grants were cancelled, forcing the complete closure of the centre on Jarvis Street. Observers commented that in addition to financial problems there had been dissension within the leadership, and dissatisfaction with the attempt to operate a comprehensive programme with volunteer workers throughout the organization. The former director, however, refused to permit the project to collapse completely, and has organized a new board of directors, mainly anglophones, and rented a large, older house not far from the former centre in order to resume activities. Representatives of La Chasse-Galerie attended some of the initial meetings of Le Conseil Francophone des Organismes de Toronto Métropolitaine, but since the October closure of the former centre and the opening of a new one, it remains uncertain whether cooperation with the new umbrella organization, Le Conseil, will continue or not.

The francophone working class has remained peripheral to the above discussion of a cultural centre for the French in Toronto. The comment was frequently heard and confirmed by the evaluation reports, that neither MFT nor La Chasse-Galerie served the needs of the francophone working class, who had

---

[22]A guided tour of the federal property refurbished for the use of ethnic groups in Toronto at Harbour Front, 235 Queen's Quay West, was provided by an MFT executive member which was much appreciated.

shown little interest in the various activities sponsored by the two umbrella organizations. A study of the role of the parish of the Sacré-Coeur in relation to the working class was undertaken in 1975.[23] It was evident from the data and conclusions of the study that the Sacré-Coeur was still the only French organization dedicated to serving the needs of the francophone working class. In addition to its religious and welfare roles, the parish sponsored regular social events such as dances, card parties, bingos, picnics, bazaars, recreation such as a bowling league, and also organized sports such as hockey, which were more in line with the general interests of members of this class than the cultural programmes organized by middle-class associations. Without these activities there would be a virtual vacuum in terms of working-class participation within a French-speaking environment.

But it has been an impossible task for a single working-class parish in downtown Toronto, remote in terms of distance from members of the working class scattered throughout the metropolitan area, to serve the largest segment of the francophone population, at least two-thirds of the projected 100,000 francophones within the area. Virtually isolated, therefore, from institutional channels for maintaining their own language and culture, and exposed to the assimilating influence of English parishes, neighbourhoods and employment, the working class constitute the critical area in the attempts to create cultural unity within the francophone population.

The French Communications Media

Respondent after respondent mentioned French radio, television, and a recently published newspaper, *Courier Sud*, as playing a decisive role in the maintenance of the French language and culture. The radio facilities certainly expanded during the decade. A booklet issued in 1975 on the tenth anniversary of the transfer of radio station CJBC to the French-language network describes the extensive changes in programming, staffing, extended hours of operation, use of mobile radio teams and vans throughout the province, and other sophisticated refinements.[24] Originally importing programmes from Quebec, CJBC had developed its own local skills and talents with greater emphasis upon francophone life in Ontario.

Growth of the radio audience has paralleled the expansion of facilities. As was noted earlier, the *Globe and Mail* in 1966 reported that CJBC had an

[23]Claire Pageau, *Etude sur les besoins socio-culturels de la minorité francophone de la classe ouvrière située au centre-ville de Toronto, en général, et du rôle de la paroisse du Sacré-coeur, en particulier*, Rapport soumis au programme des groupes minoritaires de langue officielle, Secrétariat D'Etat (Toronto, April, 1975). Permission has been given to the author to use a copy of this confidential document and to quote from it. Parish priests and members of both parishes, Le Sacré-Coeur and St. Louis de France, have been interviewed and the parishes visited.

[24]Pamphlet, CJCB 860, issued by La Société Radio-Canada, Les Relations Publiques, C.P. 500, Succursale "A", Toronto.

audience of only around 1,000 at the 8:00 to 8:15 hour in the morning when English-language stations numbered their audiences in the tens and hundreds of thousands. At that time there were more anglophones listening than franco-phones. But this has all changed, according to the present director of CJBC. Around 20,000 form the listening audience at the eight o'clock morning hour, and the total listening audience is around 59,000. But who are they? The inten-sive survey of the Toronto listening audience, promised by the CBC, is still in the future. Without an explicit survey of individuals and families, such as was conducted with a representative sample in 1965, one does not know who and how many are involved with certain mass media. The 1971 census lists 159,000 in Toronto who speak both French and English, but only 91,975 of these are French. In addition, francophones admit that one-half of their number do not claim French as mother tongue, and fewer speak it most of the time in the homes. So it is difficult to know who among the francophone population listen to and are influenced by CJBC.

The assessment is made even more difficult when it is realized that CJBC is a powerful station which reaches most of Southern Ontario, and with the aid of sixteen low-power relay transmitters in strategic centres provides extensive coverage of Northern Ontario as well. The potential francophone audience in Southern Ontario alone is around 200,000 with many more in Northern Ontario. So without an explicit audience survey the validity of the claim that CJBC plays a decisive role culturally cannot be determined. Perhaps the acid test of its influence is the level of French spoken in the homes of francophones in Metro-politan Toronto.

Television in French on a permanent basis by the CBC was inaugurated in 1973. At present, only two forty-minute programmes a day and two other programmes a week originate in Toronto, while others are imported from Quebec, France, or from the other provinces. A major asset of the French network, unlike English television, is that programmes cannot be imported from the United States, with the salutary effect of developing to a high degree French talents and skills in creating and producing programmes for francophones. According to observers, television has had a marked effect upon francophone involvement with their own language and culture in Southern Ontario. The Public Relations Department of the CBC has estimated the French television audience in Southern Ontario as around 72,000 but this includes francophones throughout the southern area of the province where relay transmitters are located in Kitchener, London, Chatham and Windsor. So its viewing audience embraces much more than Metropolitan Toronto.[25] Without audience research data, as yet unavailable, the impact of television on francophones in Metro-politan Toronto must await census data on the level of French spoken in the homes.

At the beginning of the decade, five attempts to establish a French-language newspaper had already failed, mainly for lack of circulation and consequent

[25]Information supplied by the Public Relations Department of the CBC.

financial problems. In June, 1973, several interested francophones cooperated in founding the *Courier Sud* with a bank loan to provide capital. It had eventually reached a peak circulation of 3,500, with an average size of twelve pages, assisted by the provincial government which purchased 200 copies for circulation to French-language schools. But as one staff member lamented, lack of personal knowledge of journalism, the purchase of expensive machinery, initial over-staffing, and lack of market projections, made it difficult for the paper to survive. The 50 per cent paid advertising necessary for solvency was not always available, and voluntary help in distribution was not always efficient.[26] So in spite of practising stricter economy in production, the paper ceased to publish in October, 1976. A staff member of the paper, a French-speaking European, was convinced that the paper had a future if it were run as a strictly commercial enterprise. He changed the name to the *Toronto Express*, and soon had a circulation of 3,000, and added a satellite paper, the *Hamilton Express,* with a similar circulation. The future remains uncertain.

In 1965, there was a single bookstore devoted to French publications, but it closed its doors soon afterwards. Subsequently two major outlets were established, La Librairie Champlain on Church Street and La Librairie Garneau on Bay Street. The growth of the francophone population encouraged several English book stores to stock a limited supply of French publications. The Toronto Public Library responded to increased demand by enlarging its holdings of French literature, books, magazines, newspapers, and other types of periodicals, most of which were housed at the library Languages Centre on College Street.[27] A number of branch libraries arranged to provide French-speaking staff for the assistance of francophones. The availability of French publications has thus been increased substantially during the decade. The director of the Language Centre pointed out, however, that the major problem is to acquaint francophones with what is available, while the predominance of the working class within the French population militates against a large circulation of French literature.

One casualty during the decade was the demise of the Ciné Club which had imported French films over a number of years and reached a membership of over one thousand. But the growing metropolitan atomosphere of Toronto encouraged public theatres to screen French films on a regular basis which made the activities of the Ciné Club superfluous. It was subsequently revived under the name, Ciné Club Français, with different objectives, the supplying of French films to French-language schools, and the preparation of television documentaries, especially for francophone children. But in parallel fashion to the other French communications media, the impact of French films cannot be deter-

[26]Information supplied by a member of the editorial board of *Courier Sud,* and the editor of the *Toronto Express.*

[27]Stansfield, *How to Live French in Toronto*, pp. 12-14.

mined without a specific survey of francophone families in Toronto. The French communications media present a challenging field for future research.

French as Mother Tongue

It is universally accepted that language is the most important vehicle for the transmission and maintenance of a particular culture. French Canadians have emphasized this fact throughout the history of their relations with the rest of Canada. This was the issue which gave impetus to the establishment of the Royal Commission on Bilingualism and Biculturalism and the passing of the Official Languages Act. It was also reflected in the legislation which provided for French-language public secondary schools in the Province of Ontario, and the passing of Bill 22 making French the official language in the Province of Quebec. Consequently it has become a critical indicator of the extent to which francophones identify with French culture.

The proportion of the French population acknowledging French as mother tongue has risen from 42.3 per cent in 1961 to 49.5 per cent in 1971, showing that many of the French newcomers came from areas where French was the predominant language in the home. But an even more revealing question was inserted in the 1971 census questionnaire when it was asked, What language is spoken most often at home? In the table below are tabulated the growth rates between 1961 and 1971 of the six largest minority ethnic populations in Metropolitan Toronto listed in order of mother tongue as spoken most often in the home.[28]

Table 35

Table Showing Growth Rates of the Six Largest Minority Ethnic Populations in Metropolitan Toronto in Order of Mother Tongue Spoken Most Often in the Home

Ethnic Group	Population		Increase		% Use of Mother Tongue in the Home
	1961	1971	Number	%	
Italian	140,378	271,755	131,377	93.5	69.7
Polish	58,578	51,185	-7,393	-12.6	38.2
Ukrainian	46,650	60,755	14,105	30.2	37.1
German	80,300	116,640	36,340	45.2	25.9
French	61,421	91,175	30,554	49.7	22.3
Netherlands	33,434	44,430	10,996	32.88	9.04

Source: 1961 and 1971 Censuses

[28]*Census of Canada,* 1961 and 1971.

It is readily apparent that only the Italians have maintained the use of mother tongue spoken in the home most of the time to a high degree. The French, in spite of the rise in the acknowledgement of French as mother tongue, are the fifth on the list. An examination of the settlement patterns of these two populations reveals significant differences. It must first be acknowledged that the Italians have almost doubled their population in Metropolitan Toronto during the census decade. This tide of newcomers, coming mainly from a single homeland where English is a foreign language, would have promoted the use of Italian in the home to a greater degree than is prevalent among the French to whom English is one of the official languages and was spoken by many of them prior to migrating to Toronto.

Both populations have scattered to some degree but there the resemblance ends. The highest concentrations among the French are scattered among 107 census tracts across the city while the Italians are concentrated almost solidly in north-west Toronto. The contrast is heightened when the highest densities of the five major areas of concentration in each ethnic group are compared. For the French, only eight census tracts had densitites of over 10 per cent and the highest of these was 16.3 per cent, with the average density 12.54 per cent. In contrast, the Italians in their areas of concentration had 63 census tracts with a density of over 10 per cent, with the highest density 76 per cent, and the average density 39.6 per cent. The accompanying map shows quite clearly the closely-knit community structure of Italian residential settlement in contrast to the dispersed nature of French settlement. When the high densities of Italian settlement are coupled with the extended family circle and the Italian love of sociability, in addition to their limited occupational diversification, such factors help account for the extensive use of Italian in the homes of that ethnic population.

Not only does the lack of higher concentrations of the French population tend to militate against more extensive use of the French language in the home, but it also weakens their participation on the civic and provincial scenes through lack of voting power to elect political representation. Thus the pattern of residence has deprived the French of influence in the power structures of the community and the province which their numbers would warrant. Italians have been much more active politically because of concentrated voting power in the city wards. The Italians do not have Italian-language schools, or a radio or television station, although they do sponsor programmes, have more ethnic parishes, and are concentrated in the construction and building trades segment of the work world. But retention of their language and culture is evidently dependent upon participation within ethnic boundaries strongly reinforced by their patterns of residential settlement and institutional organization.

The low level of French spoken most of the time in the homes reveals a steady decline in the use of the mother tongue in spite of the background in that language among half of the francophone population. It cannot be attributed to any segment of the metropolitan area as the table below indicates.

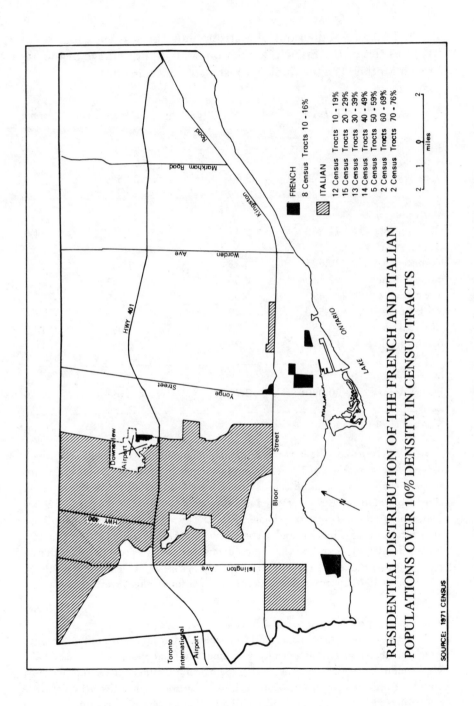

RESIDENTIAL DISTRIBUTION OF THE FRENCH AND ITALIAN
POPULATIONS OVER 10% DENSITY IN CENSUS TRACTS

SOURCE: 1971 CENSUS

Table 36

Table of Major Subdivisions of Metropolitan Toronto Showing
(A) Densities of the French Population, and (B) Percentage of the
French Mother Tongue Spoken Most Often at Home

Area	French Population	% of Total Population	French Spoken Most of Time at Home	
			Number	%
Metropolitan Area	91,975	3.49	20,580	22.3
Metropolitan Corporation	71,885	3.44	17,320	24.0
Toronto City	26,605	3.73	7,345	27.6
York Borough	3,730	2.53	915	24.5
York East	3,490	3.33	775	22.2
York North	14,560	2.89	4,195	28.8
Etobicoke	10,285	3.63	1,875	18.2
Scarborough	13,215	3.95	2,215	16.7
Metropolitan Fringe Area	20,090	3.70	3,095	15.9

Source: 1971 Census

It will be noticed that it is the residential dispersion in the fringe area which presents the lowest use of French as mother tongue in the family. Out of twenty fringe areas of one or more census tracts, use of French at home ranges in six cases from zero to 8.25 per cent, and in another twelve from 10.5 to 16.9 per cent. Only two are significantly higher, Albion Township at 52.1 percent (60 out of a total of 115 French), and Georgetown at 41.3 per cent (370 out of 895 French residents). Some of the fringe communities have grown rapidly during the 1970s, so the above statistics may be too low now, especially since French television in 1973 appeared on the scene, an item for further investigation.

The Paradox of the Invisible French

It is paradoxical that the more favourable climate in Metropolitan Toronto which has been so enthusiastically welcomed by francophones has created the very conditions which have led to loss of cultural distinctiveness and hence of visibility. Greater acceptance within the majority society has given the French a sense of security which has facilitated an increasing rate of accommodation to the host society. There has been no sign of a felt need or even a desire among francophones to dwell closely together for mutual support of their language and culture as is evident among other ethnic minorities such as the Italian or Jewish communities. Therefore no significant changes have taken place in the patterns of residential settlement during the decade. The newcomers among the francophones have joined the shift to the fringe areas and have dispersed residentially to a greater degree than previous migrants to the urban core. Thus they are more isolated than ever from contacts with other francophones while in constant interaction with the surrounding society.

The expansion of institutional structures such as the French-language schools, voluntary associations and a new parish has been a positive development in the direction of greater institutional completeness. But the contribution of such expansion needs to be qualified in two ways. It serves the small elite among the francophone middle class while contributing little to the rest of the French population. The French parish of St. Louis de France, and four of the six French-language schools are situated in predominantly middle-class areas. The present indeterminate attempt to create a cultural centre in the form of an umbrella organization, complicated by competition among regional factions for administrative control, still embraces only middle-class francophones in any significant numbers. And secondly, when the expansion is viewed in the perspective of the present size of the French population of approximately 100,000, it is hardly commensurate with the rate of growth of that population. The vast majority of francophones still have no alternative but to participate in the institutional structures of the dominant society, a continuation of structural assimilation.

It has not been possible to evaluate properly the impact of French-language radio or television, partly because both educational and regular television have had their impact since the 1971 census data was secured. Radio has in all probability slowed the loss of French as mother tongue, although this cannot be confirmed, while television would need to exert a pronounced influence upon francophone linguistic habits if the present level of French spoken most of the time in the homes is to be raised above the 22.3 per cent level of 1971.

In charting the trends of the decade, there appear to be no substantial grounds for the optimism of many francophones that significant changes have taken place that have led to a greater degree of identification of francophones with their language and culture. In fact, the opposite process has been at work, in spite of the confidence placed in the expansion of French-language institutional structures. The events of the decade have not revealed the development of a viable basis for ethnic solidarity,[29] nor a focus for ethnic identification for any but a small minority of the francophone population. One can only conclude that the French are still "invisible."

But the situation in Toronto is not unique, nor does it present an anomaly among ethnic minorities in modern, pluralistic societies. Abner Cohen in his

[29]Raymond Breton, "Ethnic Pluralism and Social Equality," in Ontario Human Rights Commission, *Human Relations*, 14, No. 22 (December, 1974), 6-11.

recent monograph, *Two-Dimensional Man*, devotes an entire chapter to a discussion of "Invisible Minorities: Some Case Studies."[30] Even though much of his research was conducted in Africa he generalizes extensively to include North American minorities. He recognizes that culture is not an independent system, consequently ethnicity can be understood only when it is analyzed within the particular community context in which it exists, an emphasis upon local circumstances.[31] Or as Breton has commented in reference to Canada, "There is not a single type of ethnic context nor a unique kind of personal situation to deal with . . . the basis of ethnic solidarity can and does vary from one ethnic group to another."[32] But in spite of such variability, Cohen maintains that there is a consistent structural pattern which is characteristic of "invisible ethnic minorities."[33]

The primary and basic element in the pattern is that members of the migrant minority are residentially dispersed among a heterogeneous urban population with consequent dilution of their cultural distinctiveness and erosion of ethnic identity.[34] The residential segregation which usually facilitates the maintenance of ethnic boundaries through communal solidarity has been lost, or has never developed. Residential dispersion makes it difficult and often impossible for members of an ethnic group who are seldom in contact with each other and continually associated with members of the host society to retain their linguistic and cultural heritage. Cohen claims that an ethnic identification is particularly difficult to maintain where the ethnic minority is formally recognized by the state, as in a federation, such as Canada, where official status is ensured and guarded by legislation.[35] Members of such minorities may not even consider themselves part of an ethnic group when they have charter group status on the national scene.

In Toronto, the variety of cultural backgrounds within the francophone population has also introduced different conceptions of what cultural boundaries are. A Franco-Ontarian migrant to Toronto who grew up in a community either partially or almost wholly anglophone in character would have a more fluid conception of ethnic boundaries than a migrant from Quebec whose past years were spent in a francophone community with only nominal contact with anglophones. Since 57.6 per cent of the francophones in Toronto were born in Ontario and only 36.6 per cent in other provinces, including Quebec, and 5.6 per cent outside of Canada,[36] the variations in the interpretations of cultural bound-

---

[30]Abner Cohen, *Two-Dimensional Man* (Berkeley and Los Angeles: University of California Press, 1974), Chapter 6, pp. 91-98.

[31]Ibid., p. 96.

[32]Breton, "Ethnic Pluralism," p. 6.

[33]Cohen, *Two-Dimensional Man*, pp. 91f.

[34]Ibid., p. 92.

[35]Ibid., p. 97.

[36]*Census of Canada*, 1971.

aries would make unlikely any degree of consensus among francophones. This divergence in the standards governing francophone behaviour has tended to isolate language as the only common bond within the French population. And when its cohesive force weakens, as is evident in the low percentage of French spoken in the homes, a final defense against assimilation has been shattered. The residential isolation of francophones remains the critical dimension in boundary maintenance.

A second characteristic of "invisible ethnic minorities" is the weakness of ethnic association in promoting the cultural survival or continuity of the minority because they are aimed, "not at the development of an exclusive ethnic polity, but, on the contrary, at promoting the successful adaptation of its members to modern urban condition." Cohen sees two reasons why migrants join such associations: temporarily in order "to get help to adjust to the new social milieu,"[37] or because such associations represent "an informal interest grouping."[38] Cohen maintains that this characteristic is part of the changing role of ethnicity in modern societies. Ethnic groups in the contemporary world are less concerned with the perpetuation of traditional cultures than with the mobilizing of interests which will give them greater access to employment, education, and influence in the power structures at the local and national levels, a political role. The traditional symbols are there, giving the impression of conservatism, but are utilized in a different way,[39] to tie members of the group together in the pursuit of power, privilege and prestige within the host society.[40]

Glazer and Moynihan, in the Introduction to their volume on *Ethnicity: Theory and Experience*, concur with Cohen that the emphasis within ethnic groups upon "religion, language, and concrete cultural differences . . . as specific foci for attachment and concern,"[41] has declined in recent decades, especially in the western world. They consider this development innovative as it redefines ethnic group objectives "in terms of interest, or an interest group."[42] Thus Cohen, Glazer and Moynihan and most of the contributors to their volume, appear to share the view that ethnic groups are "forms of social life rather than survivals from the past, as mobilizers of interests rather than bearers of cultures or traditions."[43]

---

[37]Cohen, *Two-Dimensional Man*, p. 93.

[38]Ibid., p. 97.

[39]Ibid., p. 96.

[40]Glazer and Moynihan, eds., *Ethnicity: Theory and Experience* (Cambridge, Mass.: Harvard University Press, 1975), p. 19. Also in this volume, Daniel Bell, "Ethnicity and Social Change," p. 169.

[41]Ibid., p. 18.

[42]Ibid., p. 7.

[43]Burnet, "Ethnicity," p. 199. Burnet discusses the relevance of Glazer and Moynihan's approach to Canadian multicultural programs and is of the opinion that it is closer to federal objectives than the full perpetuation of ancestral customs and cultures. " . . . during the first

This different and as yet tentative point of view casts fresh light on some French associations. Ostensibly they aim to provide a French milieu for their members, but actually they attract not only francophones, but French-speaking anglophones and European migrants from other countries. A second reason why this interpretation has relevance is that such associations have remained small and class oriented in spite of the growth of the population. They emphasize a sharing of common interests on a cultural level with the French language as the common medium of communication rather than provide a means to perpetuate an ancestral culture. Perhaps this is why they are content to accept the multicultural programme as it meets their financial needs without requiring substantial internal support.

Francophones who feel that cultural survival is crucial, resent this situation. One respondent complained that government grants mean that someone, usually outside of the ethnic minority, is responsible for setting the guidelines and evaluating the success of associational programmes, which deprives members of the ethnic minority of adequate control over their own organizations. Another respondent added that those supervising the grant programme are French-speaking but often are not francophones, so in his estimation they lacked insight into how the French "would do their own thing." One executive commented somewhat bitterly that the procedure placed the French in the same category as Canadian Indians, unable to determine the policies of their own organizations. The pursuit of class-oriented cultural interests, subsidized by government at a very nominal cost to francophones, rather than the pursuit of cultural survival organized and financed from within, has apparently divided rather than united French leadership in its quest for a common identity.

A third characteristic of an "invisible ethnic minority," according to Cohen, is the occupational diversification of the minority labour force to the extent that economic differentiation introduces class cleavages which cut across ethnic boundaries, weakening the distinctiveness of the ethnic culture.[44] This characteristic was particularly significant during the original study of a decade ago, when most francophones admitted migrating to Toronto for economic reasons. The displacement of cultural values by the economic values prevalent within the host society has been a major stimulus for assimilation to the dominant, host community. It has not been possible to document the progress of this process during the last decade, but continued residential dispersion, the slow development of institutional structures, the restriction of cultural activities to an elite among the middle class, and the continuing loss of French as mother tongue, all point indirectly to the preoccupation of francophones in Toronto with economic security rather than ethnic identity.

four years the programmes have stressed folk culture and linguistic maintenance. They have stressed the first more, and the latter less, than spokesmen for some ethnic minorities have wished. Both emphases can be related at least as logically to a policy of invigoration of ethnic groups as to a policy of cultural maintenance" (p. 204).

[44] Cohen, *Two-Dimensional Man*, p. 94.

In all essential aspects, the French population of Metropolitan Toronto conforms to the three-fold pattern which is characteristic of "invisible ethnic minorities."[45] As long as the favourable climate in Toronto has continued to exist the francophone population has continued to experience structural assimilation to the dominant, anglophone population.

But the climate has begun to change. According to the Canadian Press, early in 1977 the impact of the victory of the Parti Quebecois on November 15, 1976, with its avowed separatist tendencies, has begun to influence the attitudes of Toronto residents toward francophones. The atmosphere has cooled noticeably, according to francophones interviewed by the press. One resident of Toronto for eleven years is quoted in a newspaper article as saying, "Since the election, people have become nasty again. There has been such a change, such backlash since November. People have become very cold and distant. I've been experiencing that Quebec has put us in a funny situation here." The editor of a French-language weekly newspaper apparently shared this impression, and is quoted as saying, "A wall went up between the English and the French in Toronto and we have been able to feel it ever since." He told the reporter that if Quebec separates many in Toronto would return to that province. A former director of La Chasse-Galerie indicated in the article that "things are worse for French-Canadians in Toronto now than they have been for years." A student of York University was reported as having been told to "speak white" when she speaks French, and her reaction was, "It's more than resentment, it's hate." The remark in the article which seems to capture the shared feeling among francophones interviewed was the comment, "People in general would become quite anti-French in their attitudes towards us if Quebec separates."[46]

The status quo is being threatened. But it must be remembered that the most definite reactions have come from migrants from Quebec, who constitute only one-third of the francophone population. Whether other francophones will react in the same way or remain indifferent to the issues raises speculation about what will happen to the French population of Toronto as the course of events in Quebec unfolds.

[45]In coming to this conclusion, the census records of 1961 and 1971 have been analyzed, numberous interviews conducted with francophone respondents in every area of investigation, and an analysis of a considerable collection of documentary, descriptive, and publicity materials which are concerned with francophone life and institutions in Toronto.

[46]*Kitchener-Waterloo Record*, May 14, 1977, p. 51. Names omitted, but are in the article.

Bibliography

Books

Banton, Michael. *Race Relations.* New York: Basic Books, Inc., 1967.

Barth, Fredrick. *Ethnic Groups and Boundaries.* Boston: Little, Brown and Company, 1969.

Bell, Wendell. "Social Change and Elites in an Emergent Nation." *Social Change in Developing Areas.* Edited by H. R. Barringer, G. I. Blanksten and R. W. Mack. Cambridge: Schenkman Publishing Company, 1965.

Brazeau, Jacques. "Quebec's Emerging Middle Class." *French-Canadian Society.* Edited by Marcel Rioux and Yves Martin. Toronto: McClelland and Stewart, 1964.

Breton, Raymond. "Institutional Completeness of Ethnic Communities and the Personal Relations of Immigrants." *Canadian Society.* Edited by Bernard Blishen, *et al.* 3rd ed. Toronto: Macmillan of Canada, 1968.

Brunet, Michel. "French Canada and the Early Decades of British Rule, 1760-1791." Canadian Historical Association Booklet No. 13.

Canada. Dominion Bureau of Statistics. *Census of Canada, 1961; 1971.*

————————. Royal Commission on Bilingualism and Biculturalism. *Preliminary Report.* Ottawa: Queen's Printer, 1965.

Carlton, Richard A. "Differential Educational Achievement in a Bicultural Community." Unpublished Ph.D. dissertation, University of Toronto, 1968.

City of Toronto Planning Board. *Don Planning District Appraisal.* September, 1963.

————————. *Ethnic Origins of the Population of Toronto, 1960.* Toronto, 1961.

————————. *A New Plan for Toronto.* Toronto, 1966.

Clark, S. D. *The Developing Canadian Community.* Rev. ed. Toronto: University of Toronto Press, 1968.

————————. *The Suburban Society.* Toronto: University of Toronto Press, 1966.

Cohen, Abner. *Two-Dimensional Man.* Berkeley and Los Angeles: University of California Press, 1974.

Cohen, Percy S. *Modern Social Theory.* London: Heinemann Educational Books Ltd., 1968.

Cyr, Roger. *La Patente.* Montreal: Les Editions du Jour, 1964.

Dashefsky, Arnold. *Ethnic Identity in Society.* Chicago: Rand McNally College Publishing Company, 1976.

De Jocas, Yves, and Rocher, Guy. "Inter-generational Mobility in the Province of Quebec." *Canadian Society.* Edited by Bernard Blishen, *et al.* 2nd ed. Toronto: Macmillan of Canada, 1964.

Dofny, Jacques, and Rioux, Marcel. "Social Class in French Canada." *French-Canadian Society.* Edited by Marcel Rioux and Yves Martin. Toronto: McClelland and Stewart, 1964.

Dumont, Fernand, and Rocher, Guy. "An Introduction to a Sociology of French Canada." *French-Canadian Society*. Edited by Marcel Rioux and Yves Martin. Toronto: McClelland and Stewart, 1964.

Duncan, Otis Dudley. "A Socio-economic Index for all Occupations." *Occupations and Social Status*. Edited by Albert J. Reiss, Jr. Glencoe, Ill.: The Free Press, 1961.

Durkheim, Emile. *The Division of Labour in Society*. New York: The Free Press, 1933.

————. *Suicide*. Translated by John A. Spaulding and George Simpson. Glencoe, Ill.: The Free Press, 1951.

Durokawa, Minako. *Minority Responses*. New York: Random House, 1970.

Fairchild. *Dictionary of Sociology*. Paterson, N.J.: Littlefield, Adams and Co., 1961.

Falardeau, Jean-Charles. "The Changing Structures of Contemporary French-Canadian Society." *French-Canadian Society*. Edited by Marcel Rioux and Yves Martin. Toronto: McClelland and Stewart, 1964.

————. "The Parish as an Institutional Type." *Canadian Society*. Edited by B. R. Blishen, *et al.* Toronto: The Macmillan Company, 1961.

Firth, Edith G., ed. *The Town of York, 1793-1815, A Collection of Documents of Early Toronto*. Toronto: The Champlain Society for the Government of Ontario, 1962.

Fosselman, D. H., C.S.C. "The Parish in Urban Communities." *The Sociology of the Parish*. Edited by L. J. Nuesse and T. J. Harte. Milwaukee: The Bruce Publishing Company, 1951.

Fregault, Guy. "Canadian Society in the French Regime." Canadian Historical Association Booklet No. 3.

Gans, Herbert. *The Urban Villagers*. Glencoe, Ill.: The Free Press of Glencoe, 1962.

Garigue, Philippe. "The French-Canadian Family." *Canadian Dualism*. Edited by Mason Wade. Toronto: University of Toronto Press, 1960.

Glazer, Nathan, and Moynihan, Daniel P. *Beyond the Melting Pot*. Cambridge: The M.I.T. Press, 1963.

————, eds. *Ethnicity: Theory and Experience*. Cambridge, Mass.: Harvard University Press, 1975.

Goffman, Erving. *Stigma*. Englewood Cliffs, N.J.: Prentice-Hall, Inc., 1963.

Gordon, Milton F. *Assimilation in American Life*. New York: Oxford University Press, 1964.

Graham, Victor E. *How to Learn French in Canada*. Toronto: University of Toronto Press, 1965.

Gross, Edward. *Work and Society*. New York: The Thomas Y. Crowell Company, 1958.

Guindon, Hubert. "The Social Revolution of Quebec Reconsidered." *French-Canadian Society*. Edited by Marcel Rioux and Yves Martin. Toronto: McClelland and Stewart, 1964.

Hale, Katherine. *Toronto*. Toronto: Cassell and Co. Ltd., 1956.

Hall, Oswald. "The Canadian Division of Labour Revisited." Ed. by Richard J. Ossenberg, *Canadian Society*. Scarborough, Ontario: Prentice-Hall of Canada, 1971.

Handlin, Oscar. *The Newcomers*. Cambridge: Harvard Univerity Press, 1969.

Harte, T. J. "Racial and National Parishes." *The Sociology of the Parish*. Edited by L. J. Nuesse and T. J. Harte. Milwaukee: The Bruce Publishing Company, 1951.

Herberg, Will. *Protestant, Catholic, Jew*. New York: Doubleday and Company, Inc., 1955.

Hitchman, Gladys. *La Maison Française de Toronto: An Evaluation Study*. Report submitted to the Social Action Branch of the Secretary of State's Department. Toronto, July, 1973.

————————. *The Chasse-Gallerie: An Evaluation Study*. Report submitted to the Department of the Secretary of State, Social Action Branch. Toronto, August, 1972.

Hughes, Everett C. *French Canada in Transition*. Chicago, 1943.

————————. "Ethnic Relations in Industry and Society." *Man, Work, and Society*. Edited by Sigmund Nosow and William H. Form. New York: Basic Books Inc., 1962.

————————, and Hughes, Helen M. *Where Peoples Meet*. Glencoe, Ill.: The Free Press, 1952.

Hughes, David R., and Kallen, Evelyn. *The Anatomy of Racism: Canadian Dimensions*. Montreal: Harvest House Ltd., 1974.

Hunt, Chester L., and Walker, Lewis. *Ethnic Dynamics*. Homewood, Ill.: The Dorsey Press, 1974.

Johnson, W. D. H. An unpublished report on the position of the French population in Rouyn-Noranda.

Jones, Richard. *Community in Crisis*. Toronto: McClelland and Stewart, 1972.

Joy, Richard J. *Languages in Conflict*. Toronto: McClelland and Stewart, 1972.

Kahl, Joseph. "Some Social Concomitants of Industrialization and Urbanization." *Readings in Industrial Sociology*. Edited by William A. Faunce. New York: Appleton-Century-Crofts, 1967.

Lachapelle, C. "La vie française à Toronto." *Documents Historiques*. No. 13. Sudbury: La Société Historique du Nouvel–Ontario.

Lamarche, A., O.P. "La Paroisse du Sacré-Coeur, 1887-1933." Pamphlet issued by the parish in 1933.

Lamontagne, Léopold. "Ontario: The Two Races." *Canadian Dualism*. Edited by Mason Wade. Toronto: University of Toronto Press, 1960.

Lee, Danièle J. "The Evolution of an Ethnic Parish." Unpublished M.A. thesis, Department of Sociology, University of Toronto, 1967.

————————, and Lapointe, Jean. "Conflict Over Schools in a Multi-Ethnic Society: A Case Study." *Education, Change and Society: A Canadian Reader*. Edited by Richard A. Carlton, Louise A. Colley and Neil J. McKinnon. Toronto: Gage Educational Publishing, 1977.

Lee, John A. "The Greendale Canadians: Cultural and Structural Assimilation in an Urban Environment." *Canadian Society*. Edited by Bernard Blishen, *et al.* 3rd ed. Toronto: Macmillan of Canada, 1968.

Lazarsfeld, P. F. "Audience Research." *Reader in Public Opinion and Communications*. Edited by Bernard Berelson and Maurice Janowitz. New York: The Free Press of Glencoe, 1950 and 1953.

Lerner, Daniel. *The Passing of Traditional Society*. Glencoe, Ill.: The Free Press of Glencoe, 1958.

Leventman, Seymour. "Minority Group Leadership: The Advantages of the Disadvantaged." *Mass Society in Crisis*. Edited by Bernard Rosenberg, *et al*. New York: The Macmillan Co., 1964.

Loomis, Charles F., and Loomis, Zona K. *Modern Social Theories*. Toronto: D. Van Nostrand Co., Inc., 1965.

Lower, A. R. M. *Canadians in the Making*. Toronto: Longmans, Green, 1958.

Lundberg, *et al. Sociology*. 4th ed. New York: Harper & Row, 1968.

Martindale, Don. *American Social Structure*. New York: Appleton-Century-Crofts, 1960.

Masters, D. C. *The Rise of Toronto, 1850-1890*. Toronto: University of Toronto Press, 1947.

Maxwell, Thomas Robert. "The French Population of Metropolitan Toronto: A Study in Social Participation and Ethnic Identity." Unpublished Ph.D. dissertation, The University of Toronto, 1971.

Miller, Delbert C., and Form, William H. *Industrial Sociology*. 2nd ed. New York: Harper and Row, 1964.

Miner, Horace, "Changes in Rural French-Canadian Culture." *French-Canadian Society*. Edited by Marcel Rioux and Yves Martin. Toronto: McClelland and Stewart, 1964.

————————. *Saint-Denis, A French-Canadian Parish*. Chicago: The University of Chicago Press, 1963.

Olsen, Marvin E. *The Process of Social Organization*. New York: Holt, Rinehart and Winston, 1968.

Ontario. *Report of the (Bériault) Committee on French-Language Education in Ontario*. November 28, 1968.

————————. *The (Symons) Ministerial Commission on French Language Secondary Education*. February 17, 1972.

Pageau, Claire. *Etude sur les besoins socio-culturels de la minorité francophone de la classe ouvrière située au centre-ville de Toronto, en général, et du rôle de la paroisse du Sacré-coeur, en particulier*. Rapport soumis au programme des groupes minoritaires de langue officielle, Secrétariat D'Etat. Toronto, April, 1975.

Porter, John. *The Vertical Mosaic*. Toronto: University of Toronto Press, 1965.

Price, Charles. "The Study of Assimilation." *Sociological Studies 2: Migration*. By J. A. Jackson, Cambridge: Cambridge University Press, 1969.

Quinn, Herbert F. *The Union Nationale*. Toronto: University of Toronto Press, 1963.

Remillard, Lionel. *Development of the French Language School System and Its Financing.* Report prepared for E. J. Ridout of the Ontario Institute for Studies in Education. April 14, 1975.

Rioux, Marcel, and Martin, Yves, eds. *French-Canadian Society.* Vol. I. Toronto: McClelland and Stewart, 1964.

Rocher, Guy. "Research on Occupations and Social Stratification." *French-Canadian Society.* Edited by Marcel Rioux and Yves Martin. Toronto: McClelland and Stewart, 1964.

Rosen, Bernard C. "Race, Ethnicity, and the Achievement Syndrome." *Minorities in a Changing World.* Edited by Milton L. Barron. New York: Alfred A. Knopf, 1967.

Shibutani, Tamotsu, and Kwan, Kian M. *Ethnic Stratification.* New York: The Macmillan Co., 1965.

Smiley, Donald V. *The Canadian Political Nationality.* Toronto: Methuen Publications, 1967.

Sorokin, P. A. *Social Mobility.* New York: Harper, 1927.

Stanley, George F. G. "French and English in Western Canada." *Canadian Dualism.* Edited by Mason Wade. Toronto: University of Toronto Press, 1960.

Stansfield, David. *How to Live French in Toronto.* The Ontario Educational Communications Authority, 1975.

Stearns, Peter N. *European Society in Upheaval.* New York: The Macmillan Co., 1967.

Taylor, N. W. "The French-Canadian Industrial Entrepreneur and His Social Environment." *French-Canadian Society.* Edited by Marcel Rioux and Yves Martin. Toronto: McClelland and Stewart, 1964.

Theodorson, G. A. and Theodorson, A. G. *Modern Dictionary of Sociology.* New York: Thomas Y. Crowell & Co., 1969.

Theriault, George F. "The Franco-Americans of New England." *Canadian Dualism.* Edited by Mason Wade. Toronto: University of Toronto Press, 1960.

Vallee, Frank G., Schwartz, Mildred, and Darknell, Frank. "Ethnic Assimilation and Differentiation in Canada." *Canadian Society.* Edited by Bernard Blishen, *et al.* 3rd ed. Toronto: Macmillan of Canada, 1968.

Wade, Mason, ed. *Canadian Dualism.* Toronto: University of Toronto Press, 1960.

————————. *The French Canadians, 1760-1967.* Rev. ed. Toronto: Macmillan of Canada, 1968.

Wilkins, James Robert. "The French-Canadians of Sarnia." Unpublished undergraduate thesis in Geography, Waterloo Lutheran University, 1967.

Williams, Robin M., Jr., with Dean, John P., and Suchman, Edward A. *Strangers Next Door.* Englewood Cliffs, N.J.: Prentice-Hall, 1964.

United States. Department of Labor. *Dictionary of Occupational Titles.*

Periodicals

Angell, Robert Cooley, "Social Integration." *Encyclopaedia of the Social Sciences,* VII (1968), 380-86.

Axelrod, M. "Urban Structure and Social Participation." *American Sociological Review,* XIX (1954), 13-19.

Blishen, Bernard. "A Socio-economic Index for Occupations in Canada." *Canadian Review of Sociology and Anthropology,* IV, No. 1 (February, 1967), 42.

Breton, Raymond. "Ethnic Pluralism and Social Equality." Ontario Human Rights Commission. *Human Relations,* 14, No. 22 (December, 1974), 6-11.

Brisbois, Edward J. "The Bicultural School," *Canadian Catholic Institutions,* VII, No. 6 (November-December, 1965), 24-26.

Burnet, Jean. "Ethnicity: Canadian Experience and Policy." *Sociological Focus* 9, No. 2 (April, 1976), 202-204.

Foskett, J. M. "Social Structure and Social Participation." *American Sociological Review,* XX (1955), 431-38.

Guindon, Hubert. "Social Unrest, Social Class, and Quebec's Bureaucratic Revolution." *Queen's Quarterly,* LXXI (Summer, 1964), 150-62.

Katz, Fred E. "Social Participation and Social Structure." *Social Forces,* XLV (1966).

Murphy, Albert J. "A Study of the Leadership Process." *American Sociological Review,* VI (1941).

Pineo, Peter C., and Porter, John. "Occupational Prestige in Canada." *Canadian Review of Sociology and Anthropology,* IV, No. 1 (February, 1967), 24-40.

Queen, S. A. "Social Participation in Relation to Social Disorganization." *American Sociological Review,* XIV (1949), 251-57.

Reissman, L. "Class, Leisure, and Social Participation." *American Sociological Review,* XIX (1954), 76-84.

Watson, James B., and Samora, Julian. "Subordinate Leadership in a Bicultural Community." *American Sociological Review,* XIX (1954), 413.

Wrong, Dennis H. "Social Inequality without Stratification." *Canadian Review of Sociology and Anthropology,* I, No. 1 (February, 1964), 5-16.

Yinger, J. Milton. "Social Forces Involved in Group Identification and Withdrawal." *Daedalus,* No. 91 (1960).

Zimmer, B. G. "Participation of Migrants in Urban Structures." *American Sociological Review,* XX (1955), 218-24.

DATE DUE